T0398676

The Urban Contract

Today, the increasing mobility of capital, people and information has changed the space relations of urban societies. Contractual relations have increased in every field of social life: in the economic field, but also in the political, creative and scientific areas. Contracts are not only legal frameworks or economic aggregates of individuals, but socially embedded forms.

The concept of an urban contract proposed in this book combines the theoretical body of economic-juridical literature on the contract with that of historical-anthropological and socio-spatial literature on the city. Through a diverse range of ten city case studies, *The Urban Contract* compares European, North American and Asian urban contracts. It concludes with a theoretical proposal for understanding the deep dialectical nature of contractual cities: their reciprocity and competition, their dual trend towards growth and decay, their cyclical nature as agents of change and disruption of the social forms of urbanity.

Paolo Perulli is full professor of economic sociology, University of Eastern Piedmont, Department of Jurisprudence, Political, Economic and Social Sciences (Italy); and professor of urban sociology, Architecture Academy of Mendrisio (Switzerland). He served as a visiting scholar at the Department of Urban Studies and Planning of MIT, Cambridge (MA) in 1984–5, and as *professeur invité* at the Facultè Jean Monnet of Université de Paris Sud in 1993–4. His main research publications have included: *Metropolitan Atlas* (Bologna 1992 and Madrid 1995), *Global Networks and Nation-States* (Zurich 1999), *The City of Networks* (Turin 2000), *The City: A Socio-philosophical Lexicon* (Mendrisio 2004). His recent books have been published by Einaudi, Il Mulino and Mendrisio Academy Press.

The Urban Contract
Community, Governance
and Capitalism

Paolo Perulli

LONDON AND NEW YORK

First published 2017
by Routledge
2 Park Square, Milton Park, Abingdon, Oxon OX14 4RN

and by Routledge
711 Third Avenue, New York, NY 10017

Routledge is an imprint of the Taylor & Francis Group, an informa business

© 2017 Paolo Perulli

The right of Paolo Perulli to be identified as author of this work has been asserted by him in accordance with sections 77 and 78 of the Copyright, Designs and Patents Act 1988.

All rights reserved. No part of this book may be reprinted or reproduced or utilised in any form or by any electronic, mechanical, or other means, now known or hereafter invented, including photocopying and recording, or in any information storage or retrieval system, without permission in writing from the publishers.

Trademark notice: Product or corporate names may be trademarks or registered trademarks, and are used only for identification and explanation without intent to infringe.

British Library Cataloguing-in-Publication Data
A catalogue record for this book is available from the British Library

Library of Congress Cataloging-in-Publication Data
A catalog record has been requested for this book

ISBN: 978-1-4724-4590-2 (hbk)
ISBN: 978-1-315-61499-1 (ebk)

Typeset in Sabon
by Apex CoVantage, LLC

Contents

List of figures	ix
List of tables	x
Acknowledgements	xi

Introduction		1
1	**The global transformations of the urban world**	13
	Introduction 13	
	The new economic base of cities 16	
	Global city-regions and mega-cities 18	
	Against the 'generic city': A three-level model 23	
	The city-by-projects 26	
	The relational-contract city: Empirical evidence	
	* from the European city system 28*	
	Conclusions 33	
2	**The European urban contract**	37
	London 38	
	* Keynotes on London between past and future 38*	
	* Interpreting the urban form: City of opposites 42*	
	* Interpreting the contract form: The Greater London*	
	* Plan 48*	
	Paris 54	
	* Keynotes on Paris between past and future 54*	
	* Interpreting the urban form: A three-speed city 57*	
	* Interpreting the contract form: The 'Grand Paris'*	
	* project 61*	
	Milan 66	
	* Keynotes on Milan between past and future 66*	
	* Interpreting the urban form: City of cities 70*	
	* Interpreting the contract form: The gateway city 72*	
	Conclusion 80	

vi *Contents*

3 The North American urban contract 82

Boston 85

  A history of the Brahmins 86

  Interpreting the urban form: City of culture 86

  Interpreting the contract form: The enduring mechanism of selection 89

  The Boston Redevelopment Authority and the mechanisms of urban community building 92

New York 94

  A history of traders and sects 95

  Interpreting the urban form: Cosmopolis 97

  Interpreting the contract form: The rezoning battleground 99

Los Angeles 105

  A history of flows 106

  Interpreting the urban form: Cities by contract 107

  Interpreting the contract form: The opposed coalitions 110

Concluding remarks 114

4 The Asian urban contract 117

Introduction 117

Tokyo 120

  A history of the shogun 120

  Interpreting the urban form: The global village 121

  Interpreting the contract form: Modernization and tradition 124

Mumbai 129

  A history of colonial and postcolonial power 129

  Interpreting the urban form 1: Creating a low-density, middle-class new town 131

  Interpreting the urban form 2: Vision Mumbai 134

  Interpreting the contract form: The opaque compromise 139

Hong Kong and Shenzhen 143

  A history of diverse trajectories of modernity 143

  The Chinese urban contract: 'New towns' or 'desakota'? 151

  The Chinese urban contract: SEZ and local investment platforms 154

Contents vii

The Chinese urban contract: Shequ jianshe *(community construction) and negotiating urbanization   156*
Marx in Shenzhen: Status and contract   159
Conclusion   162

5   The urban space and deliberative democracy   166
Lefebvre and Schmitt   166
The epistemological turn   167
Nomòs *and space   168*
Space of interaction   172
Conflicts over space   173
Plenitude and plurality   174
The law of the city   175
Deliberative democracy   176

6   The common matrix   182
United in diversities   182
The many names of the city   183
Contractual technologies   188
The contemporary urban contracts   189

7   Conclusions: Tools for the globalizing urban world   202
Towards a theory of urban social contracts   202
The urban social contract   204
Conceptual, explanatory and policy tools   206
Conceptual tools   206
Explanatory tools   218
Policy tools   222

Bibliography   226
Index   239

Figures

I.1	The urban contract	7
2.1	The European urban contract	38
2.2	The London urban contract	47
2.3	The London value diamond	50
2.4	The Paris urban contract	57
2.5	The Paris value diamond	65
2.6	The Milan urban contract	72
3.1	The North American urban contract	83
4.1	The Asian urban contract	119
4.2	The Tokyo urban contract	122
4.3	The Mumbai slum interplay	138
4.4	The Mumbai urban contract	139
4.5	The Shenzhen value diamond	147
4.6	The Chinese urban contract	150
7.1	The research strategy	203
7.2	The theoretical genealogy tree	203

Tables

1.1	A three-level model	24
2.1	London value added per capita by territorial scale (1995 = 100)	42
2.2	Mix of advanced production services: Milan, Rome and New York-London (NYLON)	69
3.1	Boston Redevelopment Authority (BRA) projects (2015)	93
3.2	Los Angeles Department of City Planning projects (2015)	110
3.3	International Affordability Index (2015)	115
4.1	Urban densities in Mumbai	131
6.1	The many names of the city	184
6.2	Types of contracts	188
6.3	The Shenzhen–Hong Kong cases	188
6.4	Strategic network connectivity	190
6.5	Quality of living	190
6.6	Urban contract tools	190
6.7	Upper-middle classes vs local poor	191
6.8	National framework of contract rights	192
6.9	Property rights	192
6.10	Social and affordable housing	194
6.11	Capabilities, enabling and control	194
6.12	Governmental structures	196
6.13	Elected metropolitan mayors	196
6.14	Culture of commercial ethos	196
6.15	Legal framework	198
6.16	Governance indicators	199
6.17	Context variables	200

Acknowledgements

This book is the fruit of three years' research, exploring and comparing cities scattered over the continents. I wish to thank the many colleagues who gave support, in particular Francesco Bandarin, Neil Brenner, Gerard Frug, Patrick Le Galès, Jinnai Hidenobu, Saskia Sassen, Kala Seetharam Sridhar, Wing Shing Tang, Peter Taylor, Mizuko Ugo and Mike Wallace. I also thank my colleagues and students at the University of Eastern Piedmont, Mendrisio Academy of Architecture, the PhD programme in economic sociology and labour studies at Milan Political Science Department, and National Interest Research Project on 'Postmetropolis' directed by Sandro Balducci at Milan Polytechnic. The first drafts of some parts were published in *GaWC Research Bulletins* (led by Peter Taylor), *Glocalism* (led by Piero Bassetti) and *Imprese§Città* (led by Pasquale Alferj). Although the English text is mine, Graham Sells has provided valuable assistance in proofreading and occasional retouching.

For any remaining errors, the responsibility is, of course, solely mine.

Introduction

The city produces forms without itself having any form. This sentence by Ernst Jünger, written in the 1930s, fits well into the contemporary Asian megalopolis, the American metropolis and the European city as well. Hence the circulation and exchange of meanings, sometimes in a perturbing way. Take the case of a city with 46% of the urban population poor or at risk of falling under the poverty line: Mumbai? no, New York.[1] A city with 40% of the urban population living in illegal dwellings, only later on regularized by the municipality: Delhi? no, Rome.[2] Or a city where 47% of the total number of migrants are highly educated (i.e. graduates and postgraduates): Boston? no, Bangalore.[3] These few examples challenge our current conventional ideas and portrayals of planetary urbanization, calling for further research into what we term the urban 'social contract', the ways in which the urban populations of the world define their cohabitation. Clearly, the urban world is not monolithic, but multifaceted, and yet the traditional views of the global urban divide (North and South, East and West etc.) need fairly radical revision.

This book aims at investigating the 'contractual' forms of urban societies in Western and Eastern cities. By 'contractual' is meant here the dynamic interplay of social contract *and* private contract: the former inspiring the expressions of the legitimate power towards its constituencies of urban civic society, the latter being the endless game of market transactions over the urban realm. By forms here we mean the shaping of socio-spatial phenomena through interaction of individuals in the space (Simmel 2009).

As it evolved in the ancient Western world, the city was a divided social unit. In the 4th century AD, Rome was already a metropolis consisting of 1,782 *domus* (palaces of the wealthy elite) and 46,290 *insulae* (each including five or six apartment houses lacking water and services). Yet city forms gave direction and meaning to every individual and social action, including political expressions of power and economic activities. The *central city* was the place of normative power, both political and religious, the *circle* the ideal-typical form of every imagined urban community; the *border* (from original city wall to national frontiers) divided insiders from outsiders both physically and psychically; the *zones* (in the *polis* as later in the modern

2　Introduction

zoning of the metropolis) maintained socio-spatial limits to urban growth; the *void*, empty or disused space was left for military or ecological invasion; and the *network* was a biological concept later applied by architects and planners to technical city development.

But cities also give direction to nature, interpreted as 'world-environment' (Heidegger 1962). The built structure is always in relation to those who employ and make use of it (*Zuhandenheit* means the daily, ready-to-hand use of objects): streets, bridges and buildings represent ways of taking care of the world, discovering nature along particular directions. This is also the point in Lefebvre (1970): '*Contract law determines the frameworks of exchange and of reciprocity in exchange. (. . .) However, use, in the urban, comprises custom and privileges custom over contract.*'

These contractual visions originating in European cities have continued to influence modern urban changes (Paris, capital of the 19th century; Berlin, driven by an organizational and technical spirit; London, the global city), forming Simmelian 'spatial worlds' and a spatial basis for urbanity, social interactions and the territorial clustering of human activities. The North American city placed this European inheritance within a new context (the 'empty continent' of Tocqueville), giving rise initially to small postcolonial communities (Boston), before developing into 20th-century 'delirious' metropolitan formations (New York) and the post-metropolitan evolutions of today (Los Angeles).

How space categories were elaborated in the ancient Eastern world has been a matter of comparative research in Western social sciences at least since De Groot, Durkheim and Mauss's seminal work on Chinese religion and the structures of mythical thinking. The Chinese classification of space is apparently independent of any social organization. The classification of space and time, of things and animals is based on the *Feng-shui* (windwater) doctrine determining the orientation of buildings, the foundation of cities and so on. A convergence between ancient Chinese, Indian and Greek classifications of space is the interesting finding of Durkheim and Mauss (1902). The unanimous concurrence on significance in different religious traditions is also asserted by Guénon (1962) with regard to the symbolism of such spatial forms as a 'world axis'. The idea of a town (Rykwert 1988) is therefore rooted in a profoundly common background shared by different civilizations: Roman ritual texts have their parallels in ancient Greece, Mesopotamia, India and China. We should start from here to evaluate different historical paths of urban development.

The Eastern cities were first and foremost central capitals of empires attracting feudal lords (like Tokyo, 'the capital of the East', which already had a population of a million in the early 18th century), before becoming decentralized administrative structures of central powers, subsequently the product of 19th-century colonial city-building (Shanghai, Hong Kong, Mumbai), and currently the new protagonists of 'planetary urbanization'.

Introduction   3

A preliminary methodological point to make is about comparison. In many Western theories of urbanization, as well as in many theories of capitalism, the Eastern world has been viewed in terms of applying modernization theories to emerging urban societies. Therefore postcolonial thinking challenges the Weberian rationality-modernization assumption. According to Appadurai (2013), Weber did not foresee the seductive aspects of non-European forms of capitalism, nor did he develop a connective association of great civilizations, their religions and their economies.

Appadurai makes no real distinction between Weber's theory of modernity and the subsequent theories of modernization, probably due to the functional-structuralist heritage of his Weberian scholarship (Shils). On the contrary, Weber's theory is always *tension* between different forces, polytheism of values and polymorphism of forms. Weber's *Sociology of Religions* runs contrary to Appadurai's interpretation. India, China and Islam are constantly articulated and contrasted in terms of 'salvation religions' and their relation to economic rationality. Criticizing the Western presumption to understand the urban Eastern world through planetary urbanization concepts, Chinese urban scholars today (Tang 2014b) use the same Weberian arguments about cities: in the East they never become an autonomous and self-governing entity.

Yet over the past 50 years urbanization has shifted away from the West to South-East Asia, to India and the Persian Gulf, and today's cities are the proliferation sites of state-driven urban development. It has taken the form of the private contract, through negotiation between governments and global capitalist enterprises. However, an implicit social contract is also at work in Asian modernization processes. As Ong (2005) puts it: 'But this legitimacy has to have something behind it that nearly works. That is the understanding that the people's will places them in an implicit social contract with the state. Although these states have elected governments and are modern forms of democracy, they need to continue to have these relationships of exchange with the population. Hence this implicit agreement between the political elite and the population that the government will deliver.'

If and how the social contract will emerge as a form shaping the urban space of relations is a matter of research which will be conducted in this book. While the Weberian perspective, seeing the Western city as a unique phenomenon combining market forces with political citizenship has to be reinterpreted in the light of such developments,[4] there is a need for new insight into the hybridization of political-economic forms in the globalized urbanity of the 21st century. In other words, the city's human ontology has to be redefined in the light of spatial globalization, which directly influences its basic coordinates. The Weberian autonomy of the city as fraternal peer-group human construction, its ability to cope with larger political organizations (states, empires etc.) and its enduring role of civilization building are all variables to consider in our 'contractual' theorizing of the urban.

4   *Introduction*

From its very origins the city has constituted mutual, reciprocal exchange and recognition among different *oikoi* (houses): synekism (*syn-oikos*) is the original union of dwellings to form a city. The contractual form has been the answer to the question: how can human coexistence, linkage and obligation among different people be traced when the density of their association is no longer deducible from kinship? But the contract theories, based on a utopic vision, fail to define the spatial domain where such synthesis is produced. Sloterdijk (2003) expresses their failure well: nothing remains of such people coexisting in a specific space and time, except their plurality of abstract 'will' giving rise to 'citizens'.

Rather, taking the space of interaction seriously, we must define the autonomous spatial dynamics of societies. To avoid the spatial emptiness of contractual theories, we follow here Simmel's *Sociology* (2009): individuals are related to others by each one's role and status, as if every element was predestined to a place in the whole. This space is a matter of constant negotiation. Today the dimensions of cities like Tokyo, New York or Shanghai make it easier to accommodate different populations or social groups whose stake in the urban process of transformation is finally admitted.

More recently, the increasing mobility of capital, people and information has changed the space relations of urban societies. The city has always been a myriad of contracts, both immediate and long-lasting, formal and informal, and of a nature identical with that of the city itself: endless bargaining among and combinations of 'diverse' populations of inhabitants, users and occasional travellers, immigrants (including illegal migration and unauthorized trafficking of labour everywhere: in the United States,[5] in China, Italy or Spain). Today the rationalization imposed on social life has increased the calculative–contractual relations in every field of social life, not only in the economic, but also in the political, creative and scientific areas. Although strong informal biotic linkages survive (often associated with kinship and ethnic relations within cities), the 'contractual' dimension of the privatized city is the dominant form everywhere, in the Global North as in the Global South. Their coexistence makes the space possible (in the ontology of space elaborated by Sloterdijk): cities are neither contracts nor organisms, *because they are both*. Contracts are creating new spaces, from the interactive models of Silicon Valley to the assemblages of new 'worlding cities' in the Global South. Innovative and adaptive behaviours coexist as apprenticeship places in the 'micro-spheres' constituting the learning global. Contracts involve both individual and collective, both local and global actors: contracts between individuals and places, states and cities, multinational organizations and international institutions, multinational firms and national governments, unions of states (like the European Union), regions and cities. All these contracts see the city as protagonist: in accordance with good urban governance principles, the government, the private sector and civil society participate in the governance. Urban governance following the UN-Habitat principles would substantially change local government law

Introduction 5

around the world (Frug and Barron 2006). Sustainability, poverty reduction and historical preservation would be included among its goals. For global and globalizing, worlding cities[6] today, supranational contractual relations are perhaps more important than the relations they have with their own national governments. Chinese and Indian cities are interpreted by some scholars as sites of global 'public-private partnership': no longer financed by their central governments, cities must extract public revenues from the sale or lease of land to global capitalists. Urban land use, rent extraction and redistribution of newly created value return as key determinants of urban policy choices in current globalization.

The urban contract is not an abstract, pre-political agreement but the interplay of actors and interests in the endless urban making and remaking, which is political in its very nature. Contracts are normative and performative: by defining the agents' relation with space, they may exclude or include various segments of society in different ways. The public-private partnership is an example: it operates by selecting business interests for approval at negotiating tables and deals. The selection, sometimes tacit, sometimes explicit, involves problems of democratic legitimacy. How do the private and public sectors cooperate? Is the public, forever exposed to private interests, able to limit and have command over their influence? Can the excluded have any voice and join forces to achieve recognized local and global existence?

Contracts may be written or, more often, unwritten, incomplete and implicit as in the case of negotiations on land use, be it – as we'll see in the following chapters – in New York or in Delhi. However, contractual relations are a dialectical and negotiated concept in which economic, political, legal and cultural factors are interrelated. Contracts are not only legal frameworks or economic aggregates of individuals, but socially embedded forms. In addition, as Karl Polanyi once pointed out, today it is no longer the economy that is embedded in social relations; rather, it is social relations that are embedded in the economic capitalist system. For this reason, the social-embedded aspect of the contract needs to be considered alongside the legal-economic aspect. In approaching interpretation, four keys emerge in particular:

Contract and status

The sociological tradition has seen the contract as a result of processes of rationalization of social interactions, while in the past social relations were based on status. Whereas status was an attribute of asymmetric power linkages, contract is the basis of mutual recognition between partners.

Status and contract may, however, be destined to merge in the future, as Kojéve (1982) once suggested. The contract becomes statutory and the status contractual. So much is foreseen as a future development of humankind at a final stage of history according to the Hegelian philosophy of history. But today – in Los Angeles, in Shenzen, in Delhi – not all are citizens, and

6 *Introduction*

not all of those to the same extent – a scenario that highlights the oppressive nature of status based on heritage, caste or class and the perennial conflict to obtain it. When all have the same status, then the dialectic between status and contract will come to an end. For now, contract remains the basis for negotiation among social actors.

Contract and gift

Not all in the spatial life of societies can be reduced to contract. Since their very beginnings, cities, both Western and Eastern, have functioned as loci attracting the poor and giving them spaces for recreation and assistance (both civil and religious, as in the case of the Christian monastery and the Islamic mosque). The practices and customs are exemplary of this space of interaction which is essentially 'non-contractual'. But the main non-contractual social field lies in gift exchange, where a social orientation towards reciprocity finds expression (for the Chinese concept of gift exchange, see Keith et al. 2014). The forgotten Polanyian interpretative key can be useful to understand many socio-anthropological practices (based neither on the market nor on the state) underlying urban social life in the emerging metropolitan rural-urban regions in Asia, Africa and America, and possibly in Europe itself (southern and eastern countries in particular).

Contract and democracy

The contractarian tradition has traditionally opposed the normative tradition. The former sees the contractual agents as maximizing individuals pursuing self-interest, while the latter is marked by the sharing of norms and public reason linking individuals' behaviour in collective action. The contract proposed in this book has to do with both conceptual traditions. The contract can be seen as a self-interested obligation (I give up my liberty in exchange for protection, as in the radical Hobbesian vision). But also in cities, we will see, selfish behaviours of fragmented social actors can give rise to public good. The contract can also be seen as a socially protective institution (in fact, deities, like Mithra in the Indo-European cultures, made the pact safe for both parties involved). In contemporary liberal democracies, the basic rules of decision-making are contractually stated in a constitution. In other political regimes (like China today), civil rights are not permitted, but spaces for negotiation and civic engagement tools are. Yet the rules are constantly interpreted and rewritten in social interaction. The negotiation process underlying the contract is particularly relevant when it comes to the city. Even international local government law may help empower cities as agencies for human rights. Yet international trade agreements can have the effect of limiting city power and influencing its land use policy, favouring foreign investors engaged in privatizing cities (Frug and Barron 2006).

Contract and collective

Although in law and economics the contract is strictly a matter of contractual-individual partners, in political philosophy and sociology the contract is a collective creation whose social outcome can be Durkheimian solidarity. In urban studies we can find traces of contractual/collective dimensions in community building, and indeed (as we will see) in such different contexts as *machizukuri* in Japan, *shequ ijanshe* in China, 'occupancy urbanism' in India and various forms of neighbourhood contracts or city contracts in Europe and North America. In such cases the collective dimension of urban contracts can be promoted both bottom-up and top-down: in the former case through various forms of civic local activism, in the latter case aiming at both providing central resources and controlling the urban population.

The concept of contract, hitherto unused in urban studies literature, aims to combine the theoretical body of economic-juridical literature on the private contract with that of the historical-anthropological and socio-spatial literature on the social contract. We can therefore analytically dissect cities as variable assemblages of contractual forms intersecting two distinct axes: a vertical axis and a horizontal axis (see Figure I.1). Along the vertical axis we place the social contract linking legitimate powers in search of consensus and their constituencies. Along this axis institutions and their objective power, law and regulation of urban monopolies and markets, and locational politics, including, to use the words of Carl Schmitt, localization (*ortung*) and ordering (*ordnung*), are located. Instead, along the horizontal axis we place the private contract linking interests involved in the production and consumption of the urban. Private market contractual forms find their space of expression here.

The social contract and the private contract are in reciprocal tension, and their intersection will vary according to cultural and structural context. In the Western tradition of social contract inaugurated by Thomas Hobbes, the liberty of the subject (to buy and sell, to contract with one another, to choose their own abode) is limited to the matters regulated by a sovereign

The social contract: legitimate institutions and their constituencies
(Rules and norms of representation over space)

The private contract: interests and market forces
(Land use, growth incentives, costs and competition)

Figure I.1 The urban contract

8   *Introduction*

power. This line of thought has been defined as 'transcendental institution-alism' (Sen 2009). The Eastern tradition takes a similar approach, as the ancient Indian Kautilya's *Arthasastra* (written in the 4th century BC and rediscovered in 1904, causing a sensation among scholars around the world, including Max Weber) witnesses. This detailed, highly sophisticated manual for statecraft evoked an Asian civilization that, in Weber's words, went far beyond what was familiar and average practice for the early Italian Renaissance. In fact, regulation of the economy, labour standards and protection of the weak, law and order are acquisitions of early Indian political thought. A parallel between Eastern and Western political ethics can be traced on this common ground, towards a new global ethic (Rich 2010). In this variability implicit and informal contractual expressions also find their space, both in the East and in the West: tacit conventions and habitus, collective beliefs as expression of common needs, the multidimensional subjectivity of agents, urbanity as the result of historical civilization patterns, market forces and urban metabolism.

The *methodology of the research* to be used in the city case studies will therefore consist of:

a)   brief reconstruction of the specific path dependence of each city, its spatial relations and its economic and political geography (the *historical pattern*);
b)   collection and processing of data relating to the institutional, economic and legal frameworks in which contracts are made between local and global actors, and public and private ones (the *normative framework*);
c)   analysis of the urban sociocultural context in which such contracts are embedded and non-contractual forms of reciprocity and exchange are developed (the *social embeddedness*).

In fact, the private contract, originally a juridical instrument for agreements between private individuals, has meanwhile grown into an instrument of global negotiation between states, cities, businesses and international organizations. The social contract has also continued to be the expression of legitimate actors seeking to find consensus (and also to manipulate it) of their constituents' various forms of citizenship through pacts and agreements.

Today cities are the scene of (formal and informal) contracts involving local actors, states and global enterprises, while global cities are becoming ever less subject to national regulations and ever more similar to transnational organisms: the 'private city' (Frug and Barron 2006). In our modern era a global contract would be needed to bring together these different levels and actors, yet no convincing solution is in sight (save for some initial signs coming from international city networks in UN-Habitat, in urban heritage or in world charters for local self-government).

In the world's urban landscape metamorphic processes are occurring that have led to the appearance of new city forms; in the attempt to grasp their essential nature, they have alternatively been defined with such epithets as dispersed metropolis, generic city, neutral city, global city, post-metropolis and worlding city. Each of them has a tradition in modernity to be deciphered, and a series of current applications to be considered in both the Western and Eastern worlds.

This book will start from the new urban lexicon which is emerging from current developments: decentralized post-metropolis, urban regionalization, edge-city, mobile city, global city, global city-region, megalopolis, megaregion, city of cities, borderlands, assemblages . . . all terms that will be used. This book aims at collecting theoretical arguments and empirical evidence relating to the diffusion of such hybrid forms and of urban metabolism in Western and Eastern cities. In these hybrid forms, the extent of the influence of Western culture over Asian colonial cities will also be considered (even if it is now China that is driving urban planning in many African cities). The Eastern tradition of structuring the urban fabric (as in the case of Tokyo, 'city of villages') will be compared with the formation of 'city of cities' in the West (such as London, Paris or Milan).

This book will further develop the idea that the city produces forms without itself having any form. This pragmatism constitutes the strength of cities in the globalized world. It accounts for the diversity of paths and approaches, the emergence of differences and asymmetries in the cities' responses to global challenges. Today the cities of Europe are devising strategic plans for new centralities on a post-metropolitan and regional level, actively seeking a transnational dimension but remaining 'prisoners of the state'. The Asian cities, in contrast, are developing alternative state-driven solutions through huge business platforms, urban-rural conurbations and vast urbanization projects. The North American cities, for their part, continue their suburban sprawl which extends, foam-like, into fractal post-metropolitan formations.

This book aims to compare the urban logics underlying the French suburbs (*banlieues*), the North American ghettos and the Chinese dormitory quarters or Indian slums: all alternative solutions to the same problem of social inclusion-exclusion. Here there will also be the opportunity to compare the different social contracts between the state, the city and the fragile urban populations (immigrants, dislocated workers from the countryside, the poor impoverished by urban elite-led processes) in the different cases, and to compare the respective reforms in social housing.[7] Surprising sociocultural changes will also be analyzed: such as the case of the high-rise apartment homes in vertical towers proposed by modernism and rejected by the Western suburban middle classes in the 20th century, yet accepted as the natural habitat of the middle classes emerging in South-East Asia in the 21st century (Therborn 2011).

In the same vein, the Urban Enterprise Zones, which the British government originally created using a post–Keynesian state approach, can be compared with the Free Trade Zones, or Special Economic Zones today, conceived through pacts between central and local governments and capitalist

10 *Introduction*

enterprises in China and elsewhere in Asia. Even the new towns created in the 20th century by the urban reform movement in Europe can find paradoxical comparison with the new towns centrally planned by the Chinese government today or by city-states like Dubai. Similarly, examples will be given of the different types of urban contract in Western cities that are the result of pluralistic systems, and of those in Asian cities that are driven by the developmental state. Understanding how these urban contracts work will involve concepts like institutional density, community building, growth machine, stakeholder groups and multilevel governance: concepts that can be applied to both Western and Eastern cities only by taking into account their constitutive differences. Spatial conflicts will also be considered. Today, in fact, no territory is left free for subsequent occupation; rather, constellations of public and private actors compete to regulate the same space, including 'occupancy urbanism' (Benjamin 2014). And significant shifts and variations exist between cohesion logics and competition logics. In this respect, too, the empirical evidence of Western urban systems of multilevel governance will be compared with Eastern urban systems in which centralized state-driven governance *cum* negotiating urbanization (Tang 2014a, 2014b) is predicted (as in China), or a mix of global speculative investments (Goldman 2011), local state control and informality prevails (as in India).

Comparison will extend to legal, political and economic systems to see how societies react differently to common global inputs (a matter of economic competitiveness, pollution and climate change, or of social conflicts linked to mass immigration). To this end, a conceptual matrix will be developed to evaluate the convergence/divergence of the different urban contracts in the current conditions of globalized urbanization.

Last of all, the city of bits, virtual cities, cities of flows are phenomena that highlight a single common trend: cities are losing their solid chthonic foundation and are being built increasingly around fluid and immaterial relations. The ontology of the urban is changing due to the technical shift from material to immaterial: adapting to technology means that bodies have to adapt to virtuality and post-humanity.[8] The political implications of this historic caesura are still unclear and attempts to identify them premature. This book will, however, propose a new paradigm: cities as networks of contracts forming new post-national, postcolonial and global social orders. This book aims to contribute to the current Western–Eastern dialogue on urban globalization, offering new insight into the sociocultural forms influencing world urbanization structures.

Chapter 1, The Global Transformations of the Urban World, will open with a review of the relevant international literature on the theme (not only of a sociological nature, but also geographical-spatial, political-institutional and economic). The fundamentals of an introductory theory of city-regions will then be presented based on the contract. Essentially abstract and historical, this chapter serves as a theoretical and conceptual introduction to the empirical themes of the following chapters.

Chapter 2, The European Urban Contract, will present an historical analysis of the European origins of the urban contract, urban agency and citizenship forms, connecting municipalities and governments, local and global actors on a city-region scale: case studies will include London, Paris and Milan.

Chapter 3, The North American Urban Contract, will show how tradition and innovation symbolize the North American urban contract in which growth-machine and market-led logic prevail but the community-building aspects remain solid: case studies will include Boston, New York and Los Angeles.

Chapter 4, The Asian Urban Contract, will elaborate on the formation of cities in direct relation to the contractual forms driven by the nation-state, from the city-capital of imperial tradition to the contemporary development of new mega-cities platforms resulting from contracts between developmental states, capitalist enterprises and the emerging civil society: case studies will include Tokyo, Mumbai, Hong Kong and Shenzhen.

Chapter 5, The Urban Space and Deliberative Democracy, poses the question of global urbanization as a new phase in urban history and its implication on the scale, scope and agency of deliberative democracy constructed through the interaction of urban actors and constituencies.

Chapter 6, The Common Matrix, will outline the future of both Western and Eastern cities as interlinked chains of globality, their convergent and divergent forces, and possible scenarios for a new global order and disorder.

The conclusion will sum up the findings emerging from the relevant literature with a theoretical proposal emerging from the research for an understanding of the profoundly dialectical nature of cities: their reciprocity and competition, their dual trend towards growth and decay and their cyclical nature as agents of change and disruption of the social forms of urbanity.

This work will enter into critical dialogue with various books on urban economy (Edward Glaeser, *Triumph of the City*, 2011), urban planning (Peter Hall and Kathy Pain, *The Polycentric Metropolis: Learning from Mega-city Regions in Europe*, 2009), urban sociology (Saskia Sassen, *Territory, Authority, Rights*, 2006; Neil Brenner, *New State Spaces*, 2004), urban political science (H. V. Savitch and Paul Kantor, *Cities in the International Marketplace*, 2004), urban geography (Edward Soja, *Postmetropolis*, 2000), urban political economy (Patrick Le Galès, *European Cities*, 2002) and, more recently, the works of human geography (Peter Taylor, *Extraordinary Cities: Millennia of Moral Syndromes, World-Systems and City/State Relations*, 2013), economic geography (Michael Storper, *Keys to the City: How Economies, Institutions, Social Interaction and Politics Shape Development*, 2013), urban anthropology (Ananya Roy and Aihwa Ong, *Worlding Cities*, 2011), urban history (Daniel Brook, *A History of Future Cities*, 2013), metropolitan government (P. Kantor et al., *Struggling Giants*, 2012) and urban theory (Neil Brenner, ed., *Implosions/ Explosions. Towards a Study of Planetary Urbanization*, 2014). These and many others will form

12   *Introduction*

the reference background. The approach in the aforementioned studies is often holistic (interpreting the city as a single system), at times structuralist (interpreting the city as driven by a force like capitalism or the state). In this book, we will start from case studies on European, North American and Asian cities to interpret the capacity of cities to become, even under the pressure of capitalist imperative to growth and expulsions (Sassen 2014a), loci of permanence and reproduction of society.

Notes

1   *The Economist*, May 16, 2015, calculated on the city's very high cost of housing and living.
2   Italian PRIN-National Interest Research Project on 'Postmetropolis', 2015.
3   Centre for Policy Research, New Delhi, 2013.
4   Criticism of Weber by authors like A. Appadurai and P. Taylor will be discussed in depth in the following chapters. Both of these scholars label Weber's theory as Eurocentric but forget Weber's prediction that modern capitalism based in Shanghai would expand. More generally, Weber clearly considered the complex relations of capitalism from outside, Confucian ethics and the developmental state.
5   In agriculture, domestic work, hotels, restaurants and construction.
6   S. Sassen, N. Brenner, A. Ong and A. Roy are among the authors considered here.
7   In a comparison between the French and the Catalan cases of urban segregation, it has been observed that the lower segregation and better integration of social groups in Barcelona is also paradoxically due to the lower efficacy of the social housing policies in Barcelona, contrasted with the French case, in which the effectiveness of social housing policies has exacerbated the urban segregation of less favoured groups (Nel.lo and Blanco 2015).
8   E. Jünger (1965) is the first author to have foreseen this future trend, today developed by MIT and Stanford laboratories of virtual reality.

1 The global transformations of the urban world

Introduction

The aim of this chapter is to introduce the reader to the new lexicon of space and cities in globalization. Since the year 2000, the urban and regional literature has defined our global world as a formation of global city-regions – assemblages of economy and society seeking representation. For the purposes of this book, the ontology of the global city-region is necessarily *plural*: it is a 'web of contracts', different in nature and more extensive than in the times of the nation-state, involving multifaceted governments, global enterprises, services and networks. All are involved in the ownership, management and representation of different aspects of what cities are. Some are socially irresponsible and, like capitalists, use cities as investment opportunities. But others are responsible, like governments, towards their constituencies formed by citizens, social groups and localized interests. Their contracts (both written and implicit) relate to the space of places and flows, both material (housing, investments, people, goods) and immaterial (information, services, knowledge). Forming boundless functional spaces, the relational economy of flows has critical impacts on the political space: a new theory of multilevel relational contracting is therefore needed.

In 1950, the German philosopher of law Carl Schmitt wrote that Eurocentric ordering in international law was in decline and the old *Nomòs der Erde* (Law of the Earth) was at an end. A new global order was needed, based on the fact that beyond the interstate political order a new global space had been created by the free, stateless world economy. In response to generalized delocalization the Eurocentric world was exploding, while in the economic field the old spatial ordering of the Earth was losing its structure. In the political sphere, states were losing their capacity to wield sovereignty over a given territory, and all this was an astonishing early foretaste of what we are currently experiencing in globalization.

Schmitt developed Max Weber's legacy through the polysemic concept of *nomòs*: at the same time measure, ordering and form. Here measure means occupation, division and distribution of the land; ordering means the specific order given to a territory; and form means the political, social and religious

14   *Global transformation of the urban world*

ordering of the Earth. The three meanings constitute here a concrete spatial unity. Ordering (*ordnung*) and location (*ortung*) have the same original root, hence space and power are deeply interwoven. Territory, authority and rights are divided (Sassen 2006) yet united in the same original *nomòs*.

Weber's concept of the city has the same internal complexity. It is at one and the same time an expression of economic rationality and of political freedom; it is the founding concept of modern state theory and of the economic rationalization process interpreted as the destiny of modernity.

In Weber, the concept of city was led up to from the concept of legitimate ordering, including convention and law, the concept of power, including its legal-rational foundation, and the concept of capital, including different forms of capital accumulation. Market and finance are typical only of Western societies, rational capitalistic enterprise, free labour and rational division of labour being the foundational elements. *Oikos* (domestic economy), patrimonialism and monopoly held by a king constitute the different foundations of past or non-Western societies. This Weberian framework places the Schmittian *Nomòs* of the Earth within a long-standing interpretation of the 'city' as the key institution of modernity.

Also the contractarian tradition of the city is to be reinterpreted in the same light. Note that Hannah Arendt (1995) traces the concept of contract in the Roman tradition, according to which a pact existed between the foreigners (in mythology Aeneas and the Trojans fleeing from their destroyed motherland) and the locals (the autochthonous inhabitants of Latium) that opened the way to the founding of Rome. The contract became a means of expansion for the Romans: they were able not only to subdue other peoples but to form alliances with them on the basis of a contract. Rome is therefore the first 'contract city' of antiquity. Arendt defined the contract as the structure assumed by the space of social interaction well before and in a different manner than the Hobbesian pact or covenant.

More recently, in fields like economic geography and urban studies, the literature has coined the term 'global city-region' to analyze the contemporary urban world. It is defined as an assemblage of economy and society (two Weberian concepts, in fact) seeking representation (Scott 2001). Here we can find a nexus between the two very different bodies of theories cited earlier. Both political philosophy and economic geography show us the divergence between the old state space and the emergent global economic space.

The creation of global city-regions is far too recent a phenomenon to evaluate its stability in terms of political and institutional response to the crisis of nation-states. We have to be cautious in this respect. An attempt the sociologist Charles Tilly made 20 years ago to suggest European macro-regions as a possible substitute for nation-states in the making of the European Union was not successful (Tilly 1992). Long historical processes account for formation of the state as opposed to empires, city federations, city-states and other concurrent political forms. Yet Tilly's (1991) theory of coercion

Global transformation of the urban world   15

and capital as key conflictual forces in European state-making is still crucial and can be extended to our times. State as 'coercion' and global city-region as 'capital' can be a valid conceptual tool to explain the Europe of today: on one side the union of nation-states, on the other the global economic forces concentrated in global city-regions. Thus Europe's global city-regions are constantly involved in European strategies due to their primary economic role. Yet their role in European policy-making is limited, if not irrelevant. This apparent paradox can be explained by the interest nation-states have in being considered the representative bodies of their global city-regions.

This is true of the West and the East as well. The Chinese, Japanese and Indian formations that we call city-regions, actually applying a Western concept to the Eastern world, are developing fundamental changes in their states' economies and societies. Tensions and conflicts between state-led development and cityness are destined to become (and often are already) a major political problem.

The ontologies (in the sense of the Foucauldian ontology of the present), 'the historical investigation into the events that have led us to constitute ourselves and to recognize ourselves as subjects of what we are doing, thinking, saying' (Foucault 1984), of today's emerging global city-regions are the subject matter of this chapter. We will follow the Foucauldian idea that three axes and trajectories – knowledge, power and ethics – characterize the ontology of our selves in modernity. In the current transition from nation-state to global city-region, various aspects of knowledge, power and ethics are involved. Power relations in the economy, the demands of society or of population zones, technologies and capabilities, all are changing in proportions and scope. The essential conditions under which such changes occur in the global world, East and West, North and South, are different in substance and nature from the old centralized metropoles of nation-states in the 19th and 20th centuries.

The substance of the global city-region is functional and primarily economic: it is a much wider, or indeed more global, 'web of contracts' than in the times of the nation-state. In that period the contract was in economic terms a principal-agent contract: the principal being the state, the agent being the city. It was the state that had sovereignty in articulating the physical and human natures in a given territory (Foucault 2004). The city (already a metropolis) was simply the capital of the state. It was the city's task, on behalf of the state, to exercise functions of security and control over the population and the circulation of flows. In Walter Benjamin's unfinished essay on 'Paris, the 19th Century Capital', this is well explained as a process of 'advancement of regulation in the metropolis' through technical measures supporting administrative control (Benjamin 2012). An example of this was Haussmann's city renewal, an astonishing urban reversal to make a metropolis politically safer and economically more valuable for capital investments. Later, in the 20th-century municipal welfare state era, the role of cities was to plan urban expansion by making local welfare (transport,

16 *Global transformation of the urban world*

social housing, schools, public green areas and so on) more affordable for modern citizens. Abercrombie's Greater London Plan was a key example for post–World War II cities.

Today the agglomerating substance of the global city-region is 'relational contracting' among actors that are global in many cases: enterprises, services and networks find their place in many global city-regions at one and the same time. Among them global real estate is a key actor. The best estimates for building investments in one year (2013–14) put New York first at $55 billion, London second at $47 billion, Tokyo third at $35 billion, Los Angeles fourth at $33 billion. Considering only foreign investment, the main recipients are London, New York, Paris, Shanghai, Sydney, Los Angeles.[1]

Such actors do not obey state sovereignty. A new contract of obedience between the autonomous reasons of the economic and social actors and the political principle is not in view in current circumstances. Places follow a variable geometry and geography, functionally defined as they are by the economy and no longer territorially defined in any classical administrative boundary by the state.

Relational contracts linking economic and social actors are interconnected, giving rise to connective networks. Today it is often a case of partnership contracts where the general interest is not given in advance: it has to be identified in the ongoing process by the participant actors, both public and private. New public-private partnerships emerge across and within cities not only in the economy but also in society, in fields like knowledge, technology, education, welfare and culture. However, such partnerships are selective, unable to include the multitude: social cohesion is no longer the policy aim of states and cities. Economic competitiveness is seen as their main conjoined imperative (Brenner 2004). Yet the excluded, those who remain outside redistributive policies, in many cases encompass a wide range of social groups and interests. Their political participation has weakened, and democratic legitimacy is at stake. The reasons for this are structural, as explained in the following section.

The new economic base of cities

The economic base of contemporary cities is changing. Two features, in particular, characterize the process: the internationalization of economic systems and the flexible informalization of labour markets and relations, coupled with vigorous growth in functional urban services. Hence the cities open up to new geographies of industrialization and territorial development. The crossover between these two dimensions (Storper and Walzer 1989) occurred previously in the urban environment, while today it extends over entirely new, enlarged scales.

The economy today spreads wide across territories, distributed in long, global value-chains, yet its base lies within the cities. Therefore, the first question that needs to be addressed is: Is the contemporary city still installed

Global transformation of the urban world 17

in a territory? It was certainly so in the city's history: a point constituting a centre around which a world was built. A world that could be of different dimensions, but that clearly had a centre. Is the contemporary city still such? And, since in the Western world the same word *demos* (and therefore *democracy*) came to mean both *people* and *territory*, can we go on living today separating the people from the territory? On one hand there is the city's territory, on the other there are the flows (the constant flows of activities carried out across the world by a non-resident, migrant population), and these flows seem to be growing exponentially in all directions within and between territories.

Although not all the growth of the cities is accounted for by migration (as in the case of India's cities: 60% of the population growth is due to natural increase, not migration), yet it is a global class phenomenon, forming a new class, urban and cosmopolitan in nature. It is not limited to the tiny percentage of the affluent, globalized, mobile workforce. There are 191 million migrants the world over, a small percentage of the world population (3%). But of these, 64 million are in Europe, 53 million in Asia and 44 million in America. In a country like Germany the workforce is 14% foreign, while the figure comes to 17% in Spain, 12% in France and 16% in the United States. Most of the flows are concentrated in cities: in Amsterdam, Frankfurt and Brussels between a quarter and a third of the population is foreign, in London the figure stands at 21.1%; a third of the population of New York is foreign; in Toronto and Vancouver foreigners make up more than 40% of the population (Therborn 2011). The case of Asia is so compelling that it will form part of our picture with a special focus on China and India. Flows also form permanent city networks which are the new skeleton of urban globality: making contracts for investment in China by a German firm and its Australian partner will be the task of a London law firm using expertise in Shanghai, Frankfurt and Sydney (Taylor 2013).

The second question concerns the *region*, which was in the languages of the West initially[2] the result of an act by the king (*rex*) that traced out sacred and impassable borders (*regere fines*). Interestingly, in Chinese the term *guo* means 'country' in the sense of 'the border of the kingdom'. China is the *zhongguo*, the 'country in the middle'. The border is hence of extreme importance to define a region.

Authors like Michael Storper studied today's 'regional world' 20 years ago. Can this be a 'borderless region'? When we speak of regions today, we define territories with no precise borders, where production activities are far more delocated than in the past. We can indeed say that the region has administrative borders, but these are now permeated and crossed by flows of all types and in all directions. All regions, in particular those bordering other countries, are affected by these trans-frontier dynamics. Hence, from an administrative point of view, the region has only limited effects on the socio-economic dynamics that traverse the territories. The coordination of spatial, functional and sectoral dimensions lies behind striking institutional

18 *Global transformation of the urban world*

change (Salet et al. 2003). And it is no coincidence that urban scholars have coined a new term, 'global city-region'.

What are the essential constituents of today's world? It is made up of global city-regions that are no longer *cities* or traditional *regions* in the sense defined earlier. They are an amalgam, new mixtures of economy and society (the theme of mixing, of mixed up, of a place of contrasts is typical of our times). They have no precise political or institutional representation: perhaps they are in search of it. And tendentially they are global city-regions in the sense that the flows that traverse these territories are not territorially located, neither can they be confined in a city or regional dimension; they are global in nature. Technology drives the world, immaterial and a-territorial as it is. Hence, has this process of loss of places and centres, this deployment pattern, reached the point of impeding any margin, edge or limit to the global world? Have *urbs* and *orbis* come to mean 'everywhere and no matter where', as the French philosopher Jean-Luc Nancy (2002) writes? These are the questions we must address since, wherever we are positioned or deployed, we inevitably belong to this dimension; a dimension that presents diverse characteristics according to the contexts, the continents. Clearly the European city still preserves historic-political peculiarities (Le Galès 2002), but this is the global challenge that lies before us. It is not only the Asian, African and South American megalopolises, seen in their 'catastrophic' physical and demographic expansion, that are at stake, but also the Western and European cities.

Global city-regions and mega-cities

In the text inaugurating a study of the global city-region (Scott 2001), a table listed the top 30 such regions in the world. The list was revised in 2015: Tokyo leads the way with 28 million inhabitants (37 million including Yokohama), followed by many Eastern cities (Jakarta, Seoul-Incheon, Delhi, Shanghai, Manila, Karachi, Beijing, Osaka-Kobe-Kyoto, Mumbai, Guangzhou-Foshan), some in Latin America (São Paulo, Mexico City) and a few Western cities (New York, London, Paris, Chicago, Los Angeles). Many of them are listed as mega-cities, or major agglomerations of the world, also including Kolkata, Cairo, Buenos Aires, Moscow, Dhaka, Tehran, Istanbul, Rio, Lagos.

According to some (Taylor 2013), the phenomenon of mega-cities is primarily due to the immense mega-migration flow from rural to urban. They are the leading cities of the poor countries. There is a clear distinction between such cities and the rich hub cities of the world economy. The kinds of flow are different: in one case poor population flows, in the other capital and information flows.

Two decades ago, Manuel Castells introduced the term 'spaces of flows' to challenge the conventional vision of 'spaces of places'. The possibility of defining a city appears even more remote once the world can only be

Global transformation of the urban world   19

read essentially as a world of flows, encompassing types of relations that escape control at a given point. That is to say, the city can be a point, a node or junction, but these inter-city flows can neither be identified with a spatial governance nor measured in a direct way, given the highly sensitive commercial information involved (Taylor 2013). And here perhaps lies the strongest impediment, for throughout the 20th century we thought spatial control was still possible in the metropolitan form. It was said that governance and control were entrusted to the city and its metropolitan forms, even in a highly articulated way (like the 'thousand governments' of the American city), but all the same identifiable as units. It is here that the Simmelian 'metropolitan intellect', the calculative rationality (Verstand) in terms of force capable of ordering space, is most seriously undermined. It has been substituted by the Marxian 'general intellect', which is a force transforming social life 'not only in the form of knowledge, but also as immediate organs of social practice, of the real life process' (Marx 1858), through organs of the human will over nature. Therefore today we see ever less spatial governance based on fixity, but cohabitation of flows of various kinds (of people, capital, information). Therefore what we perceive before us is an anomia, the loss of capacity of governance, the anomic traversal of flows (the constant flow of reproduction of circulating capital, according to Marx) of a physical, immaterial and virtual type moving in all directions. These flows do not follow an organized pattern, or constitute a form capable of being governed. They are the product of market forces, of anonymous matrixes, of complex interdependencies. In some cases, like telematics networks and mobility infrastructures, the most we can do is identify the actors or decision-makers who decide to invest in the building of a network. The hub cities phenomenon is relevant here: it is the outcome of knowledge enterprise networks like Google, Facebook or Amazon which are spreading around the world (Conventz et al. 2014). But the way in which the myriad of actors behave, deploy, receive signals and use these networks defies any pattern or governance.

Here there are the old and new asymmetries that characterize the contemporary city. The main asymmetry to tackle lies in information access, which is highly selective. This is a matter of the digital divide, including training and retraining and the creation of 'smart' communities not limited to privileged economic elites. In the case of Milan, recent research has calculated a high number of firms that are excluded or underrepresented in access to information and communication technologies (ICT). In comparative research among European cities, four city types are identified (Derudder 2011): cities where the Internet has made an increase in GDP possible (including London, Paris, Frankfurt and Stockholm); cities where an increase in GDP has propelled the Internet (including Brno, Graz and Turin); cities where both the Internet and GDP are correlated (Goteborg, Koln); cities where non-correlation between the Internet and GDP has been ascertained (like Milan, Vienna, Brussels, Madrid, Barcelona and Athens).

20   *Global transformation of the urban world*

The variance is probably accounted for by the different institutional and contractual structures linking the cities, enterprises and other functional and social actors. In fact, here we have to consider both Western and Eastern cities. The 'contract city' phenomenon is also seen in Internet network creation on a global scale: here a major role is played by actors like Google, 'a pioneer – or an imperialist – in being the only major firm to locate in India, Malaysia, Nigeria, and South Africa, and in Russia' (Conventz et al. 2014).

The second asymmetry concerns mobility, which is even more selective: there are those who can move and shift, and those who simply cannot. The financial markets are much more mobile than countries and enterprises, which is why global cities like London and New York, and their national governments, staunchly protect their financial markets from regulations. Multinational firms are also more mobile than the countries in which they are located, which is why they can play with territories through localization and delocalization choices (such is the case of the Silicon Valley firms in Bangalore). Among firms, big buyers can move more easily (and actively do so) than subcontractors, which are mainly local in nature; but world experts are also more mobile than their client enterprises; firms are more mobile than their contingent labour force; and so on. Here again the contractual relation among different functional and social actors is a key explanatory variable. Also the emergence of global platforms of production, as in Asia today, is a matter of disruption of long-lasting local informal enterprise networks which informed the economy of China and India in the past (often on the basis of relations of mutual trust, or *guanxi* relations) (Guthrie 1998).

All this happens within the global city-region (or its Eastern version, called a *desakota* region due to the interlinking of city and village in Asia). It is a platform where firms can land and take off according to their strategies. But it is also an interconnected network of enterprises, institutions and people reciprocally interrelated by contracts.

Who governs the global city-region? In the case of Europe, a mix of Europe, state, region, city? A governance without government (Le Galès 2011)? In the case of Asia, a variable, yet unstable mix of developmental states and global enterprises, often unable to understand one another?

On a normative level, governance mechanisms include new soft agreements and new constitutional orderings. Soft agreements are essentially unwritten, informal contracts. They are managed by territorial governments and interest associations or 'secondary citizens' (in the West: chambers of commerce, private interest groups and a myriad of citizens' associations; in the East: corporate networks and growth coalitions as in Shanghai, Hong Kong, Singapore or Mumbai) in order to create a common understanding and common rules of conduct. This is a matter of both implicit and explicit contracting among different actors and stakeholders: consider human capital (Training for which kind of labour markets, local or global? Why should local schools and universities invest in training a skilled workforce destined to migrate to other countries?), externalities (How to manage the

Global transformation of the urban world   21

environment locally around global common goods? Can localities consider larger horizons in time and space?), and networks (density of heterogeneous people within a territory was the distinctive feature of urbanity in the past; today it is the degree of global openness and participation in any kind of multinational network that makes the difference).

The attraction and regulation of material and immaterial flows is the main issue to address. This is nothing new in the history of capitalism, but what is new is the dimension of knowledge property rights circulating in the world economy. It is difficult even to measure and represent such flows because official statistics ignore them: the people and enterprises are counted and included, but not the volumes or the values of immaterial flows in transit across territories. We have not moved beyond the nation-state statistics of the 17th and 18th centuries, at the beginnings of modern sovereignty, while the contemporary world is forged by global flows.

It would be helpful to turn to a morphology of 'spaces of flow' in order to bring out these novel aspects, even though economic flows are certainly not a recent phenomenon. According to Braudel, the Europe of the Renaissance was already a circulation of flows, but these were other sorts of flows: the dimensions were different, and so too were the space–time relations.

Hence the main themes of this contemporary *problematique* are the strong signs of a spatial crisis. In the era of global flows and disjointments (Appadurai 1996), the city risks losing out as a point that orders space due to the phenomenon of de-territorialization and the creation of diasporic arenas resulting from global migration. We need, therefore, to reflect on this aspect and on what new models are emerging from the point of view of city analysis. Brenner (2010) asserts that the 'cityness' of the city is a positivist concept produced by the Chicago School–driven urban studies, and that 'city' and 'urban' are not real or empirical elements but structural projects continuously recreated during the spatial production of capitalism. The units of analysis of 'city' and 'urban' are themselves to be understood as continuously co-constructed and reconstructed: the cityness of the city is a condition that is evolving continuously on a multiscale, the object of strategic contestation in geopolitical relations, rather than an object or a territorially delineated site.

The risk of reification of the city and the problem of turning it into a collective actor can be avoided by resorting systematically to network analysis, as in the Latourian Actor-Network Theory (critically reviewed in Brenner et al. 2012). Cities are 'networks of networks' of actors: enterprises in productive networks, people in mobility and communications networks, institutions in policy networks. Hence it is only for simplicity's sake that we speak of 'city-regions': in actual fact, we are speaking of networks of networks (or 'assemblages of assemblages').

The ontology of the global city-region as a 'web of contracts' fits well into the assemblage theory. Contracts are defined here as relational contracts linking economic, political and social actors in their complex interplay.

22 *Global transformation of the urban world*

In these contracts, social relations, shared knowledge and mutual trust enter into account in economic transactions. Global firms, local enterprises, research universities, political institutions and social networks play a relational game which is not zero-sum. Agents' associations and institutional densities vary among the different contexts and need to be measured and compared. Historical and cultural factors influence the moulding of territories. Geographical scale and territorial dimension, however, are not given entities; they are constructed in a non-uniform way, depending on the scale, scope and functional entities taken into account.

The contract city concept is proposed here as a heuristic tool to investigate and aggregate phenomena pertaining to different countries, cultures and disciplines. The two axes defining the contract are: a vertical axis including institutions, rules, laws and regulations, objective power, monopolies and markets; and a horizontal axis including the agents' subjectivity and belief systems, social conventions, urbanity as a cultural artefact and urban metabolism. The two axes intersect differently according to the historical and sociocultural variable patterns of cities.

The intersection of the two axes differs between 'vertical' societies, like China, India and Japan, and 'horizontal' societies, as in the West, and particularly in Europe and the Anglo-Saxon countries. In vertical societies, group formation is not individualistic but collective: in horizontal societies, the individual (and individual 'pursuit of happiness') is the key. In vertical societies, the city is fluid and informal, while in horizontal societies, it is more clearly defined and demarcated. The ontology of the Western city is a space delimited by precise demarcations: the ark is the first archetype followed by city walls, borders, immunitarian systems (Sloterdijk 1999). Originally, the biblical ark was said to be the model of a pact between God and men, the first 'natural contract' to protect men from nature's risks; the protective space of the ark inspired the development of the city, artificial self-protection and compromise between the self-referential and the sedentary. The ontology of the Eastern world, instead, is a fluid system whose order has a double matrix (superior-inferior in the Indian *Bhagavadzita*, yin-yang as opposite and complementary principles in Daoism); hence non-duality is the rule, as in the case of the urban–rural continuum (Tang 2014b; contra Esherick 1999). The ancient Chinese city is also a case of immunitarian walled closeness; yet the modernization of Chinese and Japanese cities (Shanghai, Tokyo) seems to maintain some of the tradition of its original flexibility, producing a peculiar, amoeba-like metropolis.

The global city-region is certainly a theme on which to reflect in the fluid, extended dimension imposed by today's economy and society – a political-institutional dimension that is not widely recognized. Does the global city-region of Northern Italy, a 27-million-person agglomeration among the first in the world, have a definable connotation (Perulli and Pichierri 2010)? Is it a 'city-region'? A more interesting approach might be: rather than a city-region in the sense Californian geographers used to formulate the idea, it

Global transformation of the urban world 23

is a 'region of cities': a particular polynuclear fabric that thickens into networks and corridors that are ever less locally, ever more macro-regionally and globally defined (towards France and Germany, Eastern Europe and, increasingly, Asia[3]). But the 'global city-region' of Northern Italy is also noteworthy for its global population flows: 2.5 million foreign residents in 2008 that are growing in number (arriving from Africa and the Middle East) and putting the city form as we have traditionally known it to the test.

Two cases that are interesting to compare in terms of a 'contract city' theory are Northern Italy and California. The North American urban contract is mostly based on market forces linking enterprises and communities, institutions and social groups (immigration included) in a 'growth machine'. The European urban contract is more a balance between multilevel forces (European, national, regional and local) in which experimental governance is taking place. The free, stateless world economy plays out differently in the two contexts. In the Italian case, institutional inertia has produced a society rich in productive units and networks but weak in regulation due to the historical background to its public administration (Corò and Dalla Torre 2015). In the North American case, the institutional density of innovative businesses, universities and local communities has been based on an urban contract in which public and private, city and market had been intermeshed from the outset, and now city power is a mechanism for promoting private economic development (Frug and Barron 2006). Yet industrial fashion and the design-driven districts of Northern Italy and the high-tech, innovative, enterprise-based communities of California are both exemplary cases of new 'world-regional' economies, less dependent on the state power-container than in the past. 'Some cities may begin to dictate how nations behave rather than the other way around' (Frug and Barron 2006, p. 8).

Against the 'generic city': A three-level model

In urban theory and practice, in the fields of urban anthropology, architecture and planning, the widely used concept of the generic city sees the uniformity of the contemporary city more as an ideology than an idea. Possessing a single form, it has been classified as a 'generic city' after the term coined by Richard Sennett and Rem Koolhaas. The generic city is one that has at last freed itself from its 'centre', from the slavery of the cultural fabric of the 'city in history' (the Mumford heritage), and accepted almost as a liberation the advent of uniform, indifferent space. This is the ideology that needs to be examined. Even when faced with processes of transformation as a space of flows prevails over a space of places, we must not let go of the idea that the city is a plural phenomenon. A single form of city does not exist, there can be no uniform approach to the city. From its very origins the city has always been a place of holding back and reaching forward, a two-way entity, so we witness a continuous differentiation and creation of new models of urbanity. These models are continuously reproduced through the

24 *Global transformation of the urban world*

changing conditions of techno-economic processes. In the era of networks, city models tend to take on characteristics of the new reticular capitalism: open, decentralized models growing at the edges more than in the centre. Hence we should examine the present state of practices applied to contemporary cities, seeking to standardize and render uniform a single type of city and reproduce it around the world. Even in the positions taken by scholars like Marc Augé and Rem Koolhaas there is the risk that many considerations on the city may converge towards the ideology of 'non-places', or can be interpreted around the new vulgate of 'generic city' or 'endless city' of Ricky Burdett and Deyan Sudjic.

We can critically evaluate these theories of the city in the era of globalization with a research programme. To achieve this, we may take a model that proposes several levels of reflection (see Table 1.1).

We may take as the first level that in which we practise everyday operating in the city, living in the city, governing the city. It is the level of political action on the part of contemporary social and political agents. This first point concerns the concept of local development. We have a rather limited idea of local development because we often think that it means something small-scale, concerning the dimensions of our immediate surroundings, our neighbourhood, at most the associated urban district. We have to use a different model that considers the variety, multiplicity and plurality that is richly present in our world. From this point of view, Europe is a truly interesting permanent laboratory of local development, and one that is contagious. The models we have experimented with, from 'industrial districts' to 'enterprise networks', have propagated all around the world, yet we can also recognize other models of local development in the same key we have thematized in Europe. The local development of systems like those in California – where a highly interesting contagion between Italian and American models took place in the 1980s – is a field of observation that could produce some benchmark models with culture playing a central role. These are processes of local development drawn from cultural systems because California is only interpretable – as Castells and others have shown – in terms of generation of cultural systems that have produced forms of innovative organization of the economy, which in turn have encouraged decentralized and reticular forms of society as seen in the Californian and Italian models.

Table 1.1 A three-level model

Level of Analysis	Key Concept	Exemplary Field
Political agency	Local development vs. growth	Industrial districts, pro-growth coalitions
Epistemological reflection	Local	City ideal-types
Ontology	Contract	Connecting sites

Source: Author

Global transformation of the urban world 25

But is what was true in the recent past (the 1980s) still true today? In other words, how can we explain the path of development of the Californian model (its regional advantage, its openness to entrepreneurs and a labour force from countries like China and India, its strong networks of entrepreneurship around the Bay Area) compared to the poorer and less innovative performance of the 'Third Italy' industrial districts in the past 20 years? And how can we take into account the emerging geography of self-sustained urbanized innovation in countries like China and India, where a tradition of 'industrial districts' never existed?

A different dimension of local/global policies is at work here. But is there a different urbanity too? The closeness of Silicon Valley to Los Angeles and San Francisco is a matter of fact, including the urban culture, population and services provided. Whereas, in the Italian case, the industrial districts and cities have only partially coalesced in a modern network system, and 'anomic' social behaviour is often the rule in a poorly governed institutional framework.

In the cases of China and India's urban development, the rapidly emerging platforms of industrial production and urban-driven innovation clearly follow different patterns, such as the privatopolis of urban-integrated megaprojects in India (Shatkin 2011) and pro-growth coalitions in China's explosive new towns phenomenon (Wu 2015). An insightful account can be found in Storper (2013). He explains that the United States' metropolitan regions are highly specialized in production and innovation, whereas in Europe the regional economies are more diversified and less technologically specialized. Probably China is more like the United States and India is more like Europe. Seven forces combine in accounting for such outcomes: codes and communication, channels, clustering, communities, context or local genius, coordination and competition. Tacit knowledge flows through channels which are often locally and globally defined, and innovations cluster into communities, which again are both locally specific and globally oriented; context is still important in the age of decontextualized factors of change, and coordination and competition are both driving forces of innovation.

There is a second analytical level to consider in relation to the theme of the urban research programme proposed here, namely an epistemological reflection on what is meant by 'local'. Here perhaps we have reached a turning point, a new way of defining the word. It is the idea that 'local' is a structure that in itself contains elements of 'globality'. In other words, local is not a small-scale structure, but something that in itself already contains the global scale. The theme of the city from this point of view constitutes an extraordinary field of application. Actually, it has always been so: we should not forget that in Western culture, following the Tower of Babel, the founding of cities and the multiplication of languages proceed hand in hand. Hence from the theme of local development we inevitably reach the theme of the city. Perhaps here we can redefine themes of policy, of political action, and dig deeper to see what families of models can be found and fielded.

26   *Global transformation of the urban world*

What is in fact needed is a pluralistic approach to the issue of the city that questions the idea of the uniform city towards which we are all heading in these times of planetary urbanization.

Thus we should examine and reflect on the generation of models that we have behind us and reconsider the theme of the plurality of city models, starting from Weber's ideal-types of cities: cities of production and consumption, for example. This reflection is also prompted by research, like that of Davezies (2008) on France, with the main focus on the income that sustains cities. Alongside one type of 'entrepreneurial' city oriented towards international competitiveness that engenders a sizeable income in market activities, another type of city exists whose income is mainly based on the transfer of public funds, public expenditure and pensions (a new version of Weber's 'pensionopoly'). Indeed, now that it has abandoned its origins, the way the city is representing itself calls for special attention.

Also the theme of rapid urban growth in the East has to be taken into account. The changing scale of urbanization in a country like China has made the production vs. consumption cities a topic of 'socialist' urban transition. The past nature of cities as administrative and consumption loci has been subverted by a rapid, growth-oriented production shift. The current market-oriented phase in China has maintained strong growth machine characteristics.

The third and final level of analysis of the city concerns its ontology. In the approach followed here, the classical dimension of 'being' a city (the ontological dimension of the city) is transformed into one of 'having' the nature of connecting sites. If we pass from the nature of place as the *genius loci* in classical urban theory to one of flows – the *space of flows* in the latest urban theory – the essential nature of the city is now contractual. Contracts are texts, objects, products written or tacitly produced by interlinked actors. In the reticular, but far from flat, world of today, the essence of society is to be a network where nodes are intertwined but many elements are not (yet) connected. As Latour puts it, a network is made up firstly of voids (Latour 2005). The power of connection in all its constitutive forms (technical, functional, expressive, political and cultural) is the essential nature – the real ontology – of cities (Tilly 1974).

The city-by-projects

By 'city-by-projects' we mean that urban representation is redefined by contractual interactions taking place in the city, following a path based on the idea of the project (Pinson 2009). We are emerging from a crisis in the planning models of modern rationality, when we thought that we would be able to launch a network in the future and then turn back from there to see what needs to be done today. This planning dimension has deteriorated over the past few decades. However, a dimension for city projects can still be conceived, but of what type? This is the theme of strategic planning.

Global transformation of the urban world 27

It concerns cities which appear able to withstand the impact of standardization, the 'generic city' that tends to trivialize any form of construction, any form of urban thought. It is basically the city that manages to become a reflexive and self-reflexive structure. But how do you make a city reflexive? During the past 20 years in Europe, many city-regions have attempted to adopt strategic plans (Salet et al. 2003). These attempts at creating strategies and structures and installing deliberative democracy may involve groups and interests not normally participating in public decision-making, or else subjected to the decisions of technocratic elites, attaining new horizons in terms of planning capability. But the idea that we can build future scenarios and then adjust them back to the present is substituted by more process-oriented policies. Instead of elaborating traditional directive plans, the new strategic plans try to render social actors capable of effectively interacting and self-regulating.

In so enabling direction, more recent European trends towards 'smart cities' are expected to introduce new contractual mechanisms: for example, subsidizing pre-investment proposals for new activities that relate to the economy of the city (smart urban technologies for an ageing population, green energy and new environmentally friendly production, venture capital for start-ups, education and support services). We need to rethink the project from a different perspective, one of self-sufficiency: a project that does not have an 'ex-ante' scenario to be fulfilled, but that is self-sustaining – what Albert Hirschman in the past and Dani Rodrik (2004) today call 'self-discovery', a journey in development where entrepreneurs discover that certain goods and technologies, already well established on the world market, can be adapted and produced locally at competitive costs.

How does a city, an urban economy on its own, effectively participate in the processes of distribution and growth in a global context? Cities can reassemble and connect with larger systems. Here reference is to the literature dealing with clusters. It is a theme that originates from industrial economics, but one that is also very relevant for those concerned with cities. Territorial clusters may be established that do not have *matryoshka*-like (state, region, province, municipality) dimensions: in fact, those structures do not mean anything in the era of the space of flows, although they are still our institutions. The idea is that territorial systems can reassemble themselves using cluster logic, contained in a word that descriptively circulates in S. Sassen's book (2006): assemblages. We should consider the present transformation processes as assemblages that border on the global and the local dimensions. Actually, they are neither local nor global, but part of both. An author who writes at a more theoretical level about 'reassembling the social' is Bruno Latour (2005). What does social re-assemblage mean? Latour emphasizes the importance of rethinking society in general as a set of local sites. Latour, a sociologist of science, has taken a direct interest in the theme of the city (especially Paris, an 'invisible city' made possible by the working of invisible forces and objects). He writes of local sites where so-called global structures

28 *Global transformation of the urban world*

have been devised. His is thus a criticism of the idea of global uniformity. Here the importance of local sites is highlighted. According to Latour, the macro and micro scale, the larger and smaller scale, no longer exist. Even the macro site connects with other micro sites. Both sites are actually formed in the same way, even if we think in terms of one of them being macro and the other micro. The scale, this dimension we call scale, is today predefined: a macro or micro, global or local scale. Latour states: no, the scale is defined by those who enact the scale and the space; they contextualize each other, thanks to the transport of specific traces which travel by specific vehicles. This metaphor is rather close to the concept of network, but with an important difference. Latour proposes to disassemble the social, starting from localization of the global. The global is a modelled terrain where tangles and hybrids will form. And departing from this localization of the global there will be a redistribution of the local. The local structure in reality has also been pre-formed by other elements: sites, times, actors. So in the end, rather than starting off from the place itself, we start off from the circulation between places. We are not starting from the place, from *this* place, but we start from the fact that this place has been made possible because it has been pre-formed by a number of other places, sites, actors, moments that have formed it: what we see is not so much the place itself in its definition, but the systems of movement between places that have made each of these places possible.

The result is a proposal which overturns discussion on the construction of society, beginning from the idea of assemblage. Assemblages not only of territories, but of policies too: variable packages which are congruent with differentiated development strategies regarding local opportunities and constraints.[4] Here, I believe, lies a significant question to consider when talking about cities, namely whether the city can still be a point from which we reassemble society, abandoning the *matryoshka*-like system of institutions contained within each other, and restructuring new forms of society, interaction and cities. And whether we can bridge the gap between cities established by institutions, and cities defined by functions: the former ever more distant from the latter (Calafati and Veneri 2010).[5] The scale of the city – medium, large or small – does not mean much if compared to the system of flows which become a major factor for territorial development.

The relational-contract city: Empirical evidence from the European city system

The new direction of research proposed here concerns the connectivity of cities and the social systems they represent. We have been looking too long at cities as stocks of resources, comparing their relative importance in terms of endowment of economic, social and cultural capital. We must now look at cities as connectivity nodes within networks of tendentially global relations. Following this approach, which is inspired by the lesson given by

Global transformation of the urban world   29

Jane Jacobs, the world is represented as a 'blizzard of transactions', and this representation of flows enables us to go beyond the old image of the world as a mosaic of local systems. Peter Taylor (2004) has studied the network connectivity between global cities starting from the advanced services (accounting, advertising, finance, insurance, legal and consulting) of 100 global companies located in 315 cities around the world, all exposed to globalization whether in central, peripheral or semi-peripheral locations. The degree to which one city is connected to another, and to which city, is the dependent variable of the research study. This approach takes in three network levels: a net level of interacting cities in the world economy; a nodal level of cities through which the network is produced; and a sub-nodal level of advanced service producer firms which are the network-makers.

In the case of Italy, what emerges from Taylor's research is the strong position of Milan, which had been 8th (now it is 13th, behind Mumbai) in world cities in terms of global network connectivity, revealing an economic strength that is disproportionate to its weak capacity of metropolitan governance (Gualini 2003). By contrast, Rome was only 53rd (now it is 46th), confirming its identity as a political and religious capital lacking a strong global economic role. The map based on interfirm relations also shows that Milan is more interconnected to North America and Asia than to other European cities.

On this basis, each global city-region develops a 'domestic policy' and a 'foreign policy' through alliances with, and not only in competition with, other global city-regions: we may well be seeing a future Milan-Turin global city-region.[6] Or Barcelona-Valencia-Balearic Islands. Or Marseille-Provence. Linked together, these global city-regions form a new platform structuring the main South European axis and corridor. Potential also lies in Paris and Brussels, the Baltic region, the Danubian region and so on. A new economic and political geography of Europe would emerge based on cross-border, transnational alliances. When it comes to global city-regions, policy makers have yet to understand the field of multilevel governance from European to urban levels. Yet in other cases, alliances among cities are not based on geographical proximity, but on strategic global influence: London-New York-Washington, Beijing-Shanghai-Hong Kong (Taylor 2013).

Thus the relational-contractual capacity of the city is the key element to develop on the analytical front. It is a question of understanding the entirety of the contractual relations of the city: 'many-to-many' contracts, both formal and informal, both explicit and implicit, as well as complete or incomplete. In economic language (following Oliver E. Williamson) we speak of 'relational contracts', in which the identity of the contracting parties is crucial, the contract is open-ended, the documents are records to renegotiate the agreement, and conflict resolution is based on social norms and codes of shared conduct. In philosophical language, they correspond to 'strange community contracts' (Jacques Derrida) in which the different participants involved know that their business is necessarily incomplete and unfinished

30 *Global transformation of the urban world*

and that, like the Tower of Babel prototype, the city is an incomplete, never-ending construction.

These contractual relationships are not typical only of global city-regions, although here they are of the utmost importance. Medium and small cities can also be interpreted in a relational-contractual approach.[7] Indeed, both large and small cities can be studied as complete local societies, recalling Simmel's (2011) lesson that the whole is a fragment, but the fragment can also be a whole.

The contractual relationships to investigate here are more diverse than those between the nation-state and the city. Moreover, it is not a question of horizontal relationships (between local participants and community-based) versus vertical relationships (between the central state and the city). These two dimensions are intertwined and are together present in forms which are often mixed, trans-local and transnational (Grote 2012).

If developed to their potential, these trans-local and transnational contractual relations can free the city from what Charles Tilly (1992) has called 'the prison of the nation-state'. Tilly is the leading author (along with S. Rokkan) on European nation-state building. Historically, the state has provided the ground for enlarging market forces. In contemporary globalization, observing the dynamic relationships among cities of large transnational areas will open the way to create new contractual economic and power relationships. It will also enable us to revise our understanding of the logics of influence, attraction and competition that guide the behaviour of local participants and, to some extent, on a different scale, the behaviour of the global players who operate on that territory.

The contractual networks to investigate are represented by businesses, groups, associations, supply chains, institutions, specialized centres, universities, charities, churches and so on. The flows that feed these contractual networks are measurable flows of people, knowledge, material and immaterial resources, and services for profit and non-profit. Contractual relationships between firms, shared research projects, industrial co-design and contracts that feed the knowledge flows can all be analyzed and represented. Examples include flows of human capital in training driven by contracts between European and Chinese universities, knowledge flows through cooperation agreements established between industrial research centres located in different regions and countries, and global immigration flows linking different countries. In these studies, we discover the power of the appeal of and relations between places, often difficult to measure. Prevalently qualitative research can then increase our understanding of the interaction mechanisms between the actors in these relations. The importance of localization can also be measured by the presence of actors in networks that have been defined, referring to the Italian industrial districts, as new 'hybrid collectives' (Parolin and Mattozzi 2013). Many actors are involved in the creation of new industrial objects as a result of the assemblages of practical knowledge and heterogeneous theories, and thus contribute to the

Global transformation of the urban world   31

development of a new product: the networks are made up of designers, market analysts, vendors and buyers, developers from research and development departments, craftsmen and suppliers. These hybrid collectives are interrelated and in constant interaction, both local and remote.

But we could also consider illegal flows of capital, goods and persons involved in globalization processes: from drugs to tax havens or the illegal transport of people from remote regions to central cities. This relational basis helps us towards a clearer understanding of the geography of territorial governance, and the players involved. In this dimension the flows are easier to understand and measure than the stocks, building illustrative models similar to those guiding the most recent research on networks in other disciplines. These studies demonstrate that a wide variety of network systems feature a shared law: that of being 'scale-free' (Barabási and Bonabeau 2003). Nodes emerge that are infinitely more connectable than others, veritable 'hubs'. Without actually translating computer science research into social sciences, we may find similarities that help us better understand how cities work globally. City networks in this perspective are networks of nodes that have different roles and varying importance. Only a few nodes have sufficient critical mass and endowment of territorial capital (understood as a set of tangible and intangible assets) to maintain global relations or develop extensive networks. Other nodes are undersized or shrinking. These latter nodes, however, can relate to the former, exchanging resources with them on a more limited scale, but going further thanks to the main node represented by the 'hub'-city. The contracts between hubs and nodes are worth studying. The hub-city has various functions that favour the exchange of resources: they can be related to accessibility (road and rail, airport and port connections), receptivity (universities or specialized centres attracting students, tourists, visitors attracted by trade fairs, exhibitions and events) and international openness (various services). The combination between these different dimensions is what counts: the first places among the top European cities are held by those that have managed to combine a range of infrastructural, integrated transport services and attractiveness for businesses and individuals. In this respect, the resources of creative activities and services different local labour systems offer can also be compared. But we must look further, studying the relationships between different nodes, or possibly the lack thereof.

In logistic terms, cities are 'gates', nodes of 'extended gates' which include ports and inland terminals. Similar flow analysis is to be made for airports, tourism, visits to cultural heritage sites, universities and the like. In cognitive terms, cities can participate in smart grids – offering a way to investigate the networks between and among companies. These networks are expressed in measurable relationships-partnerships between research centres and technological innovation (departments, associations, foundations, public research institutions, business centres, private research companies and service centres) that help us understand in which direction the flows are moving on their way to other cities, regions and countries.

32   *Global transformation of the urban world*

Systematic relationships of companies with their suppliers and specialized service providers can thus be observed, along with the geographical origins of their management teams. Let us take the manufacturing companies, for example, or the service industry, beginning with the financial and credit sectors. Or business services (what is the market for these services in the presence of a developed manufacturing sector, or in the absence of one?). These are areas that are often part of multinational groups, providing an additional constituent to our understanding of extended networks in areas where businesses are located. We can also consider intermediaries and development agencies in the same framework, as they are promoted and financed by the public sector in various capacities with the normative objective of proposing corrections and reinventions, to make good use of *second-best* instruments instead of using *first-best* ones badly (Rodrik 2004).

Qualitative data enable us to understand the growth of localized firms, especially the SMEs: their growth may not be in size, for it may in fact also be of a relational-contractual type based on knowledge sharing via relationships of various kinds with other companies possessing complementary knowledge.[8] But these same data, referring to different contexts such as those in southern Italy or Indian cities, can lead to a better understanding of the dimension of *crony capitalism*, the contiguity between the economy and politics and the capture of the public sector by interest groups. On a normative ground, in order to counteract these degenerative contractual phenomena, a central-local industrial policy could work as a coordination tool for stimulating investment and socializing risks through appropriate safeguards.

The enterprises involved in new information and communication technologies play a particularly important role in the economy of flows. These concerns are by their very nature network-linked. The cities of southern Europe clearly suffer from insufficient growth in this sector, and this imbalance urgently calls for North–South re-equilibrium. This is also true in terms of global North–South relations.

The studies on contractual relations and flows will provide us with the tools to better understand the 'stickiness' of cities or industrial districts, 'sticky places in slippery spaces', according to the geographer Ann Markusen (1996). We will gather facts to better understand the (in many ways mysterious) capacity of cities to attract (Storper and Scott 2009), create and add value (Taylor 2004). By rereading cities, territories and regions in this new relational-contractual focus, we will be able to understand and reposition each city and the networks through which it participates in the global system. Our task will then be to map out the possible, without overriding the institutional arrangements that will facilitate development – what Rodrik (2004) calls 'the multiple ways of packing these principles into institutional arrangements'. The capabilities to develop meaningful initiatives and agency amongst and between the actors mentioned here represent a central aspect. In some urban situations, such agency capacity has been more

Global transformation of the urban world   33

developed than elsewhere (as is the case of Barcelona amongst European cities), while in other cities in Southern Europe it is much less developed. In the latter cases, it may be useful to encourage the development of contractual-relational cities focusing on flows produced by exogenous shocks (direct foreign investment, tourist flows, the operations of a company-hub and so on). These flows could create opportunities for cities to react against decline, freeing up hidden local resources yet to be recognized and exploited. Yet in Asian cities, like in India, the flows of foreign investment and the physical and social infrastructures go hand in hand with increased slums and illegal or unauthorized colonies, and, like in Bangalore, technological progress doesn't alleviate urban poverty (Paul et al. 2012).

Conclusions

As a conclusion we anticipate here the most recent, and promising, theorizing on the urban as elaborated by Neil Brenner reconstructing the thinking of Lefebvre. The urban is going to substitute the city as the protagonist of contemporary society: from the city to urban society. There is a shift of social reality towards the urban, along a space-time axis from zero point (the foundation of the ancient city) to the terminal point (the planetary urbanization).

In this respect the planetary urbanization is seen as the product of forces, financial, corporate and state interests, able to extend the Haussmannization of the past cities on a global scale. What is interesting here is that we can understand almost every transformation of the Earth as a product of 'the urban': from the oceans to the deserts, from land grabbing to population expulsions, evictions, enclosures and dispossessions. Brenner and colleagues invite us to realize that a new category, operational landscapes, is able to reunite different phenomena under a common understanding of contemporary urban condition. This is a novelty, and at the same time a continuity of former theory of state spaces elaborated by Brenner a decade ago. It is towards a reconsideration of the latter that I turn now in my conclusion.

A possible limitation in Brenner's (2004) analysis is his attribution of the rescaling to the state – it is the state that articulates, uses and spaces the territories for the exercise of its power, its possibilities for manoeuvre in the face of global capitalism. In his 2004 book Brenner clearly states that:

> [I]n contrast to analyses that forecast a linear denationalization of statehood (. . .) this book underscores the continued importance of spatially reconfigured national state institutions as major animateurs and mediators of political-economic restructuring at all geographical scales. As deployed here, therefore, the notion of state rescaling is intended to characterize the transformed form of (national) statehood under contemporary capitalism, not to imply its erosion, withering, or demise.
>
> (Brenner 2004, p. 4)

34 *Global transformation of the urban world*

This is the most problematic side of Brenner's theory, as the signs of state erosion have multiplied during the last decade also due to the financial crisis of 2007–2008 and its consequences. Going more in depth theoretically, the statehood as a "precise basis for describing modern political institutions" and "the distinctive ensemble of social relations embodied in, and expressed through, state institutions" (ibid.) is clearly an obsolete conceptualization. But this is also true if we consider the new approach that Brenner follows in his 2014 book. How can the term 'statehood' in fact include within its boundaries what is imploded/exploded at planetary scale? As Brenner (2014, p. 18) explains it:

> [T]his newly consolidated, planetary formation of urbanization has blurred, even exploded, long entrenched sociospatial borders—not only between city and countryside, urban and rural, core and periphery, metropole and colony, society and nature, but also between the urban, regional, national and global scales themselves.

In such an explosion it is impossible to maintain the 'statehood' as the guiding principle, although in a policentric, multiscalar configuration. In Brenner's (2004) view, the state presents itself as the fundamental unity underlying the differences, while we see the unity as the product of the differences in long-lasting state conflictual representation processes.[9] The current crisis of statehood, global polycentrism, the multiplication of the levels and arenas of territorial governance and global disorder are all indications that we must leave the state-centric view behind us. What we see is a *polyarchic* global world where *archè* (the Greek word means both 'beginning' and 'command') no longer pertains to the nation-state.

The new polycentrism without *archè* is well covered by the French term *mondialisation*. But the world is lacking an institutional design capable of combining forces, and risks *anarchy*. We are faced with a sort of world 'without any reason' other than the permanent production of value as a sole sense-making.[10]

The proposal contained in this chapter aims at seeking out an analytical perspective other than statehood, based on its crisis and the emerging forms of 'larger spaces' (a reminder of Carl Schmitt's *Nomòs der Erde*) in the current polycentrism of networked global city-regions. These city-regions have been interpreted as networks of relational contracts. Such contracts are both formal and informal, implicit (like the 'framework programmes' between the EU, states, regions, cities and companies on such areas as knowledge, technologies and human capital), incomplete and open to the future (like the multilevel and multi-agent agreements on environmental goods and global commons). In all these contracts, we are dealing with relational contracting among urban actors (both governmental and functional), states, global networks and supranational governments. In legal terms, a trinity of world-state-localities emerges (Blank 2006). As international law scholars have put it: 'Parties negotiating international trade agreements, international tribunals arbitrating commercial disputes, United Nations' rapporteurs investigating

Global transformation of the urban world   35

compliance with human rights obligations, and international financial institutions formulating development policy have all begun to express interest in the legal relationship between cities and their national governments' (Frug and Barron 2006). The outcome could be the 'private city' as a mechanism for promoting private economic development.

In this evolving scenario, European cities, North American cities and Asian cities will be examined and compared in the following chapters. Europe's cities have had a major role in urban governance, land use laws and planning. The cities of North America have tried to emulate them, obtaining local zoning powers, but not the same planning powers as their European counterparts. The Asian cities have maintained a limited role as autonomous and self-governing entities.

The state seeks to have a voice in these urban contracts: its role is strong in Asia, weaker in Europe and North America and globally declining. Hence, in order to maintain its political power, the state is now trying to recentralize, whereas in the recent past it was required to decentralize. A comparison of 10 North American and European cities in the international marketplace (Savitch and Kantor 2004) has shown both convergence and continuing diversity among cities in their bargaining power vis-à-vis market and state powers. Some world cities, like London, New York and Tokyo, have been defined as global cities as their independence from national and regional powers and their interdependence in terms of global capitalism functions seem to prevail. Also the world cities of Asia, like Mumbai, have been attributed to the same framework: they concentrate both wealth and poverty in a contradictory manner, yet they are part of a networked global economy (Appadurai 2001). And finally, contractual powers in creating urban economic development can be, as in Shanghai, the result of a strong state power elite, a small group taking big decisions, much like the cases of Colbert's France or Prussia in past European history (Lorrain 2011). This is a new kind of pro-growth coalition, in which a small group has the cumulative power of politics, finance and industry without the limits of the market economies, namely property rights, accounting rules and a free press.

A multilevel contract theory should then take into account an extremely wide range of contractual regimes, as well as the strength and weakness of the state and local governments, global forces having variable impact on the urban, the emergence of local civicness in some emergent countries and the need to find new governance structures in areas like:

- new forms for governing the commons (water, pastures, fisheries, woods and agriculture)
- new forms of economic and functional networks (basic urban infrastructure and transport, energy, digital infrastructures and services)
- new forms of global governance (covering, for example, environmental issues, human rights, internal and foreign immigration).

36　*Global transformation of the urban world*

This need for governance is a sign of the post-national prospects that have opened up, in which the role of 'larger spaces' (supranational, macro-regional) in formation could be even more important than that of the old nation-states.

Notes

1 Data collected by Saskia Sassen in the LSE research project on 'Who owns the city?'.
2 The etymology of the word 'region' among Indo-European institutions has been studied by E. Benveniste and discussed by P. Bourdieu.
3 Since 2004, China has overtaken Romania as the leading supplier for industry in north-east Italy.
4 Rodrik (2004) explains that first-order economic principles – protection of property rights, market-based competition, appropriate incentives, sound money and so on – do not map into unique policy packages. Reformers have substantial room for creatively packaging these principles into institutional designs that are sensitive to local opportunities and constraints.
5 Calafati and Veneri (2010) distinguish between 'de jure' and 'de facto' cities, pointing out that the former type, made up of laws and institutions, is becoming ever more insufficient to include design for economy and society.
6 Soja and Kanai (2014) take a different line in representing the rise of the massive city: Urb-Italy (Milan-Rome-Turin), with a population of 46.9 million, doesn't exist in reality, it is merely an urban abstraction.
7 Tosi and Vitale point out that in the study of local communities, 'you cannot avoid studying the interaction taking place, local and translocal on multiple scales, with specific attention to the power relations which are formed' (2011, p. 23).
8 Research carried out on medium-sized companies in Northern Italy (Perulli and Pichierri eds., 2010) provides the empirical basis for these theoretical suggestions.
9 On political theory of state representation, see Hofmann (2003).
10 See Nancy (2002). The French term 'mondialisation' had already been used by Lefebvre.

2 The European urban contract

First of all, I need to choose a point of departure to define the European contract in the political realm, where citizens meet in a deliberative way. It is not the Hobbesian pact (1651), in which the multitude gives way to a sovereign state: in the meta-historical covenant Hobbes imagined, people do not constitute a political subject, but only a multitude who do not think, but follow orders. Against this view, civil society was to emerge in the 18th and following centuries. My choice, rather, falls on the Kantian text 'What is Enlightenment?' (1794), in which Kant defines it as a realm of reason, whose use must be free and public. As Foucault puts it, 'there is Enlightenment when the universal, the free, and the public uses of reason are superimposed on one another.' On one hand people use reason in the public form Kantian Enlightenment requires, while on the other individuals obey the political power as scrupulously as possible. 'Kant, in conclusion, proposes to Frederick II, in scarcely veiled terms, a sort of contract[,] what might be called the contract of rational despotism with free reason: the public and free use of autonomous reason will be the best guarantee of obedience, on condition, however, that the political principle that must be obeyed itself be in conformity with universal reason' (Foucault 1984).

Places where the contract took the urban form were cities like London, Paris and Milan in the 18th century. We can follow here Jürgen Habermas's view where 'public opinion', formed in what Hannah Arendt calls the 'public sphere' as opposed to 'private', can exercise criticism in the face of power.

The other side of the European contract derives from Max Weber's legacy. The plastic dualism of economy and society is illustrated in Weber's famous chapter on 'The city' in his major work 'Economy and society' (1958). In the Western medieval type of city, the urban contract was written by the new, emerging force of merchants and of free citizens. This is the seed of a 'politically-oriented capitalism' developing only in the West. Western rationality is based on this pact between the economic (market) and political (city, then state: both expressions of *polis*) spheres. The pact gave rise to rational capitalist enterprise, the monetary economy and the circulation of negotiable financial instruments. This link between economy and society is presented in a different way by Peter Taylor (2013), where a cityness model based on an agglomeration of the city's economies and its circulation in

38 *The European urban contract*

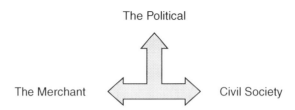

Figure 2.1 The European urban contract

a wider city network is proposed. Taylor criticizes the 'Occidental Cities' thesis of Weber, but fails to grasp the core of Weber's argument: the *plastic dualism* between economy and society and the role of the Political. 'Weber's theory relates to guardian process, but what is important is how such institutional freedom is used commercially. It is commercial autonomy that is the really important process' (Taylor 2013, p. 236).

The Political is a key partner of the urban contract, in direct relation with the Economic: they are not separate entities. The Merchant is the other fundamental partner in the urban contract. From the early stages of commercial guilds in the medieval city to contemporary forms of geo-finance in the global cities there is a strong essential continuity, but also a significant discontinuity: the guilds were encapsulated in the city and controlled through its political regulation, whereas geo-finance today is open to the globe and beyond the political control of nation-states. Even unions of nation-states, like the European Union, are unable to cope with the major problem of regaining control of the geo-financial 'anomic' will.

Hence a tripartite urban contract emerges in the European tradition: it is a pact or covenant between the Political, the Merchant and the Civil Society (see Figure 2.1). At a relatively early stage, the Political can be constituted by the local government, later by the central state, absorbing the cities' autonomy, and finally by a variable combination of the two, and the European Union in the current framework of multilevel governance. The Merchant and Civil Society were originally on the same side of the coin: the former being the market agent giving rise to the modern, rationalized economy of the cities, the latter reflecting the rising autonomy of urban society vis-à-vis political power. Later on, economic market and civil society found differentiated forms of expression and met possible forms of conflict in their (potentially rival) appropriation of the urban space. Their variable compromises and conflicts are the common ground of the European urban contract.

London

Keynotes on London between past and future

With a peak of 8.6 million people in 1939, then a decline until the 1980s and a new rise in the past three decades to 8.2 million in 2011 (+14%

between 2001 and 2011, +16% in the inner city), Greater London is the European global city, more than Paris, with a possible note: its growth was spectacular as the capital of an empire, while today it is de-territorialized and global in nature. It is more closely linked with New York than with continental Europe, while its counterparts are Tokyo and Hong Kong (a former British dominion, in fact) more than Rome or Berlin. The population growth (today's 8.2 million will probably be 9 million by 2020) is also due to a strong attraction for foreigners: 27% of the current population was born in foreign countries. Black, Asian and other minority ethnic communities are expected to grow vigorously as a result of natural growth and continued migration from overseas.

By 2036 (according to London Plan 2014), an additional 12 London boroughs are likely to have the majority of their population consisting of these groups, with Lewisham, Southwark, Tower Hamlets, Barking and Dagenham, Croydon, Ealing, Enfield, Harrow, Hillingdon, Hounslow, Redbridge and Waltham Forest joining Brent and Newham, which have had such majorities since 2001.

Immigrants no longer come from the former imperial colonies only (India, Bangladesh, China, West Indies), but increasingly from developed countries: Russia (300,000 Russians live in London), France (400,000), Italy (250,000 Italians are registered as residents in London and possibly another 250,000 are non-registered), Poland, Spain etc. (Bangladeshis number 250,000 in London). The cost of this 'implosion' is the growth in urban rent of the inner London landlords at the expense of Britain's social mix: in 2013–14 the revenue from stamp duty, a tax on houses and land purchases, increased in Kensington and Chelsea boroughs more than in all of Scotland, Wales and Northern Ireland combined.[1] Yet in the same year the Scottish referendum opted for the United Kingdom, London's capacity of attraction being a possible explanatory factor.

The 'secret' of London can be deciphered in such terms: Why has London been the only Western city to survive nation-state dominance and maintain its main attributes and autonomies over the centuries? Is there any relation with the subsequent domination of the City of London as the global financial world capital in the past two centuries? These are the questions to begin with.

The answer can be sought in the intriguing text by Thomas Hobbes, *Behemoth*, written in 1667 but remaining manuscript until 1679, according to the wishes of Charles II. It was devoted to the English Revolution of 1641. In this text, the role of the City of London as the main support of Parliament in the political conflict and civil war against Charles I is clearly evoked. The City of London (like other English trading towns) was keen to fight for a change of government following the example of the Low Countries, seeing in such change an opportunity to enhance its role. The Londoners' support to Parliament was financial and political: the City of London was the place where the House of Commons used to meet (leaving Westminster) during the conflict with the king, and the parliamentary army against the Crown was paid for by the City of London. What lay behind London's alliance

40   *The European urban contract*

with Parliament? Hobbes, a supporter of the king's sovereignty, has a clear answer: most of the subjects enriching themselves through craft and trade were men merely seeking their immediate profit. They participated in the Revolution for this purpose, and were used by Cromwell; their will was never to have a king over them, but rather to keep the king under them. When later, after taking power, Cromwell closed Parliament down, the people supported him. We can follow here the dramatic tensions between those same powers (Westminster, Whitehall, City of London) destined jointly to become the basis of modern sovereignty.

Max Weber (1958) has written that London is a special case in city oligarchy formation. Its vote was always decisive in electing the kings; London's citizens believed that the king's authority extended to their city only on the basis of their free consent. In this peculiar role the city played a decisive part: the future urban contract will be marked by its superiority. No other city in the world was to dominate its nation-state in the same way.

This is the root of London's exceptionality among European cities (Le Galès 2002). It has prevented the growth of any other regional capital in the country, centralized the economic resources, and made of the City of London a 'world city' (Hall 1984b).

The city

One of the oldest surviving traditional ceremonies still in existence today is the granting of the Freedom of the City of London. It is believed that the first Freedom was presented in 1237. The medieval term 'freeman' meant someone who was not the property of a feudal lord but enjoyed privileges such as the right to earn money and own land. Town dwellers who were protected by the charter of their town or city were often free – hence the term Freedom of the City. From the Middle Ages and the Victorian era, the Freedom was the right to trade, enabling members of a Guild or Livery to carry out their trade or craft in the square mile. A fee or fine would be charged and in return the Livery Companies would ensure that the goods and services provided would be of the highest possible standards. In 1835, the Freedom was widened to incorporate not just members of Livery Companies but also people living or working in the City or those with a strong London connection.

This paragraph[2] constitutes an interesting self-presentation of a power: London's oldest and strongest power. This is not common in urban life: often the power of a city is subject to rise and decline, or to shifting involvements of various social actors over time. In the case of London, it is the survival of the very same power through eight centuries which strikes us.

In medieval London, the guilds were at the peak of their power in the 13th century (Weber 1997). Later, in the 14th century, a separation between commercial and artisanal guilds occurred and the merchants took on the superior status of livery companies (while the poorer artisans could not afford the cost of livery). In the 16th century, the creation of a guild of merchant adventurers, engaged in foreign commerce, was first permitted. The state power was above that of the guilds' power and sought to limit it, but the guilds were represented in Parliament. The power of the guilds was based on their privilege in collecting fiscal revenue on behalf of the king – a peculiarity of the English guilds. Only those who paid taxes could be guild members. Hence the guild could give the right of citizenship to its members, assuming a 'public' role: probably the first historical case of 'private government'.

Bankers emerged from the medieval guild of goldsmiths, whose original role shifted in the 17th century to the circulation of credit within and outside London. The Bank of England owed its existence to the wealthy founders of banks like Francis Child and Richard Hoare: it exercised a monopoly granted by the Political power. A merchant adventurer like William Paterson (Scottish) and Puritan bankers like Child and Hoare joined together in the venture. It was a compromise, according to Max Weber (1922), between irrational and rational capitalism. Hence it was not so much a voluntary association of merchants as a political enterprise to finance war: its function was to stabilize the economy and at the same time to favour financial speculation.[3]

From the very outset, the goldsmiths' and then bankers' power was exceptional, unparalleled in the rest of the world. Originally bankers, like many others in the Middle Ages, they financed the wars of the Stuarts and of Oliver Cromwell as well, and their financial circuits grew. The bankruptcy of the state (1672) made it necessary to create a monopoly bank to stabilize the fluctuations of the economic cycle, and the Bank of England was established (1694). It was a political act through which the creditors giving money to the state were exempted from tributes and associated as a company with privileges guaranteed by the state. Opposition by both the Tories and the Whigs meant that a private autonomous company had to be created instead of a state bank. The many enemies of the Bank like the Tories and Whigs, the goldsmiths and the country gentry, all losers in the game, obtained no more than the creation of a private company rather than a state bank (but the state absorbed the whole stock capital). The power of the Bank resting on the commerce of bills of exchange and issue of bank notes was potentially enormous. Such is the basis of the dominance of private finance in the urban contract.

In the 18th century, the jobbers, the market makers on the Stock Exchange, were active in the Change Alley coffee shops, where 'public opinion' (according to Habermas) was born too. In the coffee shops, the newspapers circulated, forming public opinion: the first daily newspaper was published in 1702 and by the end of the century, 278 daily newspapers were circulating in London. Most of them were printed in the same place, Fleet Street, for centuries. In 1773, the New Jonathan, a coffee shop, was called the Stock Exchange for the first time. Here the living marriage between private interests and public good, evoked by Adam Smith, was first experimented.

42   The European urban contract

It was later, in the 19th century, that the global role of London emerged, led by a cosmopolitan elite where oligarchies, both economic and political, merged and were able to guide the world economy and govern its turbulences until the First World War and the crisis of 1929. This oligarchic power came to be transmitted through Westminster, the City, Whitehall, the Bank of England and the Stock Exchange (Berta 2014). No comparison is possible with any other world capital.

Interpreting the urban form: City of opposites

West and east

Taking the Great Fire of 1666 as the starting point of modern London's expansion, we can see how different urban development was in the west and east ends of the city. The western boroughs were rebuilt on the strength of the urban rent extracted by landlords, whose land was divided and developed by builders, then rented or sold: within 99 years the building became property of the lords. This mechanism was accurately planned and regulated through acts of Parliament. It was, however, the cycle of commerce, not the ambitions of legislators and administrators, that led the process. London's major buildings, from the Royal Exchange to St Paul's Cathedral, were rebuilt 'for eternity', as Christopher Wren, the leading figure behind the rebuilding of London after the Fire, expressed his architectural dream. In the western part of London rebuilt by developers like Nicholas Barbon, new streets were created and merchants and businessmen quickly moved there, abandoning the unhealthy eastern part.

By contrast, the eastern boroughs grew in an unregulated, haphazard way, based on the ancient statutes of feudal origin whose main characteristic was to limit the land concession to 31 years. Growth was therefore unplanned and underdeveloped. This very same divide was destined to become permanent in the following age of suburban expansion, lasting to the present day. If we consider the value added as indicator of wealth and quality of jobs, we have a very clear picture of London's divide (see Table 2.1).

Other maps showing the contrasts, like the maps of urban poverty and wealth, could well explain such continuity. In London's west and

Table 2.1 London value added per capita by territorial scale (1995 = 100)

Greater London	157.4
Inner London	250.6
Inner London – West	461.9
Inner London – East	129.1
Outer London	99.4
South-East	116.0

Source: A. Freeman, *London: Europe's New York*, GLA Economics, 2003.

south, the poor are highly concentrated: 23% of the working population and 41% of the children live below the poverty line. Deprivation is concentrated among the black, Asian and ethnic minorities, as well as disabled Londoners. Across London, the median house price rose 61% in 10 years (2003–13). In 2011, 786,000 households in London lived in social rented housing, 24% of the total (down from 26% in 2001). Social housing is the most unevenly distributed of the tenures; since 2001, the proportion of households in social housing has fallen in most parts of London. And social housing is now insufficient and under attack. Reforms introduced by the government have relaxed the requirement of social landlords to offer lifetime tenancies and allow for shorter fixed-term tenancies to be offered to new tenants. The government has also introduced the new Affordable Rent product, which allows social landlords the flexibility to charge rents of up to 80% of local market levels on both new social homes and a proportion of re-lets, as part of an agreement to build new homes. As the Community and Children's Services Committee documented in 2014, such agreements relate to the receipt of a development grant from the Greater London Authority. The City of London is not a recipient of such funding and therefore is not obliged to consider converting its existing stock upon re-let to Affordable Rent.

As a result, as acknowledged in the London Plan, London is an increasingly polarized city. On one hand, it has seen growth in earnings, with significant rises in both the numbers of high salary earners and in the amount they earn, leaving those on low incomes or without employment further and further behind. This polarization is associated with a range of social problems: ill health, substance abuse and crime, but firstly unemployment. Less than 40% of social tenants are employed; the majority is unemployed, retired or inactive. There are clearly spatial concentrations of disadvantage, especially in inner north-east London, from Tower Hamlets northwards through Hackney to Haringey and eastern Enfield, eastwards to Newham and Waltham Forest and on both sides of the Thames to Barking and Dagenham and the southern part of Havering, and, finally, from Lambeth and Southwark eastwards to Bexley. There is another cluster in west London, around Park Royal (London Plan 2014).

In response to the need to reduce polarization, the 2012 Olympic Games chose to invest in the eastern part of London. The London Legacy Development Corporation created to manage the post-Olympic phase is carrying out and refining the mayor's original proposals through a local plan, presented as the mayor's highest regeneration priority for the coming period. The unique status of east London, and the recognition arising from association with the Games, will be used, according to the Plan, 'to effect a positive, sustainable and fully accessible economic, social and environmental transformation for one of the most diverse – yet deprived – parts of London' (London Plan 2014).

44 *The European urban contract*

Inner and outer

Probably the most important urban plan in modern urban history, Patrick Abercrombie's Greater London Plan (1944) was at the same time the last: subsequently urban planning ended up as a doubtful, repetitive exercise, the utility of which is decreasing and ultimately becoming negligible. At the core of the London Plan is the design of four rings and a railways network and communication arterial road system linking the outer and the inner cities. The Four Rings concentrically designed are (from outer to inner): an outer country Ring, a green belt Ring, a suburban Ring and an inner urban Ring, including the Administrative County of London. In the outer ring, Garden Cities are proposed as sites for eight to 10 New Satellite Towns.

The idea of creating a green belt around the city, able to protect it and drive any future expansion outside the 'buffer zone' towards 'slumless and smokeless' new towns, is the direct heritage of Ebenezer Howard's Garden Cities of Tomorrow (1902). But it was also the last effort to make a utopia possible through design. In this sense, it represents the heritage of the entire urban culture of Europe, from Plato to Alberti. No other European city has done so well. Outside Europe, however, other cities have followed the green belt model: Toronto and its wider Ontario city-region among them.

The London urban contract was drafted by the central government and came into force through legislation (in 1955: any urban development within a band of eight miles around metropolitan London was forbidden). The central government led the process of building successfully 28 new towns (11 in the London belt) through development corporations. The result was a strong, state-driven decentralization process which enmeshed with much stronger spontaneous decentralization trends lasting until the 1980s. A new centripetal movement then set with reinvestment in London's central areas and in the west of the region (Reading, Heathrow and the M4 corridor).

The attempts (by the government and business) to reduce the green belt in recent years have not succeeded. Urban expansion has been drawn to other locations in the south-east, and the railway system opened the way to a model of intensive commuting. Central London grew in the number of inhabitants (1.5 million more in the past two decades), regaining the 2 million inhabitants lost in the 1961–81 decades; but the past loss was a statistical illusion, as London had grown in other ways in the outer metropolitan region in those same years. Post-war growth saw a new sort of London appearing – an increasingly polycentric city-region responding to the decline of the inner city (Hall 1984b). Now the centripetal forces are regaining dominance and London is responding with increasing population density in brownfield areas, where industrial-era factories and industrial services used to be located. However, the growing demand and the rise of housing prices risk creating a 'reverse brain drain': employees ready to leave London due to lack of affordable housing are estimated at 40% of the total, and 50% of the younger people (London First & Turner and Townsend 2014).

The European urban contract 45

The office metropolis

More than 1 million employees in finance, banks and insurance (400,000 in the City alone) and one-third of world financial negotiations are key figures of London today. After city expansion and the big bang of the London Stock Exchange in 1984, millions of square metres for office buildings were created. The London Plan Annual Monitoring Report shows the office starts and permits over recent decades. This is a crucial strategic indicator, as the London Plan has to ensure sufficient development capacity in the office market. Office space in London is not just more expensive than anywhere else in the world, but it is three times as expensive as the next most expensive city in Europe, Paris. This is also due to planning regulations and restrictions which make the regulatory 'shadow tax' in London much higher than in Paris or Milan (Cheshire and Hilber 2008). The London Plan is a tool with the strategic function of enabling London to remain the global city attracting business from all over the world that it has been for centuries.

The cycle of office starts and permits clearly follows the business cycle. From the resurgence of London in the 1980s after the crisis decade of the 1970s, the cycle of office starts grew up to a peak in 1993, then a slump, and again a peak in 2004, when 2.1 million square metres were commenced. A new downturn occurred in the years following the 2008–9 financial crisis and credit crunch. By volume, in the booming years the starts were concentrated in the City, where around 80% of construction was speculative.[4] The cycle is apparently endless.

Following Kantor and colleagues (2012), the rise of employment in business services in the 1971–2006 period was accompanied by a fairly static trend in financial services; on the contrary, tourism, media and cultural industries increased employment. However, from the regional, subregional and local gross value added (GVA) estimates for London in the 1997–2012 period a quite different picture emerges. In 2011, a fifth of London's output was generated by the financial and insurance industry (£60 billion). The value of this industry has grown by 159% since 1997, the second fastest rate for any industry in London, only surpassed by real estate activities, which have grown by 194% since 1997 and accounted for 10% of London's GVA in 2011. If we add construction industry growing from 4% of London's GVA in 1997 to 5% in 2011, we can conclude that finance+insurance (20%) and real estate+construction (15%) are the leading aggregate sectors in terms of gross value added, followed by information and communication technologies (ICT) and professional, scientific and technical activities, both accounting for 12% of London's gross value added (GLA Economics 2014).

We can therefore interpret the London urban contract as a tripartite pact between the financial sector and the real estate sector, with the London government in the role of implementation agency directly involved. It is true that local government in the British system acts as an agent of the central government, but in the case of London the newly created metropolitan

46   *The European urban contract*

government in 2000 (the Greater London Council and Greater London Authority) added a new tier to the urban governance system. The GLA has become a place of negotiation between the financial business sector and the mayor of London (GLA 2014). The main GLA goal is improving London's transport system to keep up with further housing expansion needs. Crossrail will connect the City, Canary Wharf, the West End and Heathrow Airport to residential areas and regional centres both east and west of London. The first services are expected to start in 2016, trains will begin running through the new core tunnel in 2018, and the whole network will be up and running in 2019. Crossrail will add 10% to London's rail-based public transport capacity, and around 230 million journeys a year by 2030. But the project will need private capital. 'The city is coming full circle,' suggests London's deputy mayor for transport: back to a model of development based on the 1900–7 expansion of the Tube. In those years, private capitalists like Charles Yerkes and John Pierpont Morgan fought to invest in London's Underground expansion. New Tube lines to Golders Green and Archway, and Great Northern, Piccadilly and Brompton opened in the space of a few years, and urban expansion and land values exploded. In 1903, Yerkel asserted: 'Cheap fares to the suburban districts is the only thing that will solve the problem of overcrowding, and other Londons must be built up on the outskirts of London.'[5] We are apparently turning to the same model of private finance. Moreover, London at the lower, local level is governed by 32 boroughs and the City Corporation, running the City of London area coterminous with the business district. It is clearly a 'special' government expression of business, now as in the past.

Private business initiative on London has since 1992 been coordinated by London First, a lobby including companies like British Airways, the Airport Authority, British Telecom, the internationally oriented business services and financial firms and the international developers involved in the biggest urban projects (Kantor et al. 2012, p. 68). Interestingly, the central government merged its own London Forum, created to promote the capital city, into London First.

The London Plan as a quasi-statutory instrument, and the strengthening of the mayor of London's role, created a new balance between central and local powers; however, the formulation and implementation of London's strategies for maintaining and enhancing its 'world city' role have been constantly influenced by private business (see Figure 2.2).

London First partners and members – as the organization declares – comprise the capital's leading businesses in key sectors such as property, infrastructure, transport, professional services, finance, retail, telecoms, media, technology, hospitality and creative industries, universities and higher education colleges. This wide sectoral coverage enables London First to represent them across a spectrum of issues, all under the shared goal of maintaining London's global competitiveness. London First aims at ensuring that national and London decision-making and implementation

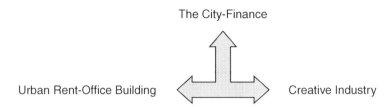

Figure 2.2 The London urban contract

are business-friendly and help maintain the capital's competitive edge. They organize campaigns, often long-term, mobilizing the expertise and experience of members to meet, debate with and persuade decision-makers. The work is done through briefings, publications and events programmes, from small-scale policy-based meetings with key ministers and officials to large-scale networking events.

The creative industry

The third party in the London urban contract is in our view the creative class, a mix of social actors from the creative professions to the community institutions able to incubate and reproduce these same social actors. In his *Creative Industry* (2002), R. Caves defines it as a contract between art and commerce. The contract is based on uncertainty (nobody knows), permanent change of crew, time factors influencing the contractual arrangements between art and commerce, artists and businesspeople. Hence the urban contract is certainly a form of insurance. Such is the contract in its economic terms, but in more comprehensive, sociological and cultural terms, the contract is between the city and the spiritual life of its inhabitants, as Georg Simmel (1903) has made clear. The endless consumption of nervous energies, the production of styles and fashions, types and ways of life is the basis of the urban contract between the city and its creative class. The theory of consumption classes and innovative networks merges in the urban fabric.

In his comprehensive work on the UK creative industry (2010), A. Freeman estimates that creative economy employment is a highly significant and growing component of the workforce as a whole, accounting for 8.7% of it in 2010. His estimates also confirm that the majority of creative workers are employed outside the creative industries in the wider creative economy; this part of the creative workforce has grown particularly vigorously, rising by 10.6% between 2004 and 2010. His work shows that the creative industries do not wholly or even mainly rely on traditional content or ICT activities alone. Rather, a new economic phenomenon has emerged characterized by a parallel application, within single industries, of ICT and other creative skills together.

This strongly suggests that any attempt to separate ICT from other creative work or to reduce the creative industries either to an offshoot of content

48   *The European urban contract*

production, or for that matter a branch of the software industry, will not succeed. On this alternative scenario, the software-related industries still contribute 213,000 jobs to the creative industries. The non-software creative industries are also very important employers of ICT labour.

Freeman estimates a growth in creative economy employment, between 2004 and 2010, of 6.8% – more than five times the growth rate of the non-creative workforce, measured on a comparable basis over the same period. In 2010, almost 2.5 million were employed in the United Kingdom's creative economy, 1.3 million of which worked in the creative industries: of these, 32% in London and 57% in south-east England.

Interpreting the contract form: The Greater London Plan

The urban contract is a strategy of fulfilment of public and private visions and interests in reciprocal tension, and giving place to variable compromises. The chief architect of London's mayor, Lord Richard Rogers, has described this strategy in terms of: compact city, return of population to urban centres, public transport, buildings attractive for families and the middle classes, and 50% of the new residential constructions reserved for affordable housing. The big businesses united in London First have referred to this strategy in terms of engaging the business community in promoting and improving London, using the vision, energy and skills of business leaders to shape and secure the capital's future. According to London First, given the long-term under-supply of housing in London, and the scale of current and future demand, the redevelopment of brownfield land alone is unlikely to meet the housing needs. Many of the brownfield sites are complex, poorly connected and will be costly to develop. There are also inevitably limits to the extent to which densities can be increased. Therefore, London First concludes, infrastructure strategy must explore the scope for urban extensions, supported by improved transport connections. If London is to build 50,000–60,000 new homes a year, some recommendations follow: 1) improving housing delivery through targets, incentives and planning reforms; 2) getting more public-sector land into development; 3) increasing housing density and building new suburbs; and 4) looking at new ways to build more homes. To achieve such increases in housing supply, the Greater London Authority (GLA), London First concludes, will have to strengthen its own ability to facilitate the delivery of new housing. The GLA is invited to enhance its capacity by bringing together its housing functions in a new housing delivery body – Housing for London – to facilitate the delivery of large-scale new house building in the capital. This new body should in the first instance work with and support the local authorities, but London First assumes that it should be willing and able to take over additional powers and responsibilities from boroughs where they are proving a barrier to delivery.

It is clear that the urban contract proposed by London First should develop new suburbs and introduce agency powers going beyond the boroughs.

Borough autonomy means fragmentation and disconnectedness, and in some cases mismanagement of public funds.

According to London First, in terms of business, a decidedly positive case can be made for the infrastructure projects needed in the capital, which will generate significant additional value for London and the United Kingdom as a whole (this is, of course, a matter of disagreement as far as northern cities are concerned). In the long run, investment in infrastructure will often pay for itself through better services for consumers, higher productivity, greater revenues to business, increased land and property values and increased tax receipts for the government.

But what about the financing of these projects? Here the business lobby openly urges fiscal devolution in favour of the London government. The first best solution would be for the London government to retain a greater proportion of the taxes raised locally than it does at present. Hence London First supports the mayor's bid for fiscal devolution to London (to both the GLA and the London boroughs). This would provide greater scope – London First continues – to borrow prudently and give the capital city greater control over its own infrastructure investments. Taking such an approach would, London First believes, lead to more timely infrastructure investment and enable stronger economic growth – and thus greater tax and other revenues – than would otherwise be the case. Fiscal devolution should not be seen as a zero-sum game for the country as a whole.

The business lobby goes on to indicate the mechanism deemed most appropriate for such a devolution policy. Recent *City Deals* have included a 'payment by results' mechanism whereby the local area will be able to keep a larger proportion of the proceeds of economic growth generated in, and around, the city than otherwise would be the case. Pending more widespread fiscal devolution, London should explore similar models for the capital.

Even with progress in devolution a funding gap will remain, according to London First. Therefore a long-term settlement with the government will still be needed, supplemented by a diverse range of other funding mechanisms, London First observes. Ironically to an observer's eye, the business lobby notes that the GLA's plan identifies a wide range of options, many of which are, unsurprisingly, similar to those outlined in the London First report on infrastructure 'Crossrail 2' funding options.

Particular attention is currently being paid to the impact that new infrastructure, particularly transport infrastructure, can have on property values in those areas it serves (see Figure 2.3). As London First's earlier report highlighted, better integration of transport and housing planning is suggested to help address London's housing shortage, and also generate additional value, a proportion of which could be captured to help pay for essential new infrastructure.

London First announces that it is undertaking further work on the potential contribution that various funding options might make towards an overall infrastructure plan and fund for the capital. One idea worth further

50 *The European urban contract*

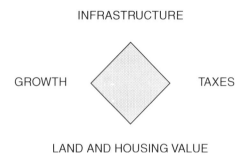

Figure 2.3 The London value diamond

consideration is whether London might create its own infrastructure fund or funds to cover those projects identified as priorities within the infrastructure plan.

The overall ideology of London First is that Londoners and London businesses will equally benefit from additional infrastructure investment and will have to pay more in the short to medium term through bills, user charges or fares, taxes or other means. Evidently, business and the middle classes, the working class, the poor and other population groups represent different 'rights to the city'. London First concludes that the potential impact of additional charges and taxes on London's overall competitiveness must be taken into account in constructing any funding package.

The task of London First is not only to indicate choices to the public government, but also to criticize its management practices when the case arises. Therefore London First addresses the need for the GLA and its agencies to continue to enhance its capability to plan, manage, fund and deliver infrastructure in London, given the scale of increased investment required. Londoners, the business lobby continues, need to be confident that they can see the distribution of costs and benefits of the programme as a whole, and that infrastructure is being managed and delivered efficiently. This is particularly critical if they are being asked to contribute more. This is not to criticize the GLA or its agencies, London First declares, but rather to make the point that meeting future challenges will mean looking beyond the ways currently followed by the London government.

In the light of the above, it is clear from this statement that London First believes it is acting as the representative agent of 'the Londoners', not only of its business community. Some questions arise. Is it legitimate? If so, where does the legitimation come from? Is London First the functional equivalent of civil society as a whole?

London First goes further, indicating the best way suggested. The delivery board the London Plan proposes is welcome and should help ensure third parties with a stake in London's infrastructure collaborate more effectively on a host of issues, but it should not be seen as the only or even the main solution. Tailored solutions, London First suggests, are likely to be needed for individual sectors – as with the proposed new housing delivery body recommended earlier – supported by enhanced cross-disciplinary planning and delivery expertise. Even the technical details are defined and proposed by the London First-agent, but it is not clear whether the London government is its principal.

The programme needs performance measures indicating the extent to which necessary outcomes are being delivered. This is particularly important given the constraints on London's ability to make the necessary investment. An annual progress report on the London infrastructure plan is called for as one good way to enhance transparency and accountability around delivery.

London First is particularly interested in privately provided infrastructure. In fact, while most of London's transport infrastructure is provided by the public sector, airport infrastructure is generally provided by the private sector. The key issue in aviation – London First asserts – is the need for an urgent, strategic government policy decision on the location of additional runway capacity in the south-east, which is critical to supporting London's status as a global hub.

London First therefore urges the GLA to plan on the basis that an additional runway be built at either Heathrow or Gatwick, led by the private sector. The business lobby encourages the GLA in its plan to follow the Airports Commission's analysis as to the likely need and cost of any associated surface transport infrastructure. This, London First holds, would greatly strengthen the plan's overall credibility, and does not mean that the GLA will no longer argue for a longer-term airport development strategy elsewhere. In parallel to supporting the Airports Commission process through to implementation, the GLA should continue to support efforts to make full and efficient use of all the south-eastern airports, particularly by enhancing the capacity and resilience of their transport links.

This part of the city strategy is highly sensitive to conflict of interests. Clearly London First has a stake, being a lobby that includes the main aviation companies and airports, but precisely for this reason it should avoid 'giving rules to the regulator'.

Another strategic sector for business is utility and digital infrastructure. Most of London's utility and digital infrastructure is provided by the private sector, paid for by customers through bills. Where there are natural monopolies, companies are regulated by independent economic regulators to ensure efficiency and allow them to recover their costs. Broadly speaking, this model has proven extremely stable and has succeeded in attracting significant private investment, while improving efficiency and driving down costs. However, according to London First, it has not always been as effective in ensuring adequate quality or indeed the timely provision of new infrastructure to support future growth.

52 The European urban contract

Therefore London First identified the following detailed areas of priority focus for the GLA: 1) Utility regulators should have a statutory duty to take account of the mayor's statutory transport, planning, housing and economic development strategies when formulating their periodic review conclusions. 2) In the energy sector, transition to a low carbon society will call for investment in electricity transmission and distribution to provide greater headroom for growth and resilience, and in gas distribution to replace ageing Victorian infrastructure. 3) The Plan suggests additional energy infrastructure that may not be economically viable – for example around decentralized energy generation; investment in such infrastructure should only be encouraged where the economic benefits are clear. 4) In the water sector, the Plan appears overly reliant on demand management measures, and neglects consideration of new infrastructure. The Plan should reflect the critical need for investment in a major new source of water to support population growth and improve the resilience of London's water supply to the small but significant risk of emergency water use restrictions in periods of extended drought. 5) In the waste sector, the London Plan sets out a clear and credible long-term strategy based on reducing, reusing and recycling waste, alongside managing as much of the capital's waste within its boundaries as practicable. The problem is not with this strategy, which commands broad support, but with its implementation, which is being undermined by a fragmented and inconsistent approach across London's boroughs. In particular, given the ongoing reluctance of the boroughs to allow the development of essential new waste infrastructure within their own boundaries, London First believes that there is a strong case for strengthening the mayor's planning powers over waste infrastructure. By providing greater confidence that existing policy will be supported and complied with, such a move could unlock significant additional private investment in new waste and recycling facilities. 6) High-quality digital infrastructure is essential for London to strengthen its position as a global leader in entrepreneurialism and innovation. Following a period of significant investment in superfast broadband in the capital, London First encourages the GLA, including through its proposed Connectivity Advisory Group, to consult broadly in identifying further actions needed to ensure ubiquitous, high-speed, secure and resilient digital connectivity in the capital, and to reduce barriers to take-up by businesses and consumers. Accommodating the scale of future growth projected in the capital is a major challenge, but it is also a great opportunity in the opinion of London First. In the long run, London First concludes, investing in additional infrastructure in London will more than pay for itself, whereas failing to invest will choke off growth and condemn London to decline. London must now plan for growth, is the resounding conclusion.

So far we have followed London First's detailed recommendations. They are based on a direct stake, and many potential conflicts of interest arise. One may wonder just how clear this is to London's public opinion, the independent media, the university community of experts, civil society in its multiple forms of voluntary associations, local communities and interest groups.

The European urban contract 53

The growth of London is the mantra of London First. But the London Plan goes in the very same direction. Projections of population growth towards 2036 are: from 8.2 million in 2011 to 9.2 million in 2021, 9.5 million in 2026, 9.8 million in 2031, and 10.1 million in 2036. The financial crisis of 2008–9 has been managed successfully: London's total employment by June 2013 (5.2 million jobs) came above the previous, 2008 peak. For the future, projections suggest that the total number of jobs in London could increase from 4.68 million in 2011 to 5.8 million by 2036 (manufacturing is projected to continue to decline, while professional, real estate, scientific and technical activities could grow from 670,000 in 2011 to 1.09 million by 2036, representing 49% of the net new job growth projected over the period).

But how was the urban contract actually implemented in the recent past? London business organizations came together in the London Business Board (LBB) and developed contacts with all levels and departments of the GLA, supported by the mayor (Kantor et al. 2012, p. 80). The current implementation structures of the urban contract were represented by bimonthly meetings of the mayor with the LBB, and daily contact between business representatives and public officials. Although consultation with other social groups, voluntary associations and civil society expressions was also implemented, clearly the main policy deliberations followed the direct influence of business interests.

We can take as an example the latest (2014) consultation process on the London Plan examining the amendments proposed. About 300 documents were produced by many local and voluntary associations and boroughs, including the City of London Corporation, big companies (like British Airways), the Port and Airport Authorities, charities and universities and so on. Some boroughs declared their concern about the new housing targets in terms of ever growing density: developing 420,000 new homes in the space of a decade will mean an increase in building activity on a scale not witnessed since the 1930s. The more deprived boroughs with highly concentrated populations, like Tower Hamlets (one-third are Bangladeshis), denounce overcrowding and ask for more social and physical infrastructure. The wealthy Kensington and Chelsea borough demands new investment in cross-rail stations as a precondition to raise the new housing target in the area. The London Forum document representing 130 community groups in the GLA shows scepticism about the target of 42,000 new homes a year, and declares that it is unlikely to deliver the quantity of social-rented homes that will be required for key workers. The City of London Corporation clearly supports the mayor's strategy and asks for more control over the 'office to home' destination changes, its objective lying in the continuous effort to produce new office space. In its critical remarks, the London Thames Forum declares that the Plan underestimates the need for industrial land and its employment and environmental consequences. On its part, London First's document is clearly supportive of the mayor's strategy. On housing, it calls for a minimum goal of 42,000 new homes a year, and declares: the more

54   *The European urban contract*

land in the development market, the more new homes will be built. It also calls for a revision of Strategic Industrial Locations and the green belt to ensure that such designations are still appropriate. It also strongly opposes the introduction of a policy to protect small and local offices, seen as an unnecessary constraint on the building lifecycle.

To understand how arbitration is conducted among such diverse interests, we can consider some major parts of the Plan. In the first strategy, the choice of developing tall buildings suited to the needs of global firms in the central areas (around the City and in Canary Wharf and Docklands) is clearly expressed. In the second strategy, the choice of developing the cross-rail infrastructure linking the financial quarters of the City and Canary Wharf with the Heathrow and Stansted Airports was the main option proposed by the London First business lobby, together with the introduction of a congestion charge – a policy supported by the citizens and opposed by small businesses but shared by the main business organizations grouped in London First.

The other strategic choice of the London Plan (2008 version), arising from both London business and developers' interests in building new urban projects and the desire to reduce spatial inequalities, was the 2012 Olympic Games project to be developed in the eastern part of London. The project was clearly very strong in terms of urban marketing and image: for the first time, the location of massive investment was the poorer eastern part of the inner city. The results in terms of reduction of social polarization characterizing the historic west/east London divide and increase of affordable housing are still to be ascertained. At the moment, the London Legacy Development Corporation is negotiating with the private companies acquiring the Olympic Village to guarantee the access of local communities to affordable homes. A local network, Get Living London, is arousing the interest of East Village residents following the slogan: Who wouldn't want to live in an area that has a new education campus, health centre and restaurants and is close to the Olympic Park?

However, the other significant implementation of the urban contract took the form of revising the inner/outer divide. The choice of reducing the divide, attributing more autonomy and attention to the outer London boroughs with respect to inner London, was launched by the new mayor of London in 2008, favouring the outer middle-class suburbia (at least at the level of political rhetoric). Here we can see how important the urban contract can be in redesigning the social alliances of the city on wider (metropolitan and regional) scales.

Paris

Keynotes on Paris between past and future

When Paris was created as a Gallo-Roman settlement, Lutetia Parisiorum, on a small island of the Seine River, it was just a minor spot on the early European map. Interestingly, in his novel *A Journey to the End of the Millennium*, Abraham Yehoshua describes Paris around the year AD 1000 as just a walled village lost in nowhere, without significant commerce and culture. In fact, with 20,000 inhabitants in AD 800, it was part of a periphery whose centres were the caliphate cities like Baghdad (700,000 inhabitants), Cordova (140,000) and Granada. Yet in the emerging Europe of cities, it was the site of a university (around 1150) and kingship (the Capetian dynasty). It was a capital ever since, and in 1200 it was already the most important European city (with a population of 110,000, followed by Venice and Milan). The economic and merchant nature of Paris does not account for its development. It is its nature as the first major 'political city' which accounts for its steady growth as the first European city since 1200: in 1300, its population was 228,000; in 1400, it was 280,000; and in 1500, it was 185,000. In the same years, London had 45,000, 50,000 and 50,000 inhabitants, respectively. The ranking of Paris in the world rank of cities is also impressive: it was fourth in 1300 and 1400, eighth in 1500 (Taylor 2013). This has all been due to political power over the last millennium. Today, in the Mori Foundation *Global Power City Index* (2014), Paris is third, behind only London and New York.

Its political role therefore lay at the very foundation of the Paris urban contract. It was so during the following centuries, when Paris was accumulating the power symbols of its kingship and, later, empire under Napoleon. This unparalleled accumulation made Paris the cultural capital of the world until the 19th century. It has been over centuries, in Walter Benjamin's urban imagery, the great hall of a library traversed by the Seine (Benjamin 2007).

In the archives forming the background for his unfinished book *Paris, Capital of the 19th Century*, Walter Benjamin collected material on 'Nature and the City', as documented by Giorgio Agamben in his monumental critical edition of Benjamin's *Charles Baudelaire* (Benjamin 2012). The chthonic nature of the city, its underground base and its submarine image are among the favoured themes of the fragments Benjamin collected. In Benjamin, the ruins are a sign of the dialectic between the technical growth of the metropolis and the destruction made possible by the technical advance itself. This was a departure from the view of Georg Simmel, where ruins are a product of man destined to become a product of nature, a cosmic tragedy. Cities (from London to Lisbon to Tokyo in the past centuries) are always in danger of destruction by water, fire and other natural catastrophic events as well as by social and technical changes, like Paris in the Haussmann urban epoch. 'The city of Paris has entered the 20th century in the form that Haussmann has given to it,' writes Benjamin (2012, p. 700). Haussmann achieved subversion of the urban image through such simple tools as spades, hoes and picks. 'What destruction – Benjamin observes – such limited tools have produced! And how since then, in the epoch of great cities, the instruments for razing them have been improved!'

In Baudelaire's text on Charles Meyron, a painter in the Paris of his time, the interconnectedness of antiquity and modernity is clearly underlined: 'Rarely have we seen represented with such poetical richness the natural

56   *The European urban contract*

solemnity of a capital city' (writes Baudelaire in *Ecrits sur l'art*): stratified stones and industrial obelisks, monumental restoration works are mixed together. Antiquity and modernity are interconnected in the new city. This vision of modernity constitutes the dialectic basis of the commercial arcades, *Passages*, which Benjamin considers both architecture and symbol, the dream of the urban community.

The protagonist here is a particular kind of urbanity, the *flâneur* in the flows of urban population. '*The man of the crowd*' of Edgar Allan Poe is the explicit model: but in Poe no *flanerie* is admitted; rather, the protagonist is permanently within the flow. Yet Benjamin ironically notes: 'The lack of housing favours the flâneur.' Again, the dialectic here is between man and merchandise. Nature is never seen as a value in Baudelaire: 'J'ai meme toujours pensé qu'il y avait dans la nature florissante et rajeunie, quelque chose d'affligeant, de dur, de cruel – un je ne sais quoi qui frise l'impudence' (quoted in Benjamin 2012, p. 153). The cruelty of nature is perhaps the reason he refused communion with nature. It is the city that attracts the poet: its labyrinth, its mosaic of ruins, its sky ('les grands ciels qui font rever d'eternité', as Baudelaire writes in *Paysage* (in *Le fleurs du Mal*, LXXXVI).

Our starting point to interpret modern Paris is therefore 1859: the first year of Haussmann's public works as a metaphor for urban change, urban renewal and urban destruction. Following Haussmann will become the dream of any 'urban growth' machine; criticizing Haussmann will become the leitmotiv of any critical approach to urban modernity.

In the short period 1848–70 we can say, following Marx, that the entire history of modernity can be detected. The European revolution-counterrevolution dialectic is incised deep into the streets of Paris. What comes first and what follows this crucial epoch is encapsulated in the image of *Paris, Capital of the 19th Century*.

Benjamin was fully aware of this, and meticulously collected evidence of Paris' urban change, its preparation and its consequences. Along a vertical axis (scc Figure 2.4), which designates the structural-technical form of the city, we can locate the following points in Benjamin's inquiry:

- in which period does the expression 'a sea of houses' make its first appearance?
- when did Haussmann's demolitions begin?
- traffic of carriages on the Pont Neuf
- first mailboxes in Paris
- arrival of the electric telegraph
- process of administrative control
- house numbering

Since then, the nature of modern metropolis is the field where all sorts of experiments in urban population control, through technical instruments and

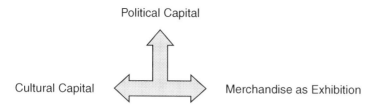

Figure 2.4 The Paris urban contract

flow regulation, are conducted. Here Foucauldian governmentality made its first appearance: during the 18th century in the pre-revolutionary *ancien regime* institutions, during the 19th century in the new forms of urban modernity. But Paris is also the city whose streets are inhabited by custom in which conservation and urbanity interpenetrate. Along the horizontal axis (see Figure 2.4), which designates the subjectivity of the urban spirit, we can therefore locate the following points in Benjamin's inquiry:

- inhabited interior
- passages
- crowd, mass, *flâneurs*
- attitude (of intellectuals, bohemians)
- psychoanalysis, phantasmagory of merchandise.

Thirdly, on the horizontal axis (see Figure 2.4) we also find the peculiar form of this phantasmagory of merchandise: *mimesis* of the febrile efforts of material production and its related form of commerce, which is realized in the crowd described by Poe and replicated by Baudelaire. The *flâneur* moves into the labyrinth of merchandise as he had been accustomed to do into the labyrinth of the city (Benjamin 2012, p. 671). Benjamin's Paris is therefore, more than any other city (including London), a laboratory of the merchandise offered as fashion, entertainment and 'universal exhibition'. It is true that the first Universal Expo took place in London in 1851; but the Paris 1855 Expo and the following ones including the Tour Eiffel legacy of 1889, celebrating the 1789 Revolution (a political symbol again), had a stronger, more permanent impact on the cultural capital of modernity.

Interpreting the urban form: A three-speed city

Following Benjamin (2000), we can interpret the urban form of Paris: the 'passages', the 'métro', the 'labyrinth'. They form the linguistic network of the city. The streets, the galleries, the fountains, the canals (also underground) are some of the key elements of its urban architecture.

The social and political actors are also clearly defined: bourgeoisie and proletariat, intellectuals and prostitutes, bankers, entrepreneurs and cocottes,

58   *The European urban contract*

doctors, lawyers and soldiers. They are topologically, not only anthropologically, defined by the very places in which they are located. The city Benjamin observes is only apparently homogeneous: it experiments border/threshold in every possible dimension (streets, parks, buildings, overpasses). This is a key point to understand the 'urban' and its transformations. The 'passages' have declined due to electric light and the changing design of pavements in the 19th century; in the 20th century, the network of highways, Boulevard Périphérique and RER (Express Rapid Transit Network) have changed the metropolitan form. The City of Paris, with its 2.2 million inhabitants (a stable datum over the decades), still stands there; but around it a new urban region has grown, with a first ring (4.1 million inhabitants) and a second ring (almost 5 million) growing fast year by year.

The social and political players have changed very much since Benjamin's Paris. According to their employment status, 50% of the French national total of senior positions (*emplois supérieurs*) live in the Paris region, as well as 30% of the scientists and researchers, and 38% of all the firms' headquarters are located in Paris (Kantor et al. 2012). In Benjamin's Paris, the working class was concentrated in the suburbs, and the political divide was clear between centre and periphery. In the mid-20th century, immigration, mostly from French-speaking countries, accounted for a considerable part of the new social housing inhabitants. Chombart de Lauwe's pivotal 1952 urban inquiry on Paris and its agglomeration was the first attempt to analyze the changing social landscape. It was a city of slums, or *ilots insalubres*, which characterized the urban space of the 'Heroic City' in the 1950s (Wakeman 2009 traces an interesting historical divide in the 1950s between the first half of the century, wars and conflicts, and the second half, modernization and a technocratic state). The ZUPs (priority urbanization zones) inaugurated by the French state numbered 195 between 1958 and 1973, creating 2 million new social housing units. The disadvantaged here, unemployed and immigrants, were twice the average for Paris. Later the same story was written by the ZFUs (urban free zones), 100 in France: here the job-creating enterprises are exempted from paying social contribution taxes, if they employ local residents as 25% of their total employees. The (unintended?) effect has been that in the ZFUs, more than in any other place, suburban riots broke out in 2005. Finally, the ZUS (sensitive urban zones) where 4.5 million live, almost a tenth of the French population, are spaces where families with high youth unemployment and recent immigrants are concentrated. Yet they are not 'ghettos' in the North American sense: the 'racial' exclusion of the ghetto is more 'social' here (Wacquant 1993).

In Paris, social exclusion has been concentrated in the suburbs (*banlieues*: literally 'places of ban'), particularly in the north and north-east of the Paris region (Seine–Saint-Denis department). This is what Pierre Bourdieu (1993), in his extraordinary journey into the French areas of relegation, defined as '*la misère du monde*' (the misery of the world). The ZUP Val Saint

The European urban contract 59

Martin, with its 14-floor abandoned tower and the survivors of the collective catastrophe of unemployment, former qualified workers from Algeria now unemployed, in the desert of closed shops and offices on the street with exotic names (Rue des Jonquilles), symbolizes the failure of the urban contract, of the social contract and of the industrial contract written by the French state in the 1960s.

In was in the 'glorious' post–World War II years, between the end of the 1950s and the beginning of the 1970s, that an attempt to reunite all social classes in a unified, homogeneous urban space was made through the '*grands ensembles*' (public housing with moderate prices, HLM) and the '*villes nouvelles*' (new towns) (Donzelot 2004). It was a movement, led by the state, which interpreted progressive urbanism in a special contract.

It was the state that decided the social distribution of different social groups over space through at least three markets: the real estate, education and labour markets. And it was again the state, as from the 1970s, that withdrew and created places of relegation where the poorer population, the unemployed and the less 'able to survive' the crisis have since been concentrated (Bourdieu 1993). Paris is divided as a result of the 'political construction of space' favouring the creation of space-based homogeneous groups. It is a twofold process, to be seen in the central selective neighbourhoods where a 'club effect' dominates, and a relegation space of '*grands ensembles*' abandoned by the state.

According to Donzelot (2004), a 'three-speed' city emerges: between the opposite spaces of gentrification and social habitat a third peri-urban middle-class city is growing, seeking separation from the 'excluded' and at the same time 'forgotten' by the upper classes of the gentrified metropolitan core. The urban social game is characterized by a triangle: the forced immobility (both social and geographical) of the social habitat, the privatized mobility of the peri-urban middle class, and the ubiquity of the globalized upper class living in the gentrified urban centre.

A study(Charmes 2003) conducted in the small municipality of Coubron, in the socially sensitive department of Seine–Saint-Denis, shows that the main preoccupation of the middle-class inhabitants is to avoid any contact with the social housing inhabitants of Clichy-sous-Bois. A sort of social apartheid tends to dominate, whereas in the past the Clichy-sous-Bois inhabitants were allowed to aspire to become Coubron inhabitants. Social and geographical mobility is therefore blocked, and the de facto urban social contract is one of exclusion. It is a contract, as the study documents, written by the behaviours of the middle class inhabitants, the mayors and the developers. The first are ready to protest; the second are ready to legitimate the social insulation; the third are ready to build gated communities for the suburban middle class.

A different, privatizing logic is driving the gentrified urban upper classes. Gentrification has led them to choose the city centre as a place of cultural and social distinction. The upper middle classes, previously content to look

60 *The European urban contract*

for larger spaces in the suburbs, are now all 'back in town', in the city centre (Bidou-Zachariasen 2003). In the neighbourhoods (like the central 9th, 10th, 11th and the more peripheral 19th and 20th *arrondissements*), they are moving into the spaces of traditional craft business, which are declining, and new spaces for living are on the real estate market. In the 19th century, these neighbourhoods were the symbolic places of intellectual elites: like Ménilmontant in the 20th *arrondissement*, a village annexed to Paris in 1860 by Haussmann, where Saint-Simon's followers used to spend their private time in gardens and '*folies*' (pleasure pavilions). In the Fordist era a place of artisans and craft shops, it is now a typical gentrified environment with cultural life, street art and small theatres mixed with immigrants' *ateliers*, dancing schools, private Catholic schools.

The newcomers in the gentrified neighbourhoods are in fact the most inclined to private education for their children. Later they could choose to move to more central *arrondissements*, where good high schools are located. Finally they may wish to send their children abroad for university studies. Their mobility is therefore fully global, yet their life in the neighbourhood is led entirely at the local level (all sorts of services are at hand, from cultural to leisure). They can spend relatively little time on their daily round, yet at the same time fly from Charles De Gaulle-Roissy airport to the rest of the world. At the central stations of the RER trains – as urban anthropologist Marc Augé has shown – on their way to the airport the upper classes will brush past, unseeing, the young people coming from the social housing of the *banlieues* in pursuit of downtown experiences. According to Donzelot (2004), Paris is the gentrification laboratory for French cities just as New York has been for the world cities.

Yet the 'back to the central city' movement, which Paris shares with many global cities, has to be correctly understood in the French framework. Donzelot considers that in gentrification processes it is the market that decides, through price mechanisms in the housing and other related markets. Yet we should remember again that the role of the state, and of urban and regional political players, has been generally stronger than in other countries. It is a less market-oriented process than, say, in New York or London. Paris has 17% of its buildings in the HLM affordable housing regime, with 34% in the 20th *arrondissement*. As an example we can take urban rejuvenation projects like La Villette, the 19th *arrondissement* park created in the 1980s by the Paris municipality: it is the site of a scientific and industrial city, of music and dance installations, theatre and cinema facilities, concerts and art activities, street festivals and so forth. Schools and social camps for children are organized, and there are 9 million yearly visitors. No other municipality in the world has done as much in a peripheral area (55 hectares) through direct public investment and management, giving its imprinting to gentrification. Is it a softer, more socially oriented gentrification? At the same time, in the 19th *arrondissement* 60% of social housing is highly concentrated and the foreign population (mostly Arab) accounts

The European urban contract   61

for 48% of the total, with ZSP (priority zoning of security) like Stalingrad-Orgues de Flandres and the cité Reverdy.

Interpreting the contract form: The 'Grand Paris' project

Formal urban contracts – an unusual tool indeed if compared to other institutional settings where political and market informalities prevail – have been largely written by the state, in the case of France, to include the various levels of territorial governments in urban governance. Starting from the *schema directeurs* and the Métropoles d'équilibre programme of the 1960s, and continuing in state-region and state-city contracts implemented after the decentralization law of 1982, the state's direct involvement in urban governance has been long-lasting in France. At least three phases can be distinguished: the 'technocratic-reformist' phase of the 1960s, Catholic and social in nature and essentially state-centric; the 'decentralization' phase of the 1980s led by socialist governments, which opened to the influence of growing cities and regions with a transition to negotiated and networked policies but maintaining the strong power of political elites (Meny 1992; Thoenig 1992); the contradictory pluralistic phase of the 2000s with a stronger emphasis on the economic competitiveness of elites ('neoliberal attempt') and at the same time the growing role of urban governance institutions in maintaining the social coordination of local fragmented interests (Pinson 2009). This is particularly important with respect to the role of Paris competing with other global cities, and the new decentralization law of 2014 reorganizing the main regional, departmental and municipal competences. In this framework, private partners have also been considered in more recent public-private partnership (PPP) schemes. A recent development of the story is assessing in which areas governments govern, in which areas some mechanisms and functional tools are implemented, and finally which areas are 'not governed' at all (Borraz and Le Galès 2010). This is particularly true today, when city borders are constantly being redefined both by demographics and urbanization, as well as political reforms.

The vision is based on the lesser constraint of the state allowing cities to develop collective actor strategies in the logic of the Weberian European city, as opposed to urban governance models based on state rescaling in relation to new demands of globalized capitalism (Brenner 2004). In this wider context, the Paris urban contract can be recognized as the permanently contingent result of conflicting forces and influences. In our scheme, the Political Capital, the Cultural Capital and the Merchandise as Exhibition are still the dominant vision-inspiring forces in reciprocal tension.

i. The Political Capital is the expression of the long-lasting strong state presence and recent 'return' (Kantor et al. 2012). Since 2008, a new ministry for 'the development of the Capital region' has been created, in spite of the decentralization process. The fragmentation of local powers in the Ile-de-France region (1,281 municipalities, 100 joint authorities, eight

62 *The European urban contract*

departments) plays in favour of the state centralizing authority. The role of the Paris municipality is of the utmost importance, yet its attempt to create its own urban plans (like the Plan Local d'Urbanisme in the crucial transport field) is in conflict with the need to coordinate the main strategic choices with the adjacent municipalities and departments. Legitimate doubt arises about the capacity to create metropolitan coalitions (Lefèvre 2009). As social and spatial inequalities grow in the wider metropolitan and regional area, new tools for social and territorial cohesion will be needed. Yet the traditional role of the state in terms of redistributive power clashes with Paris the global city, like London, New York and Tokyo. The latter strategy is made more difficult given the traditionally poor relations between the public and the private sectors in France, due to the domination of the public sector in the governance of the metropolitan area (Kantor et al. 2012). This is probably the most important difference between Paris and London emerging from comparative research: in Paris, no strong and unified economic lobby like London First has been created to influence (in the case of London, to write the agenda of) city government. Fragmentation of interests is the rule. The consultation during the production of the SDRIF (*schema directeur* Region Ile-de-France) of employers' organizations like Medef is an official, institutional process. The role the CRCI (regional confederation of the chambers of commerce) plays is monopolistic due to its public nature. For the first time in 2004, during the consultation process of SDRIF the CRCI publicly opposed the official version of the text and proposed an alternative document. The employers' organizations like Medef and Pce have conducted mobilization to modify the SDRIF in the direction of obtaining more projected growth of the region, more social housing and a third airport (Grilliat 2013). The result in terms of direct influence on the planning process agenda gives little cause for enthusiasm. However, note that Paris was home to the third-largest number of Fortune 500 company headquarters worldwide in 2013, behind only Beijing and Tokyo (Herod 2014). This means that the economic power of Paris is globally very strong and its competitiveness is less dependent on domestic entrepreneurship and national employers' associations like Medef.

In this attempt, a new project, 'Grand Paris', was launched directly by the French government under the Sarkozy presidency in 2007. It followed the argument (critically addressed to the regional planning authorities) that the *schema directeur* de l'Ile-de-France aimed not so much at boosting the competitive economic role of the capital as maintaining the regional environment and putting an end to land consumption. The spatial regional project of February 2007 of the Regional Council Ile-de-France aimed at three main objectives: promoting a more compact and dense city; developing the urban supply and the quality of life in Ile-de-France, strengthening its economic potential and international attractiveness; and protecting biodiversity, the values of natural and agricultural spaces and open spaces (green belt). It was

The European urban contract 63

against this approach, considered too timid and ecologist, that the 'Grand Paris' project was launched.

A Greater Paris Act (2010) was approved to create a new underground railway network linking the regional nodes (airports, La Defence advanced services park and Saclay new scientific and technical cluster) led by a new entity, Societé du Grand Paris, controlled by the state. It is clear that, according to the Sarkozy plan, Paris should imitate London, which is the real inspiration of the 'Grand Paris' project. We may remember that the infrastructural choice of developing a cross-rail linking the financial quarters of the city and Canary Wharf with London airports was the main option expressed by London First. The Paris strategy is evidently inspired by the same design: and the underlying fear of Paris is undoubtedly of losing ground in the endless competition with London.

The criticism many local municipalities and regional powers have expressed has reduced the impact of the project led by the state. Yet the new 2014 decentralization law introduced the 'Grand Paris' metropolitan government in 2016 joining the Paris municipality, the municipalities of Hautes-de-Seine, Seine–Saint-Denis and Val-de-Marne departments and the municipalities which are part of joint authorities with at least one municipality of the first ring (*petite couronne*) of Paris. The tool of *Contrat de Developpement Territorial* (territorial development contract) has been created to this end.

'Grand Paris' is defined as 'an urban, social and economic project of national interest to unite the major strategic territories of the Ile-de-France region and promotes the long-lasting, sustainable economic development of the capital region'. It is based on the creation of a network of public transport financed by the state. The network is articulated under territorial development contracts jointly realized by the state, municipalities and their agglomerations. The contracts participate in the objective of creating 70,000 new dwellings every year.

It is clear that the project aims at positioning Paris among the five or six global cities of the world, yet is meant to maintain both competitiveness and solidarity as guiding principles.

The Ile-de-France 23 contracts covering territories with a total population of 4.8 million have been signed or are under evaluation (end of 2014). Each contract is signed by the state and the community of agglomeration of municipalities, and regions and departments can participate. It is a 15-year strategic development plan defining objectives, projects and actions. The interaction of public players is, once more, the keynote of the contract, while private players are not included. It is a complex tool of contractual definition of each area's future role in the puzzle of 'Grand Paris'. It is also a distributive tool in terms of housing, employment, transport, schooling and so forth.

Is it a 'moral' contract, as some experts hold? Or a 'policy' tool aimed at consensus-building and cooperation among fragmented public players?

64 *The European urban contract*

Taking one contract into consideration, the Contract of Est Ensemble (Department of Seine–Saint-Denis) a socially sensitive territory of industrial tradition in the East of Paris region, we can try to answer the question. Three main axes are defined: economy, culture and housing. A total of 66 projects is proposed: 50,000 more employees are expected in the next 15 years. The sectors of the economy to be developed are defined as multimedia and video, communications, eco-building and biotech. Some leading private groups of these sectors are destined to be localized in the area. A protocol of cooperation with the Paris Municipality, articulated in 20 actions, is ongoing. A contract with the state agency EPFIF (Etablissement Public Foncier Ile-de-France) has been defined with an investment of €200 million in housing and implementation mechanisms as part of the contract. A target of 2,800 new buildings per year has been also defined. In other terms, it seems more than a 'moral' contract, yet at the moment remains a 'strategic' plan with public players as the dominant, if not exclusive, contractual agents.

ii. The Cultural Capital of the 19th century (according to Walter Benjamin) added many new assets during the 20th century: it was again the central power of the French government that supplied the major driving force as from the 1960s and through the 1990s (Défense, Centre Pompidou, Parc de la Villette, Louvre Pyramid, Bastille Opera, Bibliothèque Nationale among them). The worldwide attraction of Paris, whose first place for world tourism has been challenged by London, is today also planned in the direction of new developments like the Euro Disney 'Europe Valley' contract in the Marne-la-Vallée area. This is a PPP agreement between Euro Disney, the state and local communities to develop by 2030 a city of 60,000 residents, with hotels, offices and shops, and natural parks with an investment of €2 billion. The city-by-projects is a cultural fact, but it is also a stratified legacy. However, it is probably wrong to call Paris the 'rational city' (Herod 2014). The rationalization of space following from the French Revolution is only one sign. The modernist design of the capital has taken many different paths and is the sum of many conflicting trends. As Walter Benjamin wrote once in his Parisian journal (1929), whereas Berlin is dominated by its technical and organizational spirit, Paris is quite the contrary: the street here is the inhabited interior where conservation and urbanity coalesce. As Hannah Arendt (1968) added, it is the capacity to take tradition into account without indulging in the past but thinking of the present.

The 'contract city' is now, in the 21st century, a new effort to make Paris plural and polycentric (see Figure 2.5). Today, much more than in the past, the city's culture is linked to research, the technical and scientific domains Benjamin was ready to discover: his 'art work in the age of its technical reproducibility' is more than ever true. The Saclay project is the most important attempt to create a new research campus, a technical and scientific pole and a new town in a revised version of multipolarity. It is an ongoing process. In the first ring from the centre of Paris are some development poles, as in the southwest at Issy le Moulineaux, whereas in the north the old industrial periphery

The European urban contract 65

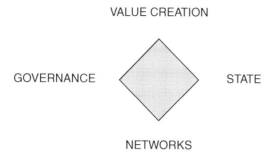

Figure 2.5 The Paris value diamond

is now a tertiary services area. In the second ring are the poles of Roissy and Saclay, destined to become new key poles in multipolar agglomerations of Île-de-France. In the south-west the Saclay project (€5 billion) has developed a joint venture of the Grandes Ecoles, the research laboratories of major French enterprises and new urban developments to create (the university campus is set for completion in 2018) a new (low density, green, scientific, integrated) environment of Paris, to be added to the centre and complementary rather than opposed to it (Veltz 2013). We will now go on to interpret the form of the urban contract underlying recent developments in Paris.

According to Pinson (2009), the main conceptual tools to interpret current urban projects (including the contractual form developed here) are: 1. differentiation of policies to create value, starting from existing urban resources or hidden resources to be mobilized; 2. anticipation of the future, due to permanent instability and the reduced role of the state, with the entry of new players (like Europe) and the proliferation of manifold actors; 3. mobilization of civil society and creation of networks, both vertical and horizontal; 4. pluralization of interests and redistribution of powers; 5. governance of the process through integration between institutional perspective and voluntary exchange among actors.

In the past, the verdict on the Parisian experience of 'planning the future' of its territory was clear. Hall (1984b) underlined the choice Paris made to grow through a single agglomeration of the centre and the new towns, seen as arms of the city itself. Twenty years later, Brenner (2004) was also clear in explaining the national commitment to promoting concentrated economic growth in the Paris region. Today we can repeat the verdict, by the 'Grand Paris' project led by the state and by integrated development of poles like Saclay, Roissy and, to a lesser extent, Marne-la-Vallée. This result is at least partially in contrast with point 2 regarding the declining role of the state: in the case of Paris, this role is strong, if we consider the permanent mobilization of the state in creating vertical networks (point 3). If we consider both the Saclay and the Roissy projects, and Val d'Europe as well, the state is the key actor in establishing the networks. Yet the network itself is, interestingly,

66   *The European urban contract*

much more pluralized (point 4) than in the past. Take Saclay: it is a project in which not only the state, the region (less than ideally) and the public sector (like the Grandes Ecoles) are involved, but also enterprises, scientific communities and technical-functional domains. Their relations are based more on horizontal networks (point 3) than on state-led vertical networks. Driving the project to an end is a matter of permanent negotiation among different interests (point 4). The key word is 'federation': including a consortium of the 23 university bodies destined to become a single university campus, characterized by a great diversity of scientific and technical fields of application. These are open ecosystems, less driven by the state's directive role – an innovation in the traditional French dirigism. A second-level 'federation' is needed between universities and enterprises: in France, the network is strong between Grandes Ecoles and enterprises (the leading professional figures in the industry coming from the Ecoles) but weak between universities and enterprises. A third-level 'federation' is among the territorial layers: city of Paris, municipalities, region and the state in their interplay with the economic, technical and scientific actors. Here we come to critical point 5: how to integrate institutional and exchange logics in the political domain. This is on one hand a problem of political leadership and cohesion, which is a questionable and rare resource today. On the other hand, it is also a problem of integrating socio-spatial groups which are led to compete more than to cooperate. In other words: How will the new projects, like Saclay, change the social composition of the population involved? How they will become more socially integrated with respect to the 'three-speed city'? How will the rejuvenation-gentrification effect not be replicated, in terms of spatial segregation of new research and university communities in a polarized space of flows?

Milan

Keynotes on Milan between past and future

Milan, 'land in the middle', according to its etymological root, is currently the functional-economic capital of a wider macro region, Northern Italy with its 26 million inhabitants. If it were also a political capital, as some Italian parties have dreamed in the recent past, it would lead a not too small state, at least by European standards.

This is far from the full story of Milan, which is a functional-economic hub and transit point much more than a political player. The city was so also in the past: Milan never created its own state, but rather connected its first-class handicraft production to European circuits of commerce. Milan was a small lordship (*signoria*) and then a duchy (*ducatus mediolanensis*) under the Visconti and Sforza families. Later, it was dominated by Spain, Austria and briefly by France under Napoleon. For half a century (1815–59), Milan was the capital of a dependent state, Lombardo-Veneto, as part of the Austrian Empire.

The European urban contract   67

All regions, and in particular those bordering on other countries, are affected by trans-frontier dynamics. Milan is located in a peculiar borderland, including Switzerland: Lugano and the Canton of Ticino are part of its direct influence. Again, the historical heritage is important: the Canton of Ticino was part of the Duchy of Milan and the Ticino River linked Italian-speaking Switzerland, Milan and Pavia in one cultural system. Pavia University was founded in the 14th century as Alma Ticinensis Universitas (University of Ticino), enjoying the same level as the universities of Bologna and Paris at that time.

Today Milan is part of a wider supranational network of European economic powerhouses including Stuttgard, Lyon and Barcelona. But the interregional links are even stronger. The regions of Northern Italy are directly linked to Milan: the Ligurian ports are points of transit to Milan, sending 60% of their worldwide imports to the city, Lombardy is a Milan-led platform for people and goods on the move across regions and businesses, and the logical hub that attracts and distributes resources and people involving the three airports of Malpensa, Linate and Orio al Serio, as it does the seven universities – Statale, Catholic, Bicocca, Politechnic, Bocconi, the International University of Languages and Media (IULM) and Pavia. The Milan fairs attract small and medium businesses from across Northern Italy as well as business visitors from around the world, as do the huge service centres of finance, logistics, law, consultancy, accountancy and advertising.

Milan is identified with the fashion industry and design worldwide; however, its diversified economy includes much more than that: the 115 municipalities of Milan's local labour market produce a wide variety of goods and services. If we consider Northern Italy as a global city-region (Perulli and Pichierri 2010), it would be counted among the first places, according to Scott (2001). Northern Italy is much larger than other city-regions in Europe (Catalunya numbers 5.5 million, whereas Bavaria comes to 12.5 million).

Who governs the global city-region (Le Galès 2011)? In the case of Milan, the recent Law on Metropolitan Cities revisited by the 'Del Rio Law' (after the name of the ministry who drew up the text in 2013) defines a province-wide government including the municipalities of the old Milan Province. This seems to be a past vision of Milan: in the 1960s, the Intercommunal Plan of Milan (PIM) indicated the very same area. But in the following 50 years very much has changed. The Milan municipality has lost population and the Milan province has only slightly increased; however, the demographic weakness of Milan is now offset by a recent trend: the 'global city-region' of Northern Italy is certainly also interesting for its global influx of immigrants (2.5 million foreign residents in 2008), forming a new (for Italy indeed) transcultural and diasporic network.

What has also changed is the economic ranking of Milan: 13th place in 2012 (it was 8th in 2007 before the global financial crisis) among world cities in terms of global connectivity as measured by multinational service firms located in Milan, revealing an economic strength that is disproportionate to

68   *The European urban contract*

its weak metropolitan governance capacity. In fact, Milan ranks only 38th in the Global Cities Index, also taking into account the political engagement of cities. The governance of Milan is based on a series of loosely connected institutionalized experiments in the metropolitan region (well examined in Gualini 2003). By contrast, Rome ranks only 53rd in terms of global connectivity, and 30th in the Global Cities Index, confirming its role as a political (and religious) capital devoid of a global economic role. The map based on inter-business relations also shows that Milan is more interconnected with North America and Asia than with certain other European cities. The research contracts of Milan with other research and innovation centres include North America, England, Germany and France more than other Italian or Southern European regions.

The importance of location in Milan can also be measured by the presence of players in networks that have been defined, alluding to Italian industrial districts, as new 'hybrid collectives' (Parolin 2010). Many players are involved in the creation of new industrial objects 'made in Italy' as a result of the assembly of practical knowledge and heterogeneous theories, and thus contributing to the development of a new product. In the case of the furniture industry, the networks are made up of designers largely based in Milan, market analysts and other metropolitan specialists, vendors and buyers from all over the world and developers from research and development departments of Milanese universities, as well as craftsmen and suppliers located in the Monza-Brianza province. These multi-localized, hybrid collectives are interrelated and in constant interaction with one another, thus being both local and remote (but without the former there cannot be the latter).

Milan is not only the golden location of the fashion and design industries as well as high-tech research centres, but it is also the new hub of illegal flows of capital, goods and persons coming from Southern Italy and worldwide involved in the dark side of globalization processes: from drugs to illegal transport of people from remote regions towards central cities. Milan is also the main Italian Internet hub, but not at a level comparable with its economic strength: it is the principal influx and departure point for the main Italian Internet infrastructures, but the role of the Internet economy is still limited in terms of GDP growth (Derudder 2011). Creativity and innovation are widespread in the Northern Italy macro region: Turin plays a special role in advanced technological research, Bologna and Reggio Emilia are strong in the research and development of advanced mechanical applications, and small ICT businesses are developing in the metropolitan area of Venice, Treviso and Padua.

The creation of Milan as a metropolitan city as of January 1, 2015, is therefore less an opportunity than a challenge given its wider socio-economic role. In fact, the level of analysis needed to fully understand the innovative socio-economic dynamics at work in Milan is not limited to the provincial territory (now identifying the metropolitan city).

The European urban contract   69

Let us begin with the empirical evidence. In socio-demographic terms, Milan has shrunk in the centre (municipality), where the population fell by 28% between 1971 and 2011. Population growth has taken place in the province (+4%), reaching around 3 million. However, Milan's population is now older both in the centre (in the period considered: +58% of inhabitants older than 65 years old) and in the province (+ 100%). People have moved towards external areas with poor welfare services, and a new welfare network at the metropolitan level is now urgently needed. Social housing is 10% of the total stock of housing in Milan, a percentage much higher than the Italian average (which is 4%), but insufficient and not well managed, and not renewed at all. Its distribution is mainly in the old peripheral quarters of the city.

The economy has gone well beyond: while the city centre hosts advanced production services (finance and accountancy above all), the metropolitan city hosts diversified quality production: manufacturing still accounts for 11% of total employment and 20% of total value added. Taken together, employment in manufacturing in Milan and Monza-Brianza (two administrative provinces, but one functional metropolitan area) reaches 20% of the total.

At the city-region level, Milan leads a network including Pavia, Piacenza, Novara, Bergamo and Lugano in term of logistics, research and other strategic functions. On one hand, Milan is a site where 3,000 foreign multinationals have their registered offices. On the other hand, the 4,000 medium-size businesses (we exclude those controlled by large Italian or foreign companies) mostly located in Northern Italy develop supply chains, managerial teams and advanced production services which have Milan as their centre. Under globalization, the enterprises' competitive chances depend on their ability to connect to global cognitive circuits of the economy, which find in Milan the interfaces between local and global environments (see Table 2.2).

Public utilities, banks, fairs and other economic infrastructures have their centre in Milan. The governance centres of the credit system, following a process of aggregation, have largely moved towards Milan: in the new development of Garibaldi-Repubblica, the towers of Unicredit, a leading

Table 2.2 Mix of advanced production services: Milan, Rome and New York-London (NYLON)

	Finance	*Law*	*Advertising*	*Accountancy*	*Managerial consultancy*
Milan	18,814	1,911	12,395	27,089	5,779
	28.5%	2.9%	18.8%	41.1%	8.8%
Rome	9,477	1,470	10,571	23,072	6,014
	18.7%	2.9%	20.9%	45.6%	11.9%
NYLON	52,982	9,302	36,290	72,589	20,942
	27.6%	4.8%	18.9%	37.8%	10.9%

Source: P. Taylor in P. Perulli, *Nord. Una città-regione globale*, Mulino 2012.

70   The European urban contract

Italian bank, are the tallest buildings in Italy. The fair industry, living in a very competitive realm, still finds in the Milan Fair its leading site even while other fairs in Bologna, Rimini, Verona, Vicenza and Padua have grown. The restructuring of *public utilities* has been led by liberalization processes – in telecommunications and energy above all – and closer integration is expected in the near future along two axes: Turin-Genoa-Milan-Brescia and Bologna-Treviso-Padua. Milan's status as a metropolitan centre is increasingly important within these infrastructures: the metropolitan city's impact will affect advanced services and enterprise locations, together with the distribution of knowledge workers and their mobility in both local and international terms.

We now come to the socio-demographic changes induced by mobility vectors: roads, highways, railways, airports, ports and logistics infrastructures can provoke both displacement and recentralization effects. Within population movement and agglomeration, the role of cities as powerful attractors emerges. The new post-metropolitan corridors linking Milan-Turin, Venice-Padua-Treviso, Milan-Bologna are such a case.

The international literature on cities tries to explain why and how cities grow, and why some cities grow while others do not. One theory is 'new production geography', which explains urban growth as a result of skilled workers' location choices and also the job opportunities for less-qualified and low-paid sectors of the workforce (including immigrants). These attempts at interpretation result in the diffusion of flexible production models distributed both within and between specific geographical settings: clusters, traditional industrial districts, new high-tech districts, localized enterprise networks and metropolitan platforms assuming the form of global cities like Milan.

Urban dynamics seems to be led by enterprises' location choices, agglomerating along corridors and nodes and interacting with the preferences and choices of individuals that are only partially free, mostly determined by factors like housing, mobility and so on. This helps explain why the urban areas which have grown most in the past 40 years in Northern Italy are middle-sized cities along corridors like Rimini, Bergamo, Vicenza, Brescia, Parma, Reggio-Emilia, Modena, Verona, Trento and Venice-Padua-Treviso. Major metropolitan areas like Milan, Turin, Bologna and Genoa are lagging behind. The need to 'organize the polycentric region' emerges: synergies and circuits among metropolitan and middle-size cities have to be created, at both the interregional and subregional levels.

Interpreting the urban form: City of cities

The city is not simply a place where some industries are located and the social classes (bourgeoisie and proletariat) reside. The city is an industry itself: its raw material is urban land and its final product is housing (Insolera 1975). These definitions can help to explain a difficult concept: urban form.

In the case of Milan, we can interpret the changing urban form between the industrial revolution and today as 'following industry'.

In the 18th and 19th centuries, the industrial revolution did not take place within the city, but in the vicinity of energy resources and raw materials. It was only after the creation of the railway network that industry could get close to the markets, that is to the city. In the case of Milan, industry grew in the outer ring including Sesto San Giovanni (north), Brianza (west) and Bergamo (east). Industrial companies such as Breda and Pirelli began life near the railway stations. In the 20th century, industry moved to Sesto San Giovanni in order to make use of larger spaces and extract urban rent in the spaces left free by the industrial move.

This is why Milan is a case of a centre without centralization: a radial model whose expansions have taken place following the railway infrastructures towards the north. Milan's 1912 urban plan is the document which followed the expansion towards the periphery, creating streets and boulevards, public gardens and squares able to bring about a parity of citizenship between the centre and the most remote peripheries (Romano 2014). In the following half century, the working class and the bourgeoisie experienced episodes of struggle and social compromise until the end of Fordism. In the last part of the 20th century, the former industrial base was deindustrialized and new urban rent was extracted by reusing the large areas abandoned by Pirelli, Falck, Breda and Innocenti. New developments were made: universities, the expansion of private hospitals, new creative industries.

What is peculiar about Milan, compared to London or Paris, is the contradiction between high-density growth (made in the past by industry and the working class, today by finance and the creative class), and low polity. Milan is based on an external source of power corresponding to a weak nation-state. The local elites have succeeded only partially in negotiating with the central government. The past and recent history of Milan is one of fragmented urban expansion and limited strategic vision.

The only strategic proposal made in the recent past was that of Milan as a 'city of cities'.[6] This was an exercise in strategic planning promoted by the Province of Milan and Milan Polytechnic between 2004 and 2009, trying to link urban sprawl phenomena (the so-called infinite city) within a dynamic and soft urban engineering vision. In particular, it was able to utilize the institutional planning resources of hundreds of fragmented municipalities in terms of territorial pacts and soft agreements, giving them a wider provincial framework. It was not based, however, on the management of hard infrastructures, whether material or immaterial (transport, highways, logistic centres, digital infrastructures), and remained an essentially cultural, yet valuable exercise. Its main value has been to show the way to future redesign of the Milan urban region, going beyond the provincial boundaries (3.9 million inhabitants) and interpreting the new processes of 'regionalization of the urban' taking place in the wider relational space. We now turn to this enlarged dimension.

72 *The European urban contract*

Interpreting the contract form: The gateway city

Milan as a node of a global network (Magatti 2005) is an urban region with a population of 8 million, a 'space of relationality' among the first 10 in the world, a 'platform' based on a 'deposit' of networks whose horizons are local-regional, national, European and global. Indices of connectivity and of positionality are therefore needed to assess the nature of Milan's globality. To find these indices, it is necessary to represent and measure the flows, both material and immaterial.

We identify seven functional systems of access-transit-exit to/from Milan feeding different but interdependent flows of persons, enterprises, merchandises, services, information and knowledge. The functions of logistics, airports and fair represent the infrastructure gateway. The functions of university and research represent the knowledge gateway. The functions of fashion and design represent the creative industry gateway (see Figure 2.6).

Milan's overall urban system can be understood in terms of governance through the (variable, even conflicting) relations within each function and linking the three selected gateways. *Infrastructures* represent the main and most powerful sector of the Milanese economy. Their systemic role is to attract heavy investments and lobbying for state public financing, assisted by the finance, insurance and banking sectors. Milan's historical role has been marked by infrastructure-building, in the past and in the present. Its position on the vertical axis of our scheme means that it is closely bound up with political and institutional decision-making. The urban contract here is between the state, the city and the business sectors, with declining influence on the part of the local government and heavy costs in terms of political intermediation, inefficiency and (more recently) even corruption.

The Milanese thinker Carlo Cattaneo was the first to include in his 'federalist' urban vision of territories the role of railways connecting cities, seen as intersecting nodes of a network (including his direct participation in the Milan–Venice railway project in 1836). Railways from Milan to the north along the Simplon axis were the first modern infrastructures created in the first half of the 19th century. In 1870, the railways from Milan to Vigevano (south-west) were financed by industrialists to connect firms like Ansaldo, GCE, Osram, Bugatti and Richard Ginori to the Simplon axis. A railway

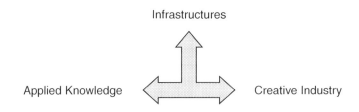

Figure 2.6 The Milan urban contract

belt was created, and the Beruto urban plan of 1887 included it in the urban design. The Milan Fair was founded at the beginning of the 20th century as a key institution of Milanese industrial and commercial capitalism: its development and following relocation in the Rho-Pero area in north-west Milan (leaving space for the much discussed private residential development of Citylife, an aggregate of insurance and financial companies) took a century of Milanese history. The underground railway network (Metropolitana Milanese) was the main achievement of the Milan municipality in the post–II World War decades: it was designed and built in a few years in the 1950s–1960s – a story of success in urban innovation. Malpensa Airport was planned in the 1970s and implemented in the 1990s to become the southern European hub at the end of the 20th century: the prolonged, conflict-torn implementation of the plan is a living symbol of the weaknesses and failures of the Milanese and regional elites in the recent past. Finally, Expo 2015, located in north-west Milan as well, represented the main infrastructural effort made by the Milanese economy at the beginning of the 21st century. When modern immaterial infrastructures serving the web economy are also taken into account, we have a complete picture of this gateway.

Applied knowledge and its institutions, that is university and research, are positioned along the horizontal axis of our scheme for their strong bottom-up ties with Milanese bourgeois society. Their past role was historically important in creating the Milanese hegemony in Italy's industrial capitalism. In 1839, Carlo Cattaneo, a key figure of Milanese civil society, founded *Il Politecnico*, a journal destined to interface intellectuals and industrialists, devoted to improvement in applied knowledge. In the same year, the Society for the Advancement of Arts and Crafts was founded, and in 1844, the School of Chemistry was born. Public and private universities were created in the following decades by the state (the Polytechnic in 1863, Statale in 1924), industrialists (Bocconi in 1902) and religious powers (the Catholic University in 1920). Since the second half of the 20th century, the Italian information and telecommunication sectors, television and web economy have been largely based in Milan. The newspaper (*Corriere della Sera*) and publishing industries (RCS, Mondadori among them), and broadcast and television industries (public and private) are based in Milan. It is a system employing a large part of the Milanese knowledge-based economy. The Milan functional urban system (FUS) is largely dominant in Northern Italy as the main service provider in the fields of information technologies, R&D, accounting, advertising, law and consultancy; life sciences and health are also excellences of Milan's knowledge system.

The creative industry is the most recent phenomenon of the Milanese economy. Born during the post-war economic boom as a result of Marshall Plan investments for reconstructing the manufacturing base, the fashion industry has become a quality production of French models at lower production costs, thanks to a highly qualified workforce. At the same time, the design industry has grown, thanks to first-class industrial designers

74 *The European urban contract*

cooperating with industrial firms in the production of quality goods for daily consumption. The role of the creative industry, supported by research institutions and universities, training schools, journals and professional groups forming a complex ecosystem, has grown year after year, eventually positioning itself on the horizontal axis (due to its strong links with Milanese society) towards the future. Milan is today considered a leading global city in the world economy, mostly thanks to its first-class ranking in the fashion and design industries. 'Made in Italy' is driven by a number of giant fashion brands (some are Italian; some have been absorbed by foreign capital groups) known worldwide, feeding a larger ecosystem of small and artisan firms and independent professionals whose crucial role is forming a natural seedbed for innovation.

The urban contract is based on the (historically variable) social relationships and compromises between these main social systems. The first system is representative of heavy capitalist and financial interests; the second represents the intellectual capital of the city; the third has the flavour of the new emerging forces of the creative class. Their ability to create a common ground, and to produce a governing class, is questionable. Yet some common features emerge.

The policy network governing Milan has never been clear-cut; the leading entrepreneurial class has never given rise to a stable political elite, nor has it formed a US-like growth machine (Vicari and Molotch 1990). Its places of formation and negotiation have often been grey: Catholic organizations, schools and lobbies have played an integrative role. After the generation of the industrial bourgeoisie, whose factories made the history of Milan before and after World War II (like Pirelli), a mostly financial and real estate coalition of interests, often aggressive and indeed debatable (Berlusconi, Ligresti), has taken power of influence. Their attempts to develop speculation in spatial structure through a suburban model of land use (like Milano 3 satellite city) have not proved successful. The interests represented by the Chamber of Commerce have proved identical, with the alliance of small commercial, retail and tertiary sectors. On the other hand, fashion, design and the emerging creative sector have never embarked upon policy initiatives 'marking' the city; the intellectuals and the professional figures have had a minor political role; political leadership has rarely emerged from civil society. Attempts to create new policy networks based on strategic coordination of different metropolitan cultures and interests (like the Association of Metropolitan Interests [AIM]) have never reached the goal of fixing the policy agenda. The metropolitan dimension has never been governed through strategic agencies, but its governance has been based on weak, fragmented negotiations (often zero-sum) among local and regional actors and interests.

Yet the urban metabolism of Milan is based on its ability to attract and create. The attraction of industrial powers (today largely multinationals) is the result of a family capitalism ready to interpret the new demands of the market. Merchant and civil society went hand in hand in the long historic interlude leading up to the urban revolution of the 20th century. Politics has never played a key role, except in some short periods (like the post-war boom and the municipal welfare phase). When industrial bases are cancelled by shifting trends, a new industry is created, often in the same place. If we consider the south-west of Milan, where light industry was created in the industrial century of 1870–1970, it is now the site of fashion and design, new activities, creative workshops, shops and showrooms. Every year, the Milan Furniture Fair attracts hundreds of thousands of international businesspeople, designers and young creatives from all over the world: it is the same site where light engineering products were produced in the industrial past by a highly qualified workforce. Planning regulation has been able to adapt flexibly to the new needs; in many cases, however, the building sector has used its political influence to 'brownfield' – rebuilding without investing in environmental quality. Incomplete urban renewal is the result.

Another example of transition is to be seen in the north axis of Milan towards Sesto S. Giovanni. Near the past sites of heavy metallurgy-siderurgy industries, new digital companies have invested in setting up headquarters, and telephone and Internet business firms have been located. On the site of Pirelli Bicocca, the main industrial family of Milan producing tyres for the auto industry, a university pole has been created: scientific faculties and humanities together in a new urban mix attracting thousands of students. Milan Polytechnic University poles have also been spun off across Lombardy and beyond (Milan Bovisa, Lecco, Lodi, Mantova and Piacenza), following a decentralized metropolitan pattern.

Turning to the north Milan site of Legnano characterized by heavy industry (textile and mechanical) plants in the past century, we can follow the implementation of the contract scheme in recent development (Tosi and Vitale 2011). The old industrial firms have given way to service and commercial developers: no creative activities have been developed; urban rents are extracted through redevelopment of deindustrialized areas by real estate groups closely connected to the region's political powers through vertical policy networks.

Peter J. Taylor, the author of the most important research on world city networks (2004), has explained that Milan is not only a place of transit, but a place where 'many things happen', and this makes it a great city. The proposed vision is ecological, composed of input, output and throughput. The throughput is a 'channel': sometimes it is only modestly active, but sometimes it creates great value. In the city, functionality is essential and each function corresponds to a channel: we have to look at what enters and what exits, and what happens in the middle. The flows crossing global Milan are sticky: they agglomerate and adhere to the city and transform it, and they in turn are transformed by the city.

Flows are generated by companies (both local and foreign), but this is not to imply diagnosis of a weak city – of dependence on external forces. It may

76 *The European urban contract*

be that the city simply attracts external functions and sectors where the local entrepreneurs are weaker. We will see that, in some cases, this does happen; in others, it does not. Flows also make clear that the traditional layering of municipal, regional and national economies no longer reflects reality. Territorial scales are less important since the city is a node, sometimes global and sometimes local: a city of cities, a city-region, a global city.

As a logistics node, Milan is a functional region including such poles as Piacenza (in Emilia-Romagna) and Novara (in Piedmont). As an airport hub, Milan is subject to flows which are global in nature. As an international fair, it is a *locus* linked to a geographic place, but it is also a function holding specialized knowledge which is global in nature; hence it is a *globus*. Turning to Milan's universities and research centres, we see a flow of foreign students, patents and knowledge. In the fashion and design industries, the city is a crossroad for visitors, designers and the creative professions, which means global, but also local in terms of artisans, businesses and services produced in the district. This is another way of looking at a city's positionality.

The Milan logistics function

The Milanese logistics region is a quadrangle including Novara, Piacenza, Bergamo and Varese (and their Piedmont, Emilia-Romagna and Lombardy regions). This can be seen, thanks to real estate data showing logistics platforms and warehouses. The data attest to the logistics' growing expansion: almost half of the enterprises are located 'out of Milan', in the wider logistics region.

Flows are increasing from and to Asia and East Europe. The main transport mode is by road, followed by water and (last and marginal) rail. Air transport is growing, but 60–70% of traders in merchandise to/from Italy prefer other European airport hubs like Munich or Frankfurt. Germany, France and the United States are Milan's main commercial partners. Milan logistics enterprises account for 14% of employees, 20% of value added and 33% of turnover of the whole Italian logistics sector.

The Milanese logistics region is connected with and utilizes Ligurian ports, North European ports, the freight platforms of Novara, Verona and Padua and the logistics gateways of Basel and Duisburg. Its strength is confirmed by 19 terminals (30% of Italian intermodal flows) and by the presence of international logistics groups (Deutsche Post, Saima Avandero, Geodis, UPS). Such groups occupy the top positions (14 out of 25) in the ranking of logistics enterprises in Milan. International openness is led here by foreign logistics companies.

The Milan Fair function

Located in the conurbation between Milan and Pero-Rho, the Milan Fair constitutes the exhibition core of 37,000 enterprises of Northern Italy. It is a world leader in mechanical, electro-technical (with 25% foreign firms) and design sectors like furniture and fashion (30% foreign firms).

The flows and cross-fertilization between the world of domestic production and global people rest on the Fair infrastructure. The Fair offers small business located in industrial districts opportunities to move (*districts on the move*) and develop negotiations, absorb change and exogenous shocks, and survive and regenerate over the long term. For the district networks, trust between individuals and groups counts more of contracts: they also need assessment through periodical monitoring. Group members receive stimuli from outside and understand their position in relation to insider partners and outsiders. They can figure out new solutions and generate new ideas. The Fair is the physical and cognitive scaffold on which to introduce innovations in products and in processes.

The Milan airport function

Malpensa, Linate and Orio al Serio are Milan's three airports, located in three provinces (Varese, Milan, Bergamo). They specialize in (respectively) intercontinental, point-to-point national and low-cost flights. Malpensa's decline from 23 million passengers in 2007 to 18 million in 2013 (but 11 million in the first half of 2014) is only partially due to the global economic crisis. In fact, in the same period, Linate only slightly reduced its flows from 9.9 million to 9 million passengers, and Orio al Serio increased from 5.7 million to 8.9 million.

Competition among Italian airports, the crisis of the national air company (finally absorbed by a Gulf Emirates company), and a lack of strategic vision by the regional and local authorities are among the reasons. Governing an international airport is a matter of strong regional vision, as in the case of the German airports (Frankfurt among others) led by the Laender. Malpensa is destined to be a second-level hub compared to London, Paris, Frankfurt and Amsterdam. The infrastructural idoneity HUB index (including the minimum connecting time) stands at 6.0 for Malpensa, 8.3 for Frankfurt, 7.9 for Paris and 7.3 for London.

The Milanese university function

Milan's seven-universities system (nine including Varese and Bergamo) is growing. In sectors like medicine, fashion and design growth, the system is also fed by private investments. The system is undergoing internationalization through the attraction of foreign students exerted by the Bocconi, Polytechnic and IULM. In postgraduate courses, one student out of six is from another country at the Bocconi, one out of 10 at Polytechnic.

The foreign students are European (mostly from Eastern Europe), but flows are increasing from Asia, the Middle East and Mediterranean countries as well. Milan could be the training gateway for the new Europe and

78   *The European urban contract*

the capital of the Mediterranean training system. These are important flows, but they are also spontaneous and disorganized: a coordinated effort to attract young people from around the world would be necessary. The critical point is that in Italy, the state is the key institution in the field of the universities, yet its role is declining and investments have dwindled in this time of crisis. Local and regional governments are not interested in taking on key roles. The result is poor performance in the crucial international ranking system of universities.

The Milan research and innovation function

Lombardy concentrates one quarter of all of Italy's research and development (R&D), yet it is only 71st among the 208 European regions of the European Regional Innovation Scoreboard. Seventy per cent of R&D regional expenditure is private, 18% is university and only 7% is public administration. The private employees in R&D number 22,000, while the public employees also come to 22,000: clearly, the public-sector productivity is very low. The balance of payments in the field (property rights, patents, know-how: in other words, all the knowledge not embodied in a product but 'disembodied') is negative. This means Milan is weak in industrial invention, patents and know-how; it is positive only in technological services.

The flows (what Milan sells in R&D) are directed to the European Union (the United Kingdom, the Low Countries, Germany), and payments too (what Milan buys in immaterial technology) go in that direction (the United Kingdom, Germany). Also in terms of research and development (R&D) capacity, the university system is internationally closed: 88% of the cooperation contracts of consortia and foundations and 57% of university department contracts are within Italy. Milan is leader at home, but dependent on outside in the crucial field of production of new knowledge.

The Milan design function

The Milanese design district is based on three pillars: fashion, furniture and the home and advertising and graphic design. It combines high-conception activities and service production, exhibition, communication, training and manufacturing. In this respect, it is probably first in the world. For example, furniture: 34,000 employees are jointly engaged in enterprises often born before World War II, in cooperation with Milan Polytechnic architects/designers in touch with North American and North European design schools.

More than one-third of Italy's furniture companies invest in design as their main competitive asset: they employ 1,141 designers, half of them foreigners. Companies are located in Milan or within 70 kilometres of the centre. Italy is the world leader in the furniture industry, following China. The main 18 companies feed 4,000 client shops, 400 directly owned by

The European urban contract   79

the company. Two hundred thirty-five showrooms or specialized shops are located in downtown Milan – more than in New York or Paris, where Italian companies are actively present.

The Milan fashion function

The peculiar nature of the fashion industry in Milan lies in bringing together what capitalism normally divides: conception and execution, big and small, design and production. The ecosystem of the fashion industry is composed of giants (stylists like Armani and Valentino, Prada and Dolce e Gabbana, Marras, Gucci and so on) and a myriad of artisans, art masters, modellers and tailors able to capture the ever changing and contradictory demands of the fashion world.

The dimensions of the phenomenon are impressive. Direct employment is accounted for by 37,500 employees distributed through 6,000 enterprises (the average size of the unit of production typically being six employees), and yet but one-fifth of the total value added of the Milanese economy is directly or indirectly connected to the fashion industry (D'Ovidio 2014).

The local constellation of fashion enterprises comprises a more extensive district including Milan, Busto Arsizio, Como, Varese, Monza and Vigevano, specialized in different products and production chains (from silk to shoes, from textile to fashion design). The miracle is that, notwithstanding the overall globalization and delocalization trends, the different phases of conception, design and production are still combined here, making the daily exchange of knowledge and rapid adjustment to demand variations still possible. Production is carried out within a range of 60 kilometres from Milan.

The spatial distribution of the fashion industry is also a matter of income polarization. The 48 enterprises with higher revenue are responsible for 94% of the total amount of revenue. The small and artisan firms producing for the giants limit themselves to a small share of the revenue.

The creative industry is largely based on family companies (Corbetta et al. 2014). The family of entrepreneurs leads 48% of the creative industry companies in Milan (with more than €20 million turnover); the remaining 41% are led by multinationals (the remainder consists of cooperatives and consortia). This is another feature of the polarization effect which makes it clear that the urban contract is a matter of both local and global players in a decidedly asymmetric game.

According to the creative class theory, led by Richard Florida and others, talented people are attracted by places where some peculiar characteristics of technology, environment and culture exist. In the case of Milan, we can see how varied the interplay is among the social actors making the creative industry viable. On one hand, we find a robust, yet limited group of giants leading the world-famous brands and sending their products out all over the world, sometimes family-driven companies, sometimes multinationals. On the other hand, we find a diffused system of small and artisan firms,

80 *The European urban contract*

scattered around the territory and interconnected in a vital ecosystem, yet holding a limited share of the revenue produced within the system.

Conclusion

City deals, contracts *de ville*, strategic plans: these are some of the forms of urban contract we have ascertained in the European experience. 'Negotiating' urbanization means here formally including local constituencies and social groups, and, overall, integrating manifold institutional levels of government in the urban governance machine.

The concept of the city's 'speech', recently formulated by Saskia Sassen as a way of directly expressing a city's collective behaviour, can be contrasted with the silence of the city (a term Antonio Gramsci used to stigmatize cities like Rome and Naples with a weak social structure, hence unable to enjoy the faculty of 'speech'). London, Paris and Milan do have speech through their collective actions (plans, programmes, deals) able to overcome the problems of social weakness and silence of the city. In the case of London, such speech is very much attuned to the voice of the city's business sectors. In the case of Paris, the speech is prevalently that of the state, and the city and regional governments. In the case of Milan, we can hear the speech of many functional sectors of economic society, as the local government is unable to utter speech at the metropolitan level.

What directions do these 'speech acts' take? A common direction and challenge has been to make the city more competitive among the European and international urban hierarchies – a rallying cry starting from the 1980s, in years of urban decline in Europe, and still alive. With London, the point is to be first in the world, a boast able to attract manifold investments and worldwide interests to the city. Using the speech of the past (colonial and imperial) to reaffirm the economic supremacy of the financial capital of the world is still a strategy adopted by the urban elites of London. But also in the case of Paris, being great ('Grand Paris') has been the mantra of urban strategies and policies led by the French government since at least 2007. As far as Milan is concerned, the 2015 Expo, 'Feeding the Planet', has constituted the primary example of a strategy to secure a prominent role in the world.

Yet what is the price to pay in terms of equality and social integration? The European urban contract cannot exclude the weaker segments of society without denying its very nature. Inclusion, as well as integration, of the lower social strata into the social pyramid has been the main outcome of two centuries of social conflicts. The Paris commune and the British municipal welfare state have been emblematic of a progressive, open spirit among European cities. Again we can quote Gramsci, seeing the city as the progressive place of modern, urban types of population.

'London first' (the motto of the lobby which includes the city's leading capitalist groups) has been able to drive London's politics and ideology in

The European urban contract   81

terms of growth in both financial capital and population: more private capital, yet social housing is still strong, placing London first also in terms of social housing stock (if not affordability). When Donald Trump, the Republican candidate for the presidency of the United States, said that Muslims should be excluded from the country, the conservative mayor of London, Boris Johnson, replied, 'As a city where more than 300 languages are spoken, London has a proud history of tolerance and diversity and to suggest there are areas where police officers cannot go because of radicalisation is simply ridiculous.'

Paris is the main competitive follower of London, yet willing to compete on different grounds: more state and public sector, more affordable housing (from 17% to 30% is the target of the new mayor of Paris, the socialist Anne Hidalgo). Yet the risk of social exclusion is a paradoxical outcome, possibly due to the efficiency of a public policy which has been able to create zones of public housing mainly for ethnic minorities. Milan is a global network node, yet unable to govern its own metropolitan area: functionally equivalent to other global cities, yet neither reflexively conscious of its role nor governed through institutional design according to metropolitan standards.

To sum up, are European cities still places of urban contracts socially oriented, more than market oriented? The answer is, at the moment, positive. The wave of globalization and finance-driven capitalism has certainly produced effects of increasing pressures towards social polarization and inequalities; the immigration of millions from the Middle East and North Africa has seen defensive walls and barriers raised in many European countries. However, the European resources for integration and solidarity have not been exhausted. They are still there.

Notes

1   *The Economist*, October 4–10, 2014.
2   Extracted from the website of the City of London at www.cityoflondon.gov.uk (visited on September 30, 2014).
3   I follow here and elsewhere in this chapter P. Ackroyd (2000), the most accurate literary account of London's endless expansion.
4   Mayor of London, London Plan Annual Monitoring Report 4, February 2008, p. 36.
5   *The Economist*, December 20, 2014–January 2, 2015.
6   For a comparison with Barcelona, see Nel.lo (2002).

3 The North American urban contract

My point of departure will be the journey of the French aristocrat Alexis de Tocqueville, one of the major modern historians, and possibly (according to Elster 2009) the first social scientist, to the United States of America in 1831. In his work *Democracy in America*, Tocqueville was the first to analyze the township as the fundamental unit of the bottom-up social fabric of the states. The new system (which Tocqueville admired and at the same time was surprised by) was entirely based on the distribution of power in a myriad of groups, factions, towns and cities. It was the Founding Fathers' legacy to avoid any power concentration and leave individuals free to pursue their own self-interest, which will eventually entail participating in the public sphere, and so on and up, to the level of state-building. This key feature of the American system – political fragmentation – is functional to the efficiency and performance of democracy. A century later, another European social scientist visiting the United States, the German sociologist Werner Sombart, observed that in American cities, trace of community was cancelled and pure organic society was demolished. A mere rationality was employed in the design of the urban fabric: the urban grid divided the whole country into squares which were always the same.

While Sombart was writing his text (1906) explaining why socialism is not possible in the United States, the new frontier was attracting millions of people from Europe and elsewhere in the world: immigrants unable to speak a word of English, workers without any industrial culture, East European Jews, Irish Catholics, Polish peasants, illiterate Southern Italians and Chinese coolies, all absorbed and blended in American cities. 'Within the span of a few decades from the late 19th to the early 20th century, the United States was transformed from a predominately rural agrarian society to an industrial economy centered in large metropolitan cities. (. . .) The decades surrounding 1900 were not only the age of industrialization in the United States, but were also the age of urbanization and immigration. The 1880s were the first decade in American history, with the exception of the Civil War decade, when the urban population increased more than the rural population (in absolute numbers)' (Hirschman and Mogford 2009).

The 'dispersed metropolis' of MIT urban planner Kevin Lynch and the 'generic city' of Chicago sociologist Richard Sennett in the late 20th century are the latest and indeed rich intellectual fruits of this heritage. In this case, we see the urban contract written with the immigration procedures allowing the new nation to be fed by unprecedented flows of people from around the world (the 'First New Nation' as American sociologist Seymour M. Lipset proudly called it).

If we look at some New England rural-urban landscapes, as are seen in Vermont, we can still understand the North American spirit Tocqueville analyzed. In his entertaining text 'South of the Northeast Kingdom' (2002), the talented dramaturgist David Mamet, born in Chicago but living in Vermont, puts it in such terms: Montpelier, the capital of the state, was a point of transit on the way from Boston to Montreal. State Street had been the old Post Road, but after the creation of the state highway, it was abandoned by commerce, farms and the urban services farmers required. It is now a place of residence, and around it a new renaissance of artisan handicrafts has flourished. Burlington's unregulated urban expansion is only 50 miles away.

We have here a sample of early urban America: individualism and locality-based networks, infrastructures (railways and highways) structuring the unlimited expansion of the urban settlements, and metropolitan poles of attraction. Bottom-up and top-down approaches to urbanization coexist. The urban contract is written here by yeoman democracy and railroad capitalism, a mixture where politics seems to play a minor role in comparison with yesterday's Europe and today's Asia. Yet the role played by Alexander Hamilton (one of the Founding Fathers of America and treasury secretary) in supporting the early development of public investment in infrastructures has merited a place in history.

A more recent scientific account of the North American urban contract is presented by new neoclassical urban economy (NNUE) literature. According to Michael Storper's (2013) critical review, it lies in an interplay between workers, firms and developers (on the horizontal axis) and the transport system (on the vertical axis) (see Figure 3.1). The workers are quite ready to move from the cold, densely populated locations in the Northeast of the country to warmer, less densely populated places in the South (Storper

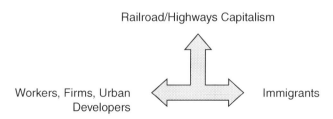

Figure 3.1 The North American urban contract

84 *The North American urban contract*

2013, p. 16). Firms change location in pursuit of lower costs (labour, energy, taxes). Builders and developers adjust housing stocks following individual capitalist self-interest but obtaining a collective outcome of general equilibrium. The interplay is made possible and in some cases even driven by investments in yesterday's railroads, today's interstate highways systems.

Nineteenth-century railroad capitalism was a combination of the major ingredients of rational and irrational capitalism, of modern routinized enterprise and huge rapacious enterprise in the financial and colonial spheres in Weberian terms. 'American railroad capitalism combined not only modern and traditional features (in Weber's sense) but also had a multi-ethnic component. It depended on international capital, mostly English and German, employed a multi-ethnic workforce, including tens of thousands of Chinese coolies, and expected its profits to come primarily from land sales to immigrants' (Roth 2000). The Northern Pacific Railroad was a case in point: created by Henry Villard, a German-born tycoon, to connect the two American coasts, it was later rescued by European-American capitalists like the Siemens, Rothschilds, Cohens, Speyers and Morgans.

In the 20th century, the political role of central/local governments was apparently limited to guaranteeing the context of freedom (of expression, religion, economy and security) Franklin D. Roosevelt proclaimed to Congress in 1941. In actual terms, the state had a role both in creating infrastructures (railroads, highways, ports) and in promoting industry (Ministry of Defense expenditure in R&D above all), boosting development in selected American cities. To take one example among many, Los Angeles was selected for major port infrastructure investments, creating in California the military research infrastructure destined to incubate the future Silicon Valley.

In the American urban contract, civil society is constantly appearing and disappearing. In 1955, citizens protested the San Francisco Trafficways Plan, inspiring similar revolts to halt freeway construction in US cities. Yet in 1956, the Federal-Aid Highway Act authorized construction of 5,000 miles of urban freeways and 41,000 miles of interstate freeways (American Institute of Architects 2012). The same can be said years later of Afro-American protests in urban America, students' movement in American campuses and so on. They are clearly important factors influencing the history of urban America, but in a way far from the European pattern: much more contingent and destructured, like the temporary assemblages of American architecture in Los Angeles's four ecologies (Banham 1971).

Gerard Frug's (1984) text on the city as a legal concept casts light on the historical roots and recent evolution of the American urban contract. In the foundational phase of American cities, the public-private identities of cities are intermeshed. In fact, the cities are similar to merchant organizations in protecting their members, almost an extension of the market, in this respect departing from the pattern of the European medieval cities. The organic, German conception of cities gives way to a liberal identity as mere location for individuals. In America, 'both cities and mercantile corporations served to protect the private investments of individual founders' (Frug 1984, p. 257). Cities and mercantile corporations were only distinguished by the scope of property rights: 'private corporations being those founded by individual contributions of property, and public corporations being those founded by the government' (ibid.). Although this did not reflect historic reality, as most cities were not founded by the government, it became the view of city status in the United States. The city authority was divided into two parts: legislation for the public good (hence subordinate to the state), and the possession of property for municipal uses (assigned to the self-determination of cities).

Only after the 1850s was the local autonomy of cities reduced in favour of state control: cities became not a miniature state, but business corporations. Owning and organizing businesses, cities were similar to enterprises and could reduce the risk of corruption due to corrupt businessmen seeking city contracts. Max Weber's analysis of city bosses in America (in *Politics as a Vocation*) comes to mind: they are political entrepreneurs receiving money from the great financial tycoons, including bribes and tips; parties are strongly capitalist enterprises making profit through political control of mostly municipal administrations.

Boston

'New England towns, at the height of their power, were religious and fraternal communities, and their ability to represent what seemed to be the fundamental interests of their citizens enabled the towns to control the state, rather than the other way around' (Frug 1984, p. 274). In this insightful picture by a brilliant scholar of local government law, no room is left to the economy. This is very interesting given the force of the market in the American view of society. On the other hand, however, Frug notes that despite their political power, cities 'would still have to depend for their survival on the goodwill of the private corporations that did business within their boundaries'.

The dilemma of the American city is well represented here: obtaining political autonomy from the state to protect their citizens, but depending, on a territorial competitive basis, on taxes and duties paid by private corporate bodies to extract revenues for the city's services, survival and growth. Private enterprises can always move towards better local conditions and leave their original communities, and citizens too can vote with their feet for much the same reasons.

Boston, the New England moral and economic capital, has undergone profound changes during its life, maintaining control over both sides of this dilemma. It has proved capable of good local government and attracting and maintaining firms and capital, labour and knowledge through a peculiar urban contract.

86 *The North American urban contract*

A history of the Brahmins

Created in 1857 in Boston, *The Atlantic* was a monthly elite-oriented magazine founded by (among others) Francis H. Underwood, Ralph Waldo Emerson, Oliver Wendell Holmes and Henry Wadsworth Longfellow. Holmes's 1860 article giving the name of 'Boston Brahmins' to descendants of the British colonists coming to America in the early 17th century traced the genealogy of the first urban elite of the United States. Interestingly, it is presented as a caste – the upper caste of the Indian social system. The literati holding the monopoly of state functions are a case of intellectual elite rather different from the bureaucratic Western model. It is a mix of civic religion, Puritan ethics and bourgeois aristocracy that could well have been the brainchild of Max Weber.

The name of the Lowell family resounds among Harvard University presidents, ministers, federal judges and even the mill city of Massachusetts. The Adamses provided US presidents, industrialists and presidents of companies like Raytheon, a technological leader in military industry. The Appletons were leaders in the Massachusetts Bay Colony, the Dudleys founded Cambridge, the Forbeses were clergymen and merchants in China but also invested in railroads, while the Winthrops provided governors and so forth. Many of them belonged to the cultivated ruling class, with a monopoly in knowledge through colleges, universities and newspapers. And indeed many of them had come over on the *Mayflower*, and signed the Mayflower Compact at Cape Cod in 1620: 'covenant and combine ourselves together into a civil body politic, for our better ordering and preservation and furtherance of the ends aforesaid'.

Interpreting the urban form: City of culture

In Kevin Lynch's *The Image of the City*, which came out in the 1960s, Boston was still a city of water, defined by its peninsula form. Water, the port and the Charles River are constituent parts of the Bostonians' image of their city. This was even more so in the 17th century, when Boston was founded and began to expand. The new land industriously gained by levelling hills and extending into the new areas was used to include and exclude. When immigrants moved in to South End Boston, the Brahmins moved out to other parts. The Bostonians, in Henry James's great literary picture, were sociologically proud of their cultural exclusivity. 'The general character of the place struck him as Bostonian; this was, in fact, very much what he had supposed Boston to be. He had always heard Boston was a city of culture.' At the same time, they were landlords and developers, the key social structure of the coming 'growth machine'. In the meantime, universities like Harvard and MIT, founded by the Boston Brahmins to create the local elite or later financed by the federal land grants of Vermont Senator Morrill's Act, became the main infrastructure of urban regeneration and growth in the 20th century (Logan and Molotch 1987).

The North American urban contract 87

Thus Jane Jacobs (1961) was on the wrong track when she interpreted the creation by the Boston Committee of Institutes of a district dedicated 'solely to institutions of an educational, scientific and artistic character', as early as 1859, as the beginning of Boston's long, slow decline. It was certainly contrary to Jacob's view of the mixed nature of cities; however, Boston's turned out to be a long-lasting success story, albeit highly selective.

The conventional image of Boston and the Bostonians is one of stability, of a settled (white, working, middle-class and WASP) population, but mobility is in fact the key to understand the city. In-migration and out-migration were very high in the 19th and early 20th centuries, with two migration streams: 'enormous numbers of newcomers continued to flow into Boston, while vast numbers of people left the community for other destinations' (Thernstrom 1973, p. 22). In the decades from 1880 to 1920, one-third of the city's residents was born outside the United States and the fraction of immigrants in the labour force was even higher, around 45%. Decline in migration started only in the 1920s due to restrictive legislation; by 1960, the foreign population was only 12% and internal (US) migrants were 18%. The stable, Massachusetts-born population accounted for 70% of the total.

These data challenge the image of America as a nation of stable, loosely connected communities. The flows of people were so massive that in a decade most of the inhabitants of the city had moved and abandoned the city for other destinations, which may account for America's labour force adjustments and great flexibility, hence continuous innovation and change. A nation of in-migrants and out-migrants opened the way to capitalism's creative destruction analyzed by Joseph Schumpeter. Actually, from the 1930s, this mobility pattern changed dramatically: a much greater stability came about, particularly in terms of white-collar and skilled workers. The less-skilled immigrants continued to move across the states: their ethnic neighbourhoods of Irish and Italian communities (like the North End studied by Herbert Gans as an urban village) were composed of internally highly mobile sub-communities. To some extent, this is contradicted by Jacobs's image of North End (1961) as a stable community investing in its housing and streets as opposed to the planners' image of a slum – birds of passage, as Michael Piore called the migrant workers. Hence their occupational mobility and the ability to advance, generation after generation, in the professional career structures. A different picture emerges in the case of the Afro-American immigrants: their chances of entering into urban life and acquiring the consequent mobility were severely limited. The racial imprinting of the American urban contract is a persistent feature, also in the case of Boston.

This imprinting remains true if we go on to consider the most recent urban renaissance of Boston, taking place between the 1970s and the 1990s. In the 1960s and 1970s, the economic and social base of the city entered into decline, essentially as a matter of the deindustrialization of America (Bluestone and Harrison 1982) and the change in the general conditions

88   *The North American urban contract*

favouring a traditional industrial urban structure. Communities like Lowell based on the mill economy were abandoned by industrial firms and fell into severe decline. It was then that Boston saw its most dramatic decline, in terms of population dynamics, mobility and occupational activities. Migration began towards California and the Southern states. The New England model based on quality production and working-class and white-collar occupations was at risk.

The following revolution (Bluestone and Stevenson 2002) was threefold – in demography, industrial structure and space – showing contemporary racial attitudes, patterns of residential segregation and the distribution of success in the labour market. The most striking change occurred in foreign in-migration. Between 1970 and 1990, the foreign population increased two and a half times, rising from 200,000 to 500,000 in the Boston regional area. Here was a new invasion: a flow of mostly South-East Asian, Central American and Caribbean populations, while Afro-Americans played a relatively minor part. Being mostly ethnocentric-white in 1970, Boston and its region rapidly became multicultural and multi-ethnic in nature in the 1990s.

In 1950, Boston's white population stood at 758,000, while in 1990, it came to 360,000: in 40 years it was more than halved. The Afro-American population increased from 42,000 to 145,000: a fairly steady rise. The Hispanic population was zero in 1950, numbering 59,000 in 1990. The Asian population rose from zero to 30,000. Other minorities accounted for 35,000 members of the population in 1990. To sum up, the minorities as a percentage of the total population rose from 5% to 40% over the decades from 1950 to 1990 (Bluestone and Stevenson 2002).

An update (2013) shows the Boston population now standing at 645,000, rising again (+ 4.6% with respect to 2010), due to the increasing attraction of the central city. The white population is still the majority with 53.9% (but whites alone, without Hispanics or Latinos, constitute 47% of the population), the Afro-American population comes to 24.4%, the Hispanic population to 17.5% and the Asian population to 8.9%. The social urban problems of the metropolitan core are clear: 21.4% of Boston's population is below the poverty level (11.4% in Massachusetts), the homeownership rate comes to 34.1% in Boston (whereas in Massachusetts it is 61.7%). The median household income is $53,000 in Boston (but it is in the region of $10,000–$30,000 in Roxbury or Mattapan), and $71,000 in the richer metropolitan area, although the single-adult family income can be less than half that figure (as is often the case of the Afro-Americans). The Boston area industrial structure developed from a mill-based to a mind-based economy in the very same two decades. At first the change was characterized by the relocation of firms in high-tech sectors from Boston to Route 128 and Route 495. This was a clear case of new capitalism based on knowledge sources (Harvard and MIT primarily) ready to capture agglomeration economies. It was also a new form of investment in infrastructures like highways, giving access to low-cost land for enterprises. The firms located along the 128 highway

The North American urban contract   89

numbered 1,200, with a total of 80,000 employees as early as 1973. The decline in manufacturing employment (-44% in Boston between 1970 and 1990) was more than offset by the expansion and relocation of new, high-tech jobs in the dozens of industrial parks along the new corridors of Route 128 and Route 495. The retail and FIRE (finance, insurance, real estate) sectors also decentralized at the regional level, whereas in central Boston the private-service sector and the public sector (from hospitals to other health institutions) accounted for the major share of urban employment.

To sum up, in the two decades 1970–90, total private employment grew both in Boston (from 405,000 to 438,000) and most strikingly in the Boston region (from 1,200,000 to 1,700,000). The old manufacturing shrank considerably in Boston (from 55,000 to 31,000), but the new high-tech manufacturing base remained stable in the Boston region (from 353,000 to 340,000). Trade shrank in Boston (from 105,000 to 74,000), but grew in the region (from 362,000 to 469,000). FIRE grew both in Boston (from 65,000 to 76,000) and, more strikingly, in the Boston region (from 99,000 to 161,000). Private services doubled both in Boston (from 119,000 to 211,000) and in its region (from 308,000 to 651,000) (Bluestone and Stevenson 2002).

The third revolution was spatial. Passing from a monocentric to a polycentric urban region, Boston was a case of successful suburban sprawl, which Harvard urban economist Edward Glaeser considers a matter of the 'triumph of the city'. School busing in the 1970s had an important role (albeit difficult to understand for non-Americans) in making urban decentralization possible. The white population leaving the central city for 'safer' suburbs also played a major role. New suburban communities doubled or tripled residents in the space of a few decades. All these changes followed the previous model Herbert Gans famously called 'urban villagers': it had been the model of white non-American immigrants, famously the West End Italian district. Boston, Cambridge, Chelsea, Lowell, Lawrence (the historic cities of the region, mostly working-class communities) all lost some of their populations. Such cities have had the role of producing wealth, but also of housing the poor population (minorities trapped in the city) and attracting daily commuters (who pay taxes in other cities, where they live). The consequence for the city was fiscal crisis (in the 1980s), while federal decentralization and fragmentation of local communities (more than 150 municipalities) reinforced this highly decentralized trend.

Interpreting the contract form: The enduring mechanism of selection

The most striking data emerging from the Greater Boston Social Survey conducted in 1995 (Bluestone and Stevenson 2002) concern racial segregation. This excellent Russell Sage research, the most complete on Boston in the past 20 years, is in fact subtitled: 'race, space and economic change in an American metropolis'.

90   *The North American urban contract*

The percentages of individuals living in segregated neighbourhoods (a majority-minority neighbourhood is a census block with more than 50% Afro-Americans or more than 50% Hispanic residents) are as follows: Afro-American 70%, Hispanic 38%, white 1%. The foreign-born population living in segregated neighbourhoods comes to 20%, whereas the US-born population stands at 4%.

These data show how the urban contract has been implemented through racial segregation. The change has been striking and concentrated over the past 40 years. A large part (40%) of the Boston urban population is now accounted for by minorities, but their places of residence are still closely defined by racial status. Moreover, the Afro-American segregation figures are twice the corresponding Hispanic figures. This means that the racial groups have limited spatial interaction, if any at all. In some neighbourhoods like Roxbury (an Afro-American ghetto, now Hispanic), Mattapan (a Haitian enclave), South Dorchester (Asian and Hispanic) and, to a lesser extent, South End (now a gentrified neighbourhood), among others, segregation is particularly marked. Also at the regional level we find segregation, or at least clustering by race: Hispanic in Lawrence, Asian in Lowell, Afro-American in Brockton and so on.

The same also applies, although to a lesser extent, in terms of occupational structures and opportunities. If we observe the three most common occupations by race, we find that 20.2% of white males are in executive, administrative and managerial positions, 20.3% in specialized professional occupations and 15.9% in sales occupations. Of Afro-American males, 23.1% are in specialized professional occupations, 15.3% in service occupations and 11.9% in protective service occupations, while 19.6% of Hispanic males are in service occupations, 22.6% working as machine operators, assemblers and inspectors and 13.7% as handlers, equipment cleaners, helpers and labourers. These data show that occupational segregation is also very marked. It is still a very rare exception (1.4%) for an Afro-American to be a manager or executive. Afro-Americans are concentrated in professions (service and protective services) where the whites represent no more than 3% of the total white occupational distribution. The Hispanic population too is concentrated in manual and service occupations where the whites represent no more than 2 or 3% of the total white occupational distribution. It seems that the social groups fail to interact, or have very limited interaction due to race segregation.

Also for the female labour force, racial segregation is a sad fact, although to a lesser extent. Of white females, 29.2% are in specialized professional occupations, 20% in administrative support and 16.9% in sales, while 30.4% of Afro-American females are in service occupations, 23.2% in administrative support and 15.8% in sales. Of Hispanic females, 41% work as machine operators, assemblers and inspectors, while 17.9% are in service and 15.6% in specialized professional occupations.

To interpret these data, we should note that historically the process of Boston's Afro-American population growth was more concentrated in the

The North American urban contract 91

1940–60 period, when that population tripled. In 1970, there were proportionally more Afro-Americans in Boston than in New York in 1960 or in Chicago in 1950, although fewer in absolute numbers, of course (Thernstrom 1973). The percentage in Boston was in fact 16.3% in 1970. The origin of most of the Afro-American population was in-migration from the South, but a large percentage was born in Boston.

The historical pattern, however, is that of permanent occupational segregation regardless of status as immigrants or born in the city. This was true in the great 1880–1900 immigration decades: in Boston, Afro-Americans of the first, second or third generations were all confined in blue-collar, unskilled occupations, whereas a very high percentage of Irish and other European immigrants were able to obtain semiskilled factory jobs, skilled trades and white-collar occupations. The Afro-Americans remained heavily overrepresented in all the poor occupations, as janitors, porters, servants and waiters. Even half a century later, in 1940, six out of seven of Boston's Afro-Americans were still confined to the same poor manual occupations.

According to Thernstrom, however, a breakthrough occurred between 1940 and 1970. Afro-Americans started to make a greater showing in semi-skilled operative jobs, and also in clerical occupations. However, the percentage did not increase in professional and managerial positions, and their occupational upgrading failed to reduce the income gap relative to other groups, and to whites in particular. Their median earnings relative to whites actually fell significantly in the 1950s, and picked up in the 1960s. In 1970, the Afro-Americans of Boston were still earning less than three-quarters of the earnings of their white counterparts.

This long-lasting social urban inequality is therefore rooted in practices of exclusion: the self-reinforcing causes are among others, lower education and residential segregation.

Regarding the former factor, education, in 1970, the median school years of Afro-Americans were 11.6. In 1995, the figure came to 13.4 for Afro-American males and 12.5 for females, a clear improvement. However, inequality in higher education is another unfortunate fact, limiting entry into the higher-level professions and bureaucratic hierarchies of both the private and the public sectors for Afro-Americans.

The same pattern regarding the Irish and Afro-American population in the past recurred in the recent Boston triple revolution. Recent immigrants, Asian and Hispanic now, are much better off than their Afro-American counterparts. The newcomers are from Latin America, Colombia, the Caribbean and Puerto Rico, and they build up their informal networks; they have been able to forge a place in the local labour market by replacing former immigrants from Italy, France or Canada, leaving their old jobs (in industries like textile) in search of new white-collar jobs. Thus the immigration chains pass from old European immigration to new Hispanic immigration, largely excluding Afro-Americans. Asian immigrants came from India, Korea, post-war Vietnam, Cambodia and Laos. Their capacity to adapt – in

92 *The North American urban contract*

terms of residential conditions and occupation – is very high, both in Boston and in the surrounding cities with an industrial tradition, like Lowell (where Wang Computers is located).

Going on, now, to the second explanatory causal factor, residential segregation, it may be impossible to assert that ghettoization is directly correlated to occupational segregation. Relevant here are the cases both of Jews living in the American ghetto but ranking high in white-collar occupations, and the Irish, among the least spatially segregated yet in bad occupational ranking. However, it is worth noting that the residential segregation of Afro-Americans has increased over time, instead of decreasing: the residential segregation index was 51 in 1880, 64 in 1910, 78 in 1930, 86 in 1940, 80 in 1950, 84 in 1960 (Thernstrom 1973).

The mechanisms of representation in the urban contract are therefore highly selective. In this respect, the Boston area has been characterized by a 'revolutionary continuity' of its elite in city building, and by an enduring mechanism of selection based mainly on race.

The Boston Brahmins have left as their heritage the world's leading university system, having its centre in Cambridge and spreading around the entire metropolitan area. The firms and spin-off companies agglomerate in central Cambridge, around MIT. The impact on a labour market made of self-employment and services (one-third of US jobs, according to the Freelance Union) is very strong. The land market and urban rent follow this strong, knowledge-based primacy. The parties to the urban contract are mostly the universities, knowledge-based firms and services and the government. Of the 49,667 firms in Boston, only 11.6% are Afro-American-owned, although this minority accounts for 24.4% of the population, employed in low-skilled sectors of the economy. Asians and Hispanics perform better.

The Boston Redevelopment Authority and the mechanisms of urban community building

The powerful Boston Redevelopment Authority (BRA), with a budget of $18 million and a staff of 86 full-time personnel in 2016, is expected – as its statute declares – to 'engage local residents, businesses, agencies and institutions in guiding the future character of Boston's unique neighborhoods and districts'. The BRA was established in 1957 to transform blighted areas, and in 1993 merged with Economic Development Industrial Corporation, gaining even stronger powers than other development agencies in the United States. It has created, in areas such as the Boston South End and the North End, the Waterfront and Charlestown, redevelopments that have attracted new population, wealth and gentrification. The paradox is that a tool entitled to 'untangle the often complicated process of redeveloping old sites, like clearing titles on parcels whose owners have long disappeared',[1] is now criticized and discussed by the local communities involved. Some communities think that the BRA's job was destined for areas now gentrified, and that it should come to an end. Others call for reduction of the huge extension of areas under the BRA.

The North American urban contract 93

The BRA is certainly a major 'owner' of the city, in the sense applied by Saskia Sassen (2014b). It can in fact buy and sell land and buildings, make plan and deals with private developers, negotiate with them and give tax breaks. It is also expected to engage local residents and neighbourhoods in enhancing city life.

The trend Sassen observed in the acquisition of buildings in cities today is from small to large and from public to private, with strong implications for local democracy and rights. This is, of course, the effect of huge privatization processes, led by strong investment groups across the world. But the process is also exacerbated by the work done by public actors, whose accountability is limited, in the city-building activities.

In the case of the BRA, it seems that many of the development projects observed are going in the same direction private developers and market forces have followed. If the public has anything to say, it is in terms of limiting and containing the spontaneous market forces. Listed in Table 3.1 is a sample of the last BRA board meetings (accessed October 6, 2015):

Table 3.1 Boston Redevelopment Authority (BRA) projects (2015)

Site	Project	Final output	Social impact
Jamaica Plain	Redevelopment Project of service area	76 residential units	12+6 affordable units
South End	Redevelopment Project of industrial area	Hotel	the hotel operator will use best effort to hire 51% Boston residents, 25% minorities, 25% women
Midtown Boston South Cove	Development Impact Project of temporary advertising unit to commercial, community and cultural space	23-story hotel, 72 residential units	
Congress Square	Development Impact Project	Retail, offices, residential, boutique hotel	
South Boston		100 condominiums, commercial space	
Pier South Boston Waterfront	Mixed use development, public and open space	Hotel + Residential units	
Midtown Coplay Place	Air rights of Mass Dept. Transportation	542 residential units, store, retail	76 affordable units
South Boston	Development Project	D Street Hotel $200 million investment	$400,000 benefit funds to 12 community organizations

Source: BRA.

94   *The North American urban contract*

The projects are located in wealthy parts of the city and introduce additional space for luxury hotels, condominiums and offices. Some compensation for affordable housing units is introduced in two of the eight projects examined. The proportion of residential/affordable units in the two cases is 4:1 and 8:1, respectively. One interesting example of compensation is to be seen in the case of a hotel, whose operator is engaged in future hiring of residents, minorities and women. An even more interesting case is the use of Community Benefits Funds for a $200 million project hotel on the South Boston Waterfront. In this case, $400,000 paid by the hotel project developer will be distributed by the BRA to 12 community organizations (charities, religious, sailing, etc.) applying for this benefit. The two cases say something about how local consensus is obtained and how the BRA involves communities.

Also astonishing is the amendment procedure the BRA followed in changing the final destination of the project. Projects approved for a destination are later amended, and the amendment is amended again, and so on to include new destinations (e.g. from community open space to residential) or to increase densities (e.g. the numbers of residential units doubled).

According to Frug (2007), a 'rule of law' for cities is needed, to make neighbourhood compliance with the projects and the city–developer negotiation more accountable and transparent. The problem is how to organize community building around projects involving the future destination of the city. The underlying question is about the projects' effects on the overall collective lives of citizens. In this respect, there is a need to discuss and deliberate on land use, but also on the wider-reaching effects of the projects: the kinds of populations attracted or excluded, side effects on social lives and so forth.

The lack of such processes for evaluation and deliberation is partly due to the procedures the public authorities, like the BRA, follow in city redevelopment.

New York

'Within the five boroughs of modern New York alone, archaeologists have identified about eighty Lenape habitation sites, more than two dozen planting fields, and the intricate network of paths and trails that laced them all together.' The fascinating beginning of *Gotham* (Burrows and Wallace 1999), tracing the origin of the settlement since prehistory, already contains a prophecy: New York is destined to be a city of networks, of unending movement of people. Yet these moves and circulations will need adequate infrastructure, a 'grid'. The modern metropolis, the world capital of the 20th century, would simply make this prediction possible. The transition from the paths of native Indian hunters to the streets of European-American immigrant capitalists is the most impressive urban transformation modern history has ever produced. We will follow it in our terms, as a history of urban contracts.

A history of traders and sects

It was, in fact, a contract that gave birth to the city. Peter Schaghen, being in charge of liaison between the Dutch government and the Dutch West Indian Company, writing in 1626 made the earliest reference to the colonial Company's purchase of Manhattan Island from the Lenape Indians for 60 guilders. In a letter now in the Rijksarchief in The Hague, Schaghen reported the arrival of the ship *Wapen van Amsterdam* from the New Netherland colony.

It is worth reading the letter:

> *High and Mighty Lords, Yesterday the ship the Arms of Amsterdam arrived here. It sailed from New Netherland out of the River Mauritius on the 23rd of September. They report that our people are in good spirits and live in peace. The women also have borne some children there. They have purchased the Island Manhattes from the Indians for the value of 60 guilders. It is 11,000 morgens in size [about 22,000 acres]. They had all their grain sowed by the middle of May, and reaped by the middle of August. They sent samples of these summer grains: wheat, rye, barley, oats, buckwheat, canary seed, beans and flax. The cargo of the aforesaid ship is: 7246 Beaver skins, 178½ Otter skins, 675 Otter skins, 48 Mink skins, 36 Lynx skins, 33 Minks, 34 Muskrat skins. Many oak timbers and nut wood. Herewith, High and Mighty Lords, be commended to the mercy of the Almighty,*
>   *In Amsterdam, the 5th of November anno 1626.*
>   *Your High and Mightinesses' obedient, P. Schaghen.*

In *Delirious New York* (1978), Rem Koolhaas remarks that the transaction was a fraud: the sellers were not the owners, had never lived there, but were only passing. It is an interesting account of the purely arbitrary nature of the contract.

The other side – real this time – of the urban contract was tolerance, particularly religious tolerance. In 1654, Ashkenazi and Sephardic Jews – some with passports, others without – arrived in New Amsterdam, and in 1655, they were admitted and granted full residency. In 1682, a Virginian visitor remarked that 'they have as many sects of religion there as in Amsterdam.' The imprinting of religious sects remains as a landmark of the modern capitalist spirit. We can follow here Max Weber in America: his 1904 journey (just a year before *The Protestant Ethic*) 'represented an opportunity for observation and illustration of a certain kind of moral and social order, and a cultural and political dynamic linked to capitalist development. To make sense of this order and trace its dynamic has the effect, whether intentional or not, of moving the American presence toward the center of Weber's thinking about the modern world' (Scaff 2011). To Weber, in his 1904 speech at St. Louis, Missouri, America was

96 *The North American urban contract*

a new nation, possessing an immense territory, in the post–Civil War era without an old aristocracy, and in that respect unburdened by the power of tradition, but having 'democratic traditions handed down by Puritanism as an ever-lasting heirloom', as well as an economy exhibiting in unparalleled ways the 'effects of the power of capitalism'. In the words of Weber: 'It was perhaps never before in history made so easy for any nation to become a great civilized power as for the American people. Yet, according to human calculation, it is also the last time, as long as the history of mankind shall last, that such conditions for a free and great development will be given.'

The words of Weber echo in Richard Sennett's account of the urban grid: 'the grid disoriented those who played upon it; they could not establish what was of value in places without centers or boundaries, spaces of endless, mindless geometric division. This was the Protestant ethic of space' (Sennett 1990). The Manhattan grid was designed in 1811 by Commissioners De Witt, Morris and Rutherford in order to favour the buying, selling and improvement of buildings that were 'cheap to build' (as the commissioners underlined): according to Lewis Mumford, it was the block, projected as a function of a traffic artery; according to Rem Koolhaas, it was a prophetic act, the affirmative nature of the speculative spirit. The city becomes a mosaic of episodes, each contrasting with the others – a perfect architectural design of the competitive, agonistic spirit of capitalism Max Weber described.

Between 1810 and 1900, the population grew from 96,000 to 1,850,000; a second expansion in the five boroughs in 1897 led the growth to 6.9 million in 1930. Since the early 20th century, the urban contract has involved the building of skyscrapers of 100 floors, multiplying the urban rent to an unprecedented extent. Urban regulations come later. In 1916, the Zoning Law (a concept imported from Europe) admitted ex-post the skyscraper logic, defining the largest admissible volume; in the 1920s, the New York Regional Plan Association finally and definitely accepted the inevitability of the skyscraper, and simply asked how to make it more beautiful and safer.

The Zoning Law was a compromise including the interests of different constituencies: the real estate developers, the merchants, the city-beautiful critics of the skyscraper and the social reformers. Harmonizing such interests was a difficult task, although the final outcome was more towards creating a safer environment for building and rebuilding than an attempt to follow the European models of urban growth control. The need to ensure that the values of the buildings were not destined to decrease was the golden rule of the Zoning Law. This was the main interest of real estate developers, of course. But the City itself, obtaining 80% of its budget from taxes on property or buildings, was interested in protecting the value of buildings. As skyscrapers would reduce sunlight and therefore the market and rental values of the adjoining buildings in the area, the Zoning Law would allow for regulation of the height of the buildings. Passed off as the end of laissez-faire

The North American urban contract   97

and of do-as-you-please policy by the *New York Times*, it was in fact the beginning of a new era of urban densification. The Zoning Law also created five area districts with different densities permitted, ranging from the 'A' classification, where industrial activities were allowed and the entire lot could be occupied by buildings, to 'B' and 'C' classifications destined for tenements, to 'D' and finally 'E', destined for detached or attached single-family houses with a maximum of 50% coverage.

In 1939, Democracity was presented at the New York World Exposition: not a utopia, but a concrete proposal for today's way of life, according to the *New York Herald Tribune*. It is democratic like the flows of visitors (farmers, miners, workers, teachers . . .) passing through the Exposition, representing the various social groups of modern society. No better comment could be found on the Simmelian pages on *The Metropolis and Mental Life*, which inspired the architects of modern America as well as the Chicago urban sociologists. Another 1939 New York Exhibition creation was Futurama, a project sponsored by General Motors envisioning an urban landscape of decentralized cities, urban satellites and highways.

Robert Moses' role in building the metropolis has been critically assessed by Jane Jacobs and discussed by urban historians from Robert Caro to Mike Wallace. In the New York municipal archives, Robert Moses' papers document the city's vast infrastructure from 1934 through 1959.

Interpreting the urban form: Cosmopolis

With 8.2 million population in 2010 and 8.6 million in 2015, New York City has recovered from the loss of population in the 1970s and 1980s (when it was 7 million) and is projected to grow to 9 million by 2040 – but it is growing faster. According to New York Municipality, 'New York City's pre-eminence as the world's leading city stems in large part from its unparalleled diversity. That diversity allows people from every imaginable background to live and work side-by-side, share aspects of their cultures, exchange ideas, then mix, match, and innovate to generate the art, literature, fashion, technology, and conceptual breakthroughs that are the envy of the world. And that diversity drives economic growth, as employers decide to locate in the City to take advantage of its incredible and multidimensional talent pool' (City of New York 2015).

Many scholars share this diagnosis, particularly those following Richard Florida's 'creative class' recipe. It means that the cultural capital of cities like New York is driven by human capital looking for appropriate and distinctive qualities of life and spaces. Diversity is therefore the product of the city's attractiveness for high-skilled segments of the workforce, particularly independent professionals (or Ipros) – the most briskly growing segment of the New York labour market in every sector of the economy – as well as talented immigrants from all over the world. Diversity is also the product of primary functions and secondary activities linked to users of the primary ones: in this

98 *The North American urban contract*

respect, New York City is a big diversity generator. It is a container of diversities: the entire world is represented in New York, Don De Lillo's Cosmopolis.

However – the New York Municipality admits – 'the City's diversity is imperiled by the fact that more and more people struggle to afford to live here. New York attracts newcomers from around the nation and from every corner of the globe in part because of the opportunities it provides for people to make better lives for themselves and their families. But our role as a beacon of opportunity is threatened because people cannot afford to give the City a try. Too many existing residents also are shut out of opportunities because they are living in a neighborhood that lacks good schools and good jobs, are homeless, or are going without medical care and other essentials in order to pay the rent.'

One reason is that New York wages have stagnated over the past 20 years, increasing by less than 15%, while the average monthly rent for an apartment in New York City has increased by almost 40%. Housing costs are an increasingly serious threat to the future of New York City. Another reason is the lack of affordable housing plans, which implies more public expenditure to overcome the problem.

New York had already overcome the fiscal crisis of 1975. According to 'The Public Interest' conservative thinking, 'relative prosperity and the illusion that a local economy can sustain the higher taxes that go with bigger government encourages weak government leaders to offer small concessions to special interests, such as municipal unions or vocal advocates for the poor. These concessions snowball over time, creating an ever-larger constituency for government spending and making it increasingly difficult to turn back the clock' (McMahon and Siegel 2005).

It seems that the opposite has occurred. New York City recovered from the fiscal crisis, thanks to cuts and fiscal restructuring, and the economy restarted – the decade of the 1970s remaining a dark side of the city's history. In the 1980s and 1990s, the growth machine, and its financial sector, regained momentum, producing a more unequal society. 'The American economy has experienced rising income and wealth inequality for several decades and there is little evidence that these trends are likely to reverse in the near term' (Pfeffer et al. 2013).

The global city (Sassen 1991) has gone through continuous growth in advanced services employment, continuing also after the 2007 recession. Employment in New York State increased in the last year observed (May 2014/May 2015) from 9,084,000 to 9,219,000.

Racial and ethnic diversity has also increased over the past 30 years in the United States in general, and the states of New York and New Jersey rank very high in the chart. This means that the economy, culture and demography are shifting to more ethnically and racially diverse community mixes. But spatial segregation has increased.

In fact, the share of the population in large and moderate-sized metropolitan areas of the United States living in the poorest and most affluent neighbourhoods has more than doubled since 1970, while the share of families living in middle-income neighbourhoods dropped from 65% to 44%.

It is the large metropolitan areas that have particularly high levels of income segregation: the 10 most segregated metropolitan areas include New York, Philadelphia, Dallas, Detroit, Houston and Los Angeles. New York–New Jersey rank first with 50.2% of families living in the poorest or most affluent neighbourhoods. Three of the four most segregated metropolitan areas are in the New York City region – Bridgeport-Stamford-Norwalk, CT; New York-Wayne-White Plains, NY-NJ; and Newark-Union, NJ (Reardon and Bischoff 2011). This means, to sum up, that more than half of New York City neighbourhoods are dominated by a single racial or ethnic group.

The 2007 recession certainly increased the distances between neighbourhoods. In New York, of the eight Public Use Microdata Areas (PUMAs) with large increases in unemployment rates, five were majority-minority communities prior to the recession. The relationship between community racial composition and the impact of the recession is even stronger in Los Angeles, which had the most majority-minority communities – 41 of 66 PUMAs. In 22 of these 41 PUMAs, the unemployment rate increased by more than five percentage points. Of the 29 PUMAs with large increases in unemployment rates, 76% were majority-minority communities (Owens and Sampson 2013).

The Asian population doubled in 20 years in New York–New Jersey, rising from 6.3% to 12.8% of the entire population. Segregation for Asians is as high as it is for Hispanics, while segregation among different Asian ethnicities is also marked. The New York-Northern New Jersey-Long Island MSA includes almost 2 million Asians, led by Chinese and Indians. Segregation of Asians from whites is even higher than in Los Angeles (Logan and Zhang 2013). Although the neighbourhoods where the Asian populations live are not always as disadvantaged as those of the Afro-Americans, spatial segregation is an undeniable fact. It can derive either from social boundaries imposed by whites, or from social boundaries determined by Asians, or both. In any case, the American city is a segregation machine at least as much as it is a growth machine. Next we provide some considerations regarding the need to implement social compromise.

Interpreting the contract form: The rezoning battleground

'New York policymakers are absorbed in finding ways to promote growth. They struggle to manage a powerful, yet very volatile, economy. Still, public policy rarely reflects unqualified boosterism; local political realities force consideration of compelling social pressures. The result: a market-led strategy that usually incorporates important compromises with a social edge' (Savitch and Kantor 2004, p. 123). This clearly formulated observation by two leading American urban political scientists will guide our attempt

100 *The North American urban contract*

to find how policy makers adopt contractual techniques for implementing social compromise in the case of New York.

In the recent past, such techniques have been mostly negotiations between the city government, community boards and private developers to protect citizens from aggressive urban development projects. The results have proved meagre, considering that in New York today 1 million households earn less than 50% of the area median income and only 425,000 housing units are available with rents suitable for them. Rent control, in-rem properties and other public regulations have clearly failed to obtain the expected results at the aggregate urban level. Between 1994 and 2012, 250,000 units of rental housing lost the protections of rent regulation. An exit strategy from rent regulation and an opt-out strategy from subsidy were implemented: 68,000 units of subsidized affordable rental housing have opted out of those programmes over the past few decades. The property tax system discourages the production of rental units and encourages conversion of units to cooperatives or condominiums. The latest available data (New York University Furnam Center for Real Estate and Urban Policy 2015) show that New York City lost more than 330,000 units of affordable, unsubsidized rental housing between 2002 and 2014. Moreover, in one year (2013), 30,000 New York City families were displaced from their homes as a result of eviction proceedings filed in Housing Court. It is also estimated that there are 100,000 illegal apartments (below the legal standards) in New York City; and 50,000 people live in shelters for the homeless.

'Knitting communities together' is the byword of the New York Ten-Year Housing Plan the City of New York launched in 2015. The goal is to create 200,000 affordable housing units (80,000 new and 120,000 preserved) for 500,000 low-income people, thereby significantly reducing the growing imbalance in affordable housing supply and demand.

It is the first time in years that the city has taken up the idea of urban strategic planning to obtain such an objective, and it is a part of a larger vision, 'One New York', launched by Mayor Bill de Blasio in 2015 to make growth, equity, sustainability and resiliency possible. The diagnosis is crude: New York is ageing, socially unequal (45% of the population is in or near poverty), environmentally fragile and fragmented in its political jurisdiction. The actions envisaged are centred along three axes: civic participation, diverse and inclusive government and regionalism. The latter is crucial: since Lewis Mumford's seminal writings on regional planning in the 1930s, the issue remains unresolved.

The Housing Plan is part of this larger effort, possibly a 'collective planner' in Mumford's terms. 'Achieving these goals will require strategic planning and intensive collaboration among City agencies and with the State and Federal governments, in partnership with community based organizations, service providers, for-profit and not-for-profit developers and property owners, and financial institutions' (City of New York 2015). The tools include a comprehensive survey of all vacant or underused public and private sites in the city, launch of new housing programmes and reform in zoning. However, federal cuts in housing programmes and housing choice vouchers for the lowest-income households have been severe in the past few years and represent a challenge to the city's strategy. A new federal urban policy (called for by urban scholars like Richard Florida) would therefore be needed to reverse the current trends of urban social polarization and implement the plan. The policy should both help people willing to stay in the city and protect the places to be converted into less socially selective uses. Moreover, the financing of the New York Housing Plan ($41 billion) is limitedly based on public resources ($8 billion by the City of New York, $2 billion by the state and federal governments) and very much based on private sources: bonds, private financing and tax credit equity should amount to $30 billion. But will these key conditions be met?

This will largely depend on the willingness of market forces to enter into social compromise. Big developers and individual property owners both apply for and negotiate subsidies, tax reductions and so forth. 'City zoning laws became so filled with complex loopholes, rights, and exceptions that builders and planners found them unpredictable and driven by capricious case-by-case judgements' (Savitch and Kantor 2004, p. 126). The aim of the new Housing Plan is to create fiscal incentives for buildings which are not covered by the existing programmes but risk being converted into condominiums or exiting rent regulation.

Tax Incentives 421-a is a programme granting tax reductions to developers constructing multiple dwellings on vacant lots. Developers receive tax exemption up to 25 years from the increase in real estate taxes resulting from the construction work. The projects must contain 20% affordable units. The market rent units fall subject to rent stabilization for the same duration. Buildings in Exclusion Areas (located in all of Manhattan, parts of Brooklyn, the Bronx, Queens and Staten Island) are not eligible unless they receive governmental assistance, contain 20% affordable units, or the owner participates in the 421-a Affordable Housing Production Program.

Critics of 421-a claim that the benefits for luxury apartments are much higher than the benefits for affordable units. According to the Association for Neighborhood and Housing Development, in fiscal year 2014, 153,121 apartments got a 421-a tax break, but only 12,748 (8%) were affordable.

How does New York City strategic planning work? It is a process involving many different agencies, including the NYC Department of City Planning. The Department promotes housing production and affordability, but also fosters economic development and coordinated investments in infrastructure and services. Its duties also include supporting resilient, sustainable communities across the five boroughs. This is probably a conflictual mandate. In fact, promoting affordable housing is a task exceeding, and possibly clashing with, the market laws which drive private initiatives for growth.

102 *The North American urban contract*

The Herculean task of the Department, in the context of the 10-year Capital Strategy of New York City, is to ensure investments in neighbourhoods able to reconcile strategic planning priorities and community needs. How is it to be done? The answer is, by coordinating neighbourhood planning studies and introducing regulatory changes, as is the prerogative of the Department. It includes mandatory inclusionary housing in newly rezoned areas. The goal is to promote economically diverse communities and housing choices for all income levels, including the lowest. But this 'minor level' strategy of micro urban change has to be reconciled with the 'major level' strategy of boosterism followed by another and indeed powerful city body.

The 'Lower Manhattan Financial Center strategy', followed by the city mayors up to Mayor Michael Bloomberg (2002–13) and implemented by the Public Development Corporation, renamed the NYC Economic Development Corporation in 2012, has been to create hundreds of large-scale projects to maintain or attract companies. Each entails intensive use of public land and finance. Such was the case in the 1980s and 1990s when tax concessions were made to major Manhattan banks and even to the NY Stock Exchange, inducing them to remain there: billions upon billions of dollars have been channelled to this end – many companies later relocated or laid off staff, while some, like Lehman, have since gone bankrupt. Later, the NYC Economic Development Corporation and the Alliance for Downtown New York launched plans to attract firms in Internet-ready spaces. Tax incentives were provided to property owners converting 50 commercial skyscrapers into 5,000 apartments. One idea being aired is to move on, beyond the Lower Manhattan Financial Center strategy, and accept regional dimensions including Jersey City, Downtown Brooklyn and Long Island City (Wallace 2002).

At the moment, more than 80 major projects are ongoing or have been concluded by the NYC Economic Development Corporation. Applied Science NYC, for example, is a $2 billion project with a 99-year lease and 10 acres of Roosevelt Island to Cornell Tech, with city financing to the tune of $100 million; Columbia's new data science campus will cost the city $15 million, energy discount and lease flexibility in exchange for the project. Many projects include the same kind of exchange.

How arbitration between 'major' and 'minor' strategies competing on land use and public finance (which are not unlimited) will be conducted is a matter of discussion. In this respect, we can evaluate the inclusive community development initiatives led by the Department of City Planning to expand quality jobs and services, expanding public access to land use and so forth.

But the main role of the Department lies in supporting the City Planning Commission in its annual review of approximately 450 land use applications for a variety of discretionary approvals. This is clearly the crucial role of the Department. Every year hundreds of permits and changes in urban land use are issued.

The Department's role is to provide technical assistance to the City Planning Commission's meetings and review sessions. They include issues like (just to take one single review session in 2015), Housing Preservation Development (HPD) sustainability policies and programmes, Riverside–West End Historic District extension, the Bronx, Queens and Brooklyn pre-hearings and so on. Each report describes the project and all of the necessary actions. It also contains an extensive summary of the public review, including the community board and borough president's recommendations, the City Planning Commission public hearing and the Commission's consideration deliberation. Interestingly, the Commission has the last word: even if the community board votes against the application, the final decision is up to the Commission. Take, for example, the case of an application regarding One Vanderbilt Avenue in Manhattan (March 30, 2015) for the development of a commercial building: the community board passed a resolution (39 in favour, 0 against, 1 abstention) recommending rejection of the application, yet the Commission resolved to approve. This shows its enormous power.

Over the past nine years, more than 9,400 blocks – equal to roughly one-fifth of the city – have been rezoned. This means that within a few decades, the entire city is destined to change land use: an outcome that would clearly be inadmissible in any European city, for example. And yet this shows a dynamism that is truly astonishing to Europeans. But the question is: are the planners of the Commission driven by the 'planning for vitality' principles Jane Jacobs (1961) advocated: stimulating diversity, promoting continuous networks of local neighbourhoods, combating border vacuums, unslumming the slums, converting self-destruction into constructive forces and clarifying the visual order of cities?

The discretionary side of the urban contract calls for thorough investigation. Since the 1961 zoning ordinance, NYC zoning has produced a variety of new techniques combining different tools: incentive zoning, contextual zoning and special districts. Density plays a crucial role: by increasing it new residential, office and service spaces can be created, multiplying the urban rent. How this increase of rent values is distributed is a matter of public choice. For example, in core high-density areas, creating high-rise developments, reusing former industrial sites, developing contextual zoning districts to preserve neighbourhoods are possible options open to the city government. In lower-density areas and suburbs destined to rapid growth, other tools have been experimented with.

Revision of the Zoning Resolution has been the main tool to obtain such results. The Zoning Resolution has been revised to achieve planning objectives across neighbourhoods. 'Affordable housing' needs incentives in order to drive operators towards socially oriented housing strategies. 'Mixed uses' zoning – one of Jacobs's key principles – has been used to help create vibrant, active neighbourhoods including residential and other activities, particularly in areas where residential uses were previously prohibited (like former

104　*The North American urban contract*

manufacturing loft spaces). Special incentives have been created to promote fresh food stores in underserved areas, and a range of zoning amendments has been adopted to ensure (following here another Jacobs principle) a more sustainable city through requirements for bicycle parking, street trees, more green space in front yards and landscaping in parking lots. New rules have also been adopted to ensure a more open, accessible waterfront. This is a key issue in Manhattan. Rezoning on Manhattan's Far West Side, which established the foundation for expansion of the Manhattan central business district, is a case in point. Zoning has also been used to catalyze investments in critical areas of the city, from Hudson Yards to West Chelsea, where the High Line project of new urban park has been successfully implemented, attracting international tourism and business. Harlem 125th Street rezoning is another case, including affordable housing units which can be part of a strategy of 'unslumming the slums' through incentives to stay put, as Jacobs advocated.

According to the City, 'the Zoning Resolution is a blueprint for the development of the city. It is flexible enough to address the advances in technology, neighbourhood transformations, changing land use patterns and emerging design.' However, what direction to take is an open question.

One possible direction is promoting the Inclusionary Housing R10 Program by offering a floor area bonus in exchange for the creation or preservation of affordable housing, both on site and off site. This programme requires that a percentage of dwellings in the new building be set aside, or new affordable units be provided in the same community district or within a half mile of the development, which is a condition for entitlement to the bonus. In special districts (Hudson Yards, West Chelsea, some parts of Manhattan and Brooklyn waterfront) a bonus is supplied if some percentage of affordable housing units is provided.

The Inclusionary Housing R10 Program was created in 1987 for the highest-density residential areas and commercial districts with the same high density: which means essentially Manhattan. In these areas, new developments providing affordable housing can receive a bonus of 20% of the maximum permitted residential floor area. The floor area ratio is 10.0 and can increase to 12.0. The bonus increase depends on whether the affordable housing is on site or off site, is a new construction or a rehabilitation, and if public funding is used for financing. In other residential districts, the density values are much lower, and the floor area ratio can be as low as 2.2.

Given the reported success of the programme, since 2005 it has been extended to other parts of the city, including the Bronx, Brooklyn and Queens, through rezoning of Inclusionary Housing R10 Program–designated areas. Developers resolving at least 20% of new buildings for affordable units can receive a bonus of up to 33% in terms of additional floor area.

Flexibility of rules can eventually be permitted for large-scale developments, which include large zoning lots or several zoning lots contiguous or separated by a street. In such cases, the City Planning Commission has the

The North American urban contract   105

power to modify the zoning rules to allow greater flexibility of bulk (the lot size, floor area ratio, lot coverage, open space, yards, height and setback determining the maximum permitted size of a building) and open space on the site. All regulations are in such cases flexibly interpreted and provision is made for special permits and authorizations.

The global city and its spaces (Sassen 1991) are a permanently contested terrain. Real estate developers and landlords, public officials and social groups are constantly engaged in the organized complexity of urban biotic ('the intimate and casual life of cities', Jacobs 1961) and urban negotiating processes. One example is to be seen in the life cycles of New York cultural districts (Zukin and Braslow 2011) and the migration of centres of artistic production from Greenwich Village in the 1920s–1950s to Soho (formerly a manufacturing district) in the 1970s, then on to East Village in the 1980s, and finally beyond Manhattan to Williamsburgh and Bushwick (formerly working-class districts in Brooklyn) in the 1990s and 2000s. The process of group migration has been accompanied by suspension of the rent control that had favoured artists in New York zoning laws, the rezoning of districts (like the waterfront in 2005) giving rise to rent increases and obliging artists to move further afield, and also defeat of infrastructural projects like Robert Moses's plan for a Lower Manhattan Expressway ('expressways that eviscerate great cities', as Jane Jacobs attacked in 1961). Actually, 'during the past thirty years, New York City has twice regularized artists' districts by adopting and revising a Loft Law that stabilizes rents in live-work buildings – first in the early 1980s and again in 2010. The first Loft Law covered loft buildings mainly in Lower Manhattan, and the revised law extended rent protection to the outer boroughs, especially Brooklyn' (Zukin and Braslow 2011). However, the unintended consequence can be increased cultural attractiveness and revitalization for the district, and hence gentrification, rent increases and evictions.

Los Angeles

From a Mexican *pueblo* of 3,000 souls to a metropolis of 3 million in one century, the first 'dispersed metropolis' of the world is now (2014 data) a city of 4 million (it was 3.4 million in 1990, 3.7 million in 2000) within an urban region of 18 million, including Los Angeles, Orange, Riverside, San Bernardino and Ventura Counties. According to Mike Davis's (1990) fascinating reconstruction of the 'City of Quartz', three power stratifications have been found in the city's history, each associated with different land-use economies. The first geological phase (19th century–early 20th century) was based on a non-Protestant elite prospering on latifondism; the second phase (mid-20th century) was characterized by dualism between two opposed elites, the new Westside elite oriented to entertainment industry and, later, to knowledge capitalism and the old downtown real estate powers competing in the context of low-density, high-immigration suburban growth; the

106   *The North American urban contract*

third, current phase (end of 20th century–21st century) is marked by Asian (Japanese, then Chinese) investments and migration to Los Angeles, now a land-scarce post-metropolis, main node – second only to the Tokyo financial pole – of the globalized Pacific Rim.

A history of flows

According to Davis, two main flows to LA occurred in the past century: the 1930s movie and entertainment industry flow, and the 1980s cultural industry flow. The first is well known: it consisted of people from the movie and entertainment industries leaving New York and making Hollywood the world capital of the movie industry. The second is more intriguing, as for the first time cultural investment has become the pull factor driven by international real estate capital. A public-private coalition has formed to build a cultural superstructure: the museum archipelago. National and international developers investing in culture, artists and the University of California, Los Angeles financed as central magnets of development, the LA municipality creating a culture tax of 1% on new developments – such are the main ingredients of the recipe. LA 2000 was the strategic manifesto (held in 1988) for a pro-growth 'regional world' coalition implemented through state agencies and Southern California economic growth dynamics. The LA School of planners and geographers has, according to Davis, represented the other side of the coin: making critical theory subaltern to (and celebrant of) the LA myth. Tract lots for rich residents only, creation of outer cities and open economic internationalization are the main features of Mike Davis's critical account of the LA miracle. Flows of people from everywhere in the country to LA have constituted a basis for neoclassical theories of urban growth.

But the history of flows to LA is more deeply rooted in the negative anthropology of today's urbanites. They are like Nietzsche's last men:

> *'We have invented happiness, say the last men and they blink. They have left the regions where it was hard to live, for one needs warmth. One still loves one's neighbor and rubs against him. . . . One still works, for work is a form of entertainment. One no longer becomes poor or rich: both require too much exertion. Who still wants to rule? Who obey? Both require too much exertion'.*

The Nietzschean last men are of course meta-historic figures out of time, but their characteristics are very similar to our LA contemporary urbanites. They moved looking for warmth, leaving the Northeastern rustbelt regions of the United States. They recreated gated communities and ghettos, clustering among themselves in isolation from the 'diverse' (be they Hispanic, Afro-American or Asian). They work for entertainment, at least in the sense that Google, Apple and other California-based companies tend to attribute

The North American urban contract   107

to the 'creative' work of their employees. They do not want to be regulated: when faced with any authoritative power, they prefer anomic, apolitical behaviour.

Interpreting the urban form: Cities by contract

The low-density–high-density alternative is at the very core of urban America, and Los Angeles is the alpha and omega of this discourse. From its very beginnings, a polycentric sprawl made of Los Angeles the 'first purely American cityspace', according to Soja (2000). It was the product of several factors, including the 'largest urban-focused domestic migration in US history', as well as of Afro-American (concentrated in the South Central area), Mexican (clustered in East Los Angeles) and Asian population migrations.

The incorporation of 140 cities into Los Angeles has been labelled (Miller 1981) 'Cities by Contract'. We will follow it shortly, taking Lakewood, a municipality incorporated in 1954, as a prime example (see Soja 2000). The incorporated municipality purchased its basic services from Los Angeles County instead of producing them internally. This low-cost service supply made it possible for municipalities to attract new metropolitan residents voting with their feet, as in the famous Tiebout model of neoclassical economics. The municipalities did so through a scheme giving rise to residential developments of different types competing with real estate, commercial and industrial investors. The model was then imitated by dozens of municipalities in the county, up to 170 in the 1980s–1990s.

Thus Los Angeles has proved the prototype of the dispersed metropolis later theorized by, among others, the MIT urban planner Kevin Lynch and the French philosopher Jean-Luc Nancy. In Lynch's (1960) urban mental maps of Los Angeles inhabitants, the recurrent term is the 'empty space' around downtown. When asked to describe and symbolize the city as a whole, they defined it as 'spread-out', 'spacious', 'without form' and 'without centres': an endless, disorienting space stretching out. Crossing it – in the vivid words of one respondent – is like wasting time to get to a certain place and discovering that, after all, nothing is there. In Nancy's (2011) philosophical account of Los Angeles, the city is circulation, vibration and mobility across a space where the centre is nowhere and the circumference is everywhere, or the other way round. We now have to rethink this clearly powerful, but possibly – given the more recent urban changes – outdated representation of Los Angeles.

According to Angel (2012), elaborating on studies by Glaeser and Kahn and Zheng and colleagues, Chinese cities are seven times denser than US cities: 162 persons per hectare compared to 23 persons per hectare. The US cities' average CO_2 emissions are 56% those of the Chinese cities. Yet among the five metropolitan areas with the highest shares of population living at public transit-sustaining densities are San Francisco (71.4 %) and Los Angeles (67.7%).

108 *The North American urban contract*

In fact, the average population density in Los Angeles today stands at 8,000 persons per square mile, as compared with 24,000 in New York, 16,000 in San Francisco and 12,000 in Boston and Chicago, but also with 3,000 in Houston and San Diego. The LA population is clearly in a process of densification: not in the sense of the compact city, but rather in the direction of a post-metropolis.

The City of Los Angeles' population of 4 million is distributed in 1,393,000 housing units: only 538,000 are single-family detached units, 845,000 are multiple family units (including apartment buildings for rent and condominiums, duplexes, artist-in-residence lofts and attached single-family housing units), and 855,000 are non-single-family units (mobile homes and so on). Therefore the image of the city as a low density, dispersed metropolis should be at least partially revised. Single-family homes are more concentrated in the North and South Valleys and in some neighbourhoods: Northeast, Northridge, South and Southeast, Arleta-Palcoma, Chatsworth–Porter Ranch and Grenada Hills–Knollwood. Multiple family homes are mostly in Central, South and West neighbourhoods. The housing ownership data also contradict the conventional image of a fully suburban single-family owners' community: the people in owner units number 1,470,000 (39%), whereas the people in rental units come to 2,139,000 (61%) – close to New York City's percentage of renters (70%).

The race and ethnicity data are also of the utmost importance. White non-Hispanics currently number (according to the 2000 Census) only 1,009,000, 30% of the total population, with a marked decrease of 18% in the 1990–2000 decade. Hispanics/Latinos are now 1,719,000, 47% of the total population, with a dramatic increase of 22% in the 1990–2000 decade. Afro-Americans only number 401,000, 11% of the total population, with a decrease of 13% in the 1990–2000 decade. Finally, Asians come to 364,000, 10% of the total population, with an increase of +13% in the same decade.

Maps of racial and ethnic distribution show a high degree of segregation: the white population is greatly concentrated in the north, Hispanics/Latinos and Afro-Americans in parts of the central, south-central, south and harbour areas, and Asians in the north and partially in the central areas. A new downtown and inner city attracting the working poor have come about within the post-metropolis (Soja 2000).

In his text on the human consequences of globalization, Bauman (1998) observed that 'the State of California, celebrated by some European sociologists as the very paradise of liberty, dedicates to the building and the running costs of prisons a budget transcending by far the sum total of state funds allocated to all the institutions of higher education. Imprisonment is the ultimate and most radical form of spatial confinement.' Actually, the Los Angeles Police Department produced an End of Year Crime Snapshot Report from January 1, 2013, through December 31, 2013, to provide statistical data on citywide crime rates. According to the Report, all eight categories of Part I crime rates (homicide, rape, aggravated assault, robbery, burglary, larceny and vehicle theft) maintained a downward trend from 2008 to 2013:

homicide fell by 34.6%; rape by 32.7%; aggravated assault by 35.8%; robbery by 41.4%; burglary by 21.6%; larceny by 6.6%; and vehicle theft by 37.6%.

The 1992 riots had a permanent effect in terms of segregation. As *L.A. Weekly* reported in 1993, some 56,000 Afro-Americans fled LA between 1980 and 1990. California State, Northridge researchers found that racial displacement drove the exodus – the mass movement of mostly illegal Latino immigrants into the city's affordable black neighbourhoods. After the riots, between 1992 and 2007, the city's black population dropped by 123,000, as households left for the Inland Empire, close-in suburbs and even for family hometowns in the Deep South. The city's Latino population grew by more than 450,000 in those years. In the Los Angeles area, unemployment is worse than in 1992. In 2010, 13.4% of Latinos and 19.5% of Afro-Americans were without work.

While the population increase between 2000 and 2010 was only 2.6%, the housing units increase was 5.7%, with the central area 9.6% and the North Valley 7%. Considering the Community Plan Areas, the Central City increase was an astonishing 78% and the Central City North was 39%. By contrast, in the south, although the population increased, new housing showed the lowest increase rate (0.3%). The permits to develop new multifamily buildings (2010–14), totalling 19.225, were highly concentrated in the central area (7.879). In the same years, non-residential development was highly concentrated in the central area: of the 6,800,000 square feet of retail space in Los Angeles, 3,000,000 are in the central area; of the 480,000 square feet of office space, 308,000 are in the central area as well. Industrial space, totalling 511,000 square metres citywide, is + 820,000 in the central area only.

Yet suburbanism and exopolis phenomena continue to feed a constant flow of population engaged in daily work travels. The 1.6 million LA commuters generate a traffic of 100 million vehicle miles travelled daily on District 7 (Los Angeles and Ventura Counties) freeways. In the process of extended regionalization of its economy under way since the 1980s, LA has experienced a multipolar distribution of industrial districts and technological poles within both the city and the metropolitan area (Scott 2008).

The interpretation proposed by Allen Scott and largely shared by urban scholars is that a new kind of cultural-cognitive capitalism has been experimented with here, giving rise to new agglomeration dynamics: 'These forms of cognitive-cultural production and work occur in cities of many different sizes, but above all in major metropolitan regions, where they often form strikingly dense and specialised clusters in the wider tissue of urban space. Clusters like these are based on the usual kinds of agglomeration economies that are to be found in urban areas, although their centripetal pull is much reinforced by their persistently transaction-intensive nature and by the high levels of economic competition and uncertainty that typify them.' This interpretation casts revealing light on the reconfiguration of the dispersed, spread-out metropolis into a more clustered, although dispersed, post-metropolitan space.

110 *The North American urban contract*

Ann Markusen (1996) was the first scholar to account for the 'sticky places in slippery space' dynamic, first in relation to traditional industrial districts, but later also to the metropolitan new decentralized mosaics and more agglomerating cultural district spaces, with special reference to LA's creative industry: America's Artist Super City (Markusen 2010; Markusen and Gadwa 2010).

The prodromes of such a process of concentrated dispersion might be traced back to the regional university model of growth already described by Lewis Mumford (1962). The University of California in Berkeley spun off a second university in Los Angeles. This process of colonization has led to the building of eight more university centres, each of them potentially the centre of a new city, or at least of an already existing small city which might take on the functions of a larger city.

Interpreting the contract form: The opposed coalitions

Davis (1990) clearly explained the dynamics of pro-growth (developers and landowners) versus slow-growth (homeowners) opposed coalitions, the former winning out almost all the way; with the vast majority of the population, for example the renters, the immigration communities and the poor, standing in the middle without any say in the matter. In the meanwhile, the city strategy has been to favour major projects for social elites in selected places of the urban area.

The *Major Projects* listed in the Department of City Planning interactive application (visited on August 26, 2015) number 52, all (except one) in the northern and western parts of the city and metropolitan area. Eight projects have already been approved, and the kind of speculative logic emerges clearly from Table 3.2:

Table 3.2 Los Angeles Department of City Planning projects (2015)

Name of the project	Main outcomes	Social content
Casten Sepulveda	Retail+ 538 residential units	59 senior-affordable units
Century City Center	Office towers	
Academy Museum of Motion Pictures	Museum spaces	
Museum Square Office Building	Office spaces	
Hollywood Palladium	731 residential units or 598 residential units+ hotel	
The New Century Plan	Retail+restaurant+luxury residential units+office space	
Hollywood Millennium	Residential units+luxury hotel+office space	
Ponte Vista	1153 residential units+park+clubhouse	392 rental units

Source: LA Department of City Planning

Even in the case of Los Angeles, a community-building strategy is possible and has been traced through the impact of a major issue, namely the environment. Environmental issues have been of the utmost importance in the recent development of LA and California State, particularly as far as water resource scarcity and CO2 emissions are concerned. The California Environmental Quality Act (CEQA) is a legislative tool able to influence urban expansion in a way that no other legislation in the United States allows for. The legislation declares, in fact, that:

(a) Maintenance of a quality environment for the people of the state now and in the future is a matter of statewide concern.
(b) It is necessary to ensure a high-quality environment that at all times is healthful and pleasing to the senses and intellect of man.
(c) There is a need to understand the relationship between the maintenance of high-quality ecological systems and the general welfare of the people of the state, including their enjoyment of the natural resources of the state.
(d) The capacity of the environment is limited, and it is the intent of the Legislature that the government of the state take immediate steps to identify any critical thresholds for the health and safety of the people of the state and take all coordinated actions necessary to prevent such thresholds being reached.
(e) Every citizen has the responsibility to contribute to the preservation and enhancement of the environment.
(f) The interrelationship of policies and practices in the management of natural resources and waste disposal requires systematic and concerted efforts by public and private interests to enhance environmental quality and to control environmental pollution.
(g) It is the intent of the Legislature that all agencies of the state government which regulate activities of private individuals, corporations, and public agencies which are found to affect the quality of the environment, shall regulate such activities so that major consideration is given to preventing environmental damage, while providing a decent home and satisfying living environment for every Californian.

The impact of such a strategy on the urban environment is clear. It will make it more difficult to tolerate environmental damage resulting from extended urbanization, and will enhance the possibilities of compact urban development. It will make it easier for community-building groups of citizens and other communities to have a say in the matter. It will make the defence of the city easier vis-à-vis both the city administration itself and the claims of private interests.

The CEQA strategy is to permit housing projects with protective measures for the land (e.g. wetlands) and historical resources, environmental risk-avoidance, while favouring housing for agricultural workers, low-income housing and unfill sites. Mitigation measures or housing project alternatives must be addressed whenever the environmental quality is damaged. The

112   *The North American urban contract*

citizens' capacity to defend the city is greatly enhanced, thanks to CEQA. Three examples can be taken from a sample of 2013 CEQA court cases to illustrate the point.

Friends of Oroville v. City of Oroville

The City Council, on appeal from the planning commission, approved the replacement of an existing Wal-Mart with a Wal-Mart Supercenter in late 2010. Friends of Oroville challenged the project's environmental impact report (EIR), alleging that the greenhouse gas emissions analysis was inadequate, and that the fair share traffic fee was infeasible, the hydrology analysis was inadequate, and the city violated CEQA's notice requirements. The trial court denied Friends' claims and held in favour of the city. The Court of Appeal reversed the verdict in part, and in part reaffirmed it. As a result, the city will be required to repair portions of the EIR.

Save Tara v. City of West Hollywood

This involved the preliminary approval of a development agreement and commitment of city funds with a condition that a CEQA review would be completed sometime in the future. The Supreme Court rejected the City of West Hollywood's approach because the city had essentially committed itself to the project by that action, regardless of its intention to take additional actions and complete a CEQA review in the future.

Comunidad en Accion v. Los Angeles City Council

In this case, Comunidad challenged the city's approval of a new 104,000-square-foot solid waste transfer station, an expanded materials recycling facility and an expanded green waste processing centre at the existing Bradley Landfill site in Sun Valley, as well as the EIR certified for the facility. Comunidad essentially argued that because Sun Valley is a largely Latino community, locating the facility there exposed residents to disparate adverse effects in a discriminatory manner. The court held that Section 11135 did not apply in this situation. The trial court dismissed Comunidad's CEQA claims on the grounds that Comunidad had failed to apply for a court hearing within the time limit established by CEQA. The Court of Appeal examined whether the failure of Comunidad's attorney was an excusable error and concluded that a simple calendaring error could be overlooked.

In the wider case of the City of Los Angeles, since 2006 a New Community Plan strategy has been followed. But in 2014, a trial court invalidated the Hollywood Community Plan Update due to inadequacies in its EIR. The LA City Administration' s response is a proposed long-range plan extending to 2035 to update all the 35 Community Plans and rezone LA: a fairly

The idea is to develop a strategy of CEQA compliance, reducing conflict over EIRs. The critical points and the strategic options are (as the LA Department of City Planning admits):

1 There has been a striking mismatch between the scale of the New Community Plan program and the resources devoted to it: the program has been underfunded and understaffed.
2 The City Planning Department has been saddled with an outdated zoning code not up to the challenge of planning for a 21st-century metropolis.
3 The citywide general plan is outdated, with many elements over 20 years old. As a result, the New Community Plan program has been expected to resolve many issues more appropriately addressed at the citywide level.
4 The New Community Plan program's CEQA compliance strategy is overbroad. The current approach could lead to the preparation of 35 stand-alone EIRs, one for each of the city's 35 plan areas – an expensive and litigious path.

The main responses are:

To update the citywide general plan

The foundation of the LA planning system is the General Plan Framework, which sets forth a directed growth strategy to channel most new development along mixed boulevards and into regional centres connected by transit. Adopted in 1996, the Framework is now two decades old. Many other citywide elements, including open space, noise, safety, conservation, air quality, infrastructure systems and public services, are similarly out of date, with some even nearing the 20-year mark. While the policies contained in the Framework and the other citywide elements are still largely relevant, they should be updated to reflect changes in state law and local circumstances. Under this approach, most of the topics of the New Community Plan programme would be addressed at the citywide level, thus freeing up community plans to focus on land use and zoning. This objective requires new resources in the next fiscal years, request for which has been included in the submitted LA fiscal year 2015–16 budget.

To implement a regional approach

The city's ultimate long-range planning goal is to see all 35 Community Plans updated and the entire city rezoned. This is an ambitious goal, but feasible if the New Community Plan programme is reorganized into a more manageable number of 11 regions. While the 35 plan areas will be retained, each with its own separate planning document, the work programme itself will be organized geographically. This new organizational structure will

114   *The North American urban contract*

allow the Department to take advantage of economies of scale, concentrate public outreach efforts in contiguous areas simultaneously, and allow for larger and more collaborative work teams that together will help complete each region's plans.

To reduce the number of potential environmental controversies

Completing 35 separate EIRs is a daunting prospect, but the current New Community Plan programme would require no less. Actually, there is a better way, namely to update the General Plan Framework's EIR. The existing Framework EIR analyzed growth from 1990 through 2010. An updated citywide EIR, one that analyzes long-range growth through 2035, is the cornerstone of the Department's objective to streamline its CEQA compliance strategy. Such an EIR has two benefits, according to the city administration. One, it allows the offloading of much of the analysis currently bogging down individual plan EIRs onto a single citywide document. And, two, it allows the preparation of only one environmental document for each of the 11 regions shown earlier, a focused EIR, an addendum to the citywide EIR or even possibly a Mitigated Negative Declaration. Developed in concert with the city attorney and some of the best outside CEQA litigators, this CEQA strategy should result in more defensible environmental documents and thus less legal exposure.

Concluding remarks

Comparing Boston, New York and Los Angeles in terms of affordable rental housing is revealing (see Table 3.3). In the 25 American largest city rankings, Boston comes first, with 22% of its total housing stock; New York City comes third with 17%, whereas LA takes its place in the low position of the rankings with 8%. The same ranking applies if we consider the International Affordability Index based on the median housing price and the median household income of the three cities. This means cities have different bodies of social endowment and can respond differently to common challenges, like capitalist developers' pressures, market shifts, foreign and domestic immigration and so forth.

Housing is also revealing in term of modes of urban social contract and forms of community building. In the case of LA, the interplay is among pro-growth developers, slow-growth homeowners and civil rights groups: the winners can use legislation, zoning, planning and the courts to their ends. Legislation of the state, like CEQA, has been used well beyond its initial environmental protection scope to address choices in land use politics and policies. Often, slow-growth owners have been able to address growth towards communities where less resistance – whether active or verbal – is offered. In this respect, community building is a matter of polarized dynamics between more affluent, less dense environments (homeowner groups with

The North American urban contract   115

Table 3.3 International Affordability Index (2015)

International Affordability Rank		Median Housing Price	Median Household Income
311	Boston	399,000	74,400
331	NYC	410,800	67,100
363	LA	481,900	60,000

Source: Demographia

strong social capital) and the denser, socially deprived environments (Latinos, non-citizens-large families) (Morrow 2013). These contrasting trends can give rise to a physically less dispersed, yet socially polarized metropolis, with more concentrated patterns of urban forms.

In the past, Davis (1990) proposed an initial explanation of the dynamics between pro-growth (developers and landowners) and slow-growth (homeowners), seeing the former as almost constantly the winners. Glaeser and Gyourko (2003) later proposed a second, opposite explanation. They used the zoning and land-use controls as explanatory tools to understand the LA growth model characterized by low-density housing and scarcity of multifamily housing. Their explanation, based on the political mobilization of homeowners, seeks to interpret the long-term model of the LA diffused metropolis, but is unable to capture the more recent urban developments.

A third, more plausible explanation is therefore proposed here. It lies in the shifting nature of community development and its creative capacity. A dynamic of increasing population and housing in central and central-north LA, mainly populated by the less wealthy, and one of multipolar clustering densification in the wider metropolitan area have been observed. Thus denser urban communities arise whose political activity regarding land-use policies has proved very limited. However, the housing crisis as from 2007–8 accounts for the fact that in the following years (2010–14), the permits to develop new multifamily buildings numbered almost 20,000, a huge number for LA, given the traditional scarcity of multifamily and affordable housing. And as a final point, CEQA – originally considered a slow-growth instrument – has become a tool useful for communities to avoid both pro-growth and slow-growth coalition pressures. This implies that more in-depth analysis is needed to interpret the communities' capacity to influence the city, and the city's capacity to react.

A different lesson is learned from the case of New York. Here rent control and affordable housing policies have eroded over the past 30 years. In 1981, 63% of rental units were subject to rent stabilization or rent control (both forms are based on rules governing rent increase in exchange for fiscal benefits to the owners). They have now dropped to 47%. Over the past 30 years, there has been a net loss of 231,000 regulated units as more units exited the programme than entered through tax incentive programmes. The

116 *The North American urban contract*

loss of unsubsidized affordable rental units grew ever greater (330,000) in the 2004–12 decade (New York University Furnam Centre for Real Estate and Urban Policy).

In NYC public housing developments, 175,000 families are served, but 270,000 more are on the waiting list. There has been a crisis in the urban fiscal pact linking the city and housing owners. This pact could be rewritten by the new NYC housing plan for 200,000 new affordable housing units. The community-building process will be marked by, among other things, the capacity of communities to engage in the zoning and rezoning battleground and to control the affordable housing programme. Resources to meet the goal of 200,000 affordable units by 2020 will be needed by the market (bonds, pension funds, charities) and the federal and state levels of government. A new social compromise is therefore expected. It will be based on communities' acceptance of denser neighbourhoods as a condition for more affordable housing units. In exchange, incentives will be allocated to landlords for restricting incomes and rents. The paradox of the current NYC tax incentives system is that the city expenditure for tax incentives is much higher than the expected outcome in terms of affordable housing units (over-subsidization). The strategic developer, landowner or homeowner can make use of legislation to obtain much more than should be reasonable in terms of incentives. And as if this paradox were not enough, the housing units receiving subsidies can include hotels and warehouses. The system is a jungle, and rewriting it by the city means using huge urban rent values created in the housing market to finance affordable units.

Boston is expected to build 30,000 new building units by 2020, according to the Boston Housing 2020 Plan. However, 20,000 will be unrestricted private rent units, 5,000 will be middle class, and 5,000 will be affordable housing units. This means that Boston's shrinking middle class is today perceived as the most challenged: this class competes with low-income groups in terms of housing affordability in more affordable neighbourhoods. This is a city where, more than in other US cities, the middle class is in danger of losing ground (Boston has a proportionally smaller middle class than the state or the nation, the Plan admits). The still growing knowledge-based economy will exacerbate these trends. The neighbourhoods that have so far proved affordable (Jamaica Plain, South Boston) are becoming increasingly selective. In the meantime, Boston colleges and universities are expected to invest in housing for students (at least 10,000 more units) in very select neighbourhoods (Fenway/Kenmore and Allston/Brighton). On the other hand, affordable housing stock is made of 12,000 units owned by the BRA, and 40,000 in private hands – and are at risk of being converted to market-rate housing. A future of more socially selective processes is foreseeable in such trends.

Note

1 The *Boston Globe*, September 17, 2015.

4 The Asian urban contract

Introduction

Amartya Sen, the Indian-born Nobel Prize winner for economics, wrote *The Idea of Justice* in 2009. Regarding the word 'justice', he notes that in Sanskrit, this word has two different meanings: *niti* and *nyaya*. The first term means: law, organization, correctness, institutions, rules. The second term means: real justice, the world as it is in reality. The double meaning returns in a fascinating urban novel, *Last Man in the Tower* (2011), by Aravind Adiga, the Indian Booker Prize winner. He noted:

> At a time when India is going through great changes and, with China, is likely to inherit the world from the West, it is important that writers like me try to highlight the brutal injustices of society (Indian). That's what I'm trying to do – it is not an attack on the country, it's about the greater process of self-examination.

He also explained that 'the criticism by writers like Flaubert, Balzac and Dickens of the 19th century helped England and France become better societies' (from an interview with Stuart Jeffries in the *Guardian*, Thursday, October 16, 2008).

In Adiga's urban novel, Mr Shah, the builder, is ready to use any law and its contrary to obtain the space he needs to develop a new high-rise tower on the fringe of Mumbai's slumland. He is also ready to use violence. Mr Masterji, the Last Man in the Tower, understands that resort to Indian law is futile and refuses demolition: he will be sacrificed by the other inhabitants of the community, eager to obtain the rich sum Mr Shah promised to sell their common property. *Niti*, the law, has not been able to protect the weak or to affirm justice. The Mofa Act, regulating the promotion, construction, sale and management of flats in Maharashtra State since 1963, has been ignored: the promoter's obligation to make full and true disclosure of the nature of the land on which the flats are constructed sounds ironical in this context. The promoter who should enter into a written agreement for sale with the owners has simply eliminated the obstacle. *Nyaya*, the practical, empirical

118   *The Asian urban contract*

justice, is in the exemplary end of the story: 'Nothing can stop a living thing that wants to be free.'

Hence the encroaching nature of the Indian city, advancing beyond any proper or former limit. Today, if 70% of the tenants in a building agree, a real estate developer can demolish their building and rehouse them in new apartments on site in exchange for the opportunity to build new market-rate units (Brook 2013, p. 345). In more sociological and anthropological terms, this is also the topic Arjun Appadurai addressed in his work on Mumbai. Before analyzing it in depth, we can start from the astonishing view of Mumbai Appadurai evoked after the 2009 terrorist attack:

> In other words, as we learn more about the deep geo-politics behind the terrifying attacks on Mumbai earlier this month, we need to rec-ognize that there is a tectonic struggle going on in and near Mumbai on at least three axes: the deepest axis (from a historical point of view) is the struggle between the Indian Ocean commercial/criminal nexus and the land-based nexus that stretches from Mumbai to Delhi to Kash-mir. The second, more recent struggle is the struggle between political and commercial interests now located in Maharashtra and Gujarat for control over Mumbai, a struggle that was superficially resolved in 1956, when Bombay was declared the capital of the new state of Maharashtra. The third, most subtle, is between a land-based, plebeian form of Hindu nationalism, best represented by the auto-rickshaw drivers and small street vendors of North Mumbai and Greater Mumbai, who would be happy to see South Mumbai destroyed; and the more slick, market-oriented face of the Bharatiya Janata Party, whose elite supporters know that South Mumbai is crucial to the mediation of global capital to India, and where business tycoons like Mukesh Ambani are building homes larger than many global hotels.
>
> (Appadurai, Is Mumbai's resilience endlessly renewable?
> *The Immanent Frame*, 2009)

The interplay between the urban complexity of a divided, yet interlinked social, religious, ethnic and linguistic multitude and the urban resilience and metabolism is the key factor to analyze.

American urban theorist John Friedmann (2014) has underlined that in current research on the urbanization of the world, especially in Asia, we should carefully investigate the diverse institutional patterns. 'Becoming urban may be the general descriptive term, but what is ultimately important resides in the detailed stories: the specific actors and institutional settings involved, the hows and whys of converging or diverging processes of the phenomena examined.'

Western observers are shocked by the fast changes occurring in Eastern societies, and notably in the cities, in the past few decades. They risk using Western conceptual tools to analyze non-Western social dynamics. Yet we should note, following the Japanese social anthropologist Chie Nakane (1972), that 'the traditional social structure of a complex society, such as Japan, China or India, seems to persist and endure in spite of great modern changes'. In her view, tradition and modernity are not antagonistic and contradictory elements: they are aspects of the same social fabric. In this respect, instead of imagining a convergence of Eastern societies towards Western schemes, we should understand the permanence of forms (socially institutionalized ideals) elaborated in the long historical process and how they support or hinder the ongoing modernization process (see Figure 4.1).

The vertical principle in Japanese society means that 'an individual or a group has only one single distinctive relation to the other' (Nakane 1972) in contrast with caste or class societies. With *Frame* analysis, (the corresponding Japanese term *ba* means locality) it is possible to encapsulate individual attributes in a wider social context, household, company or neighbourhood. In contrast, Indian society is strongly characterized by caste (occupation and kinship) attributes. In comparison with Western standards, in Japanese society, individual autonomy is minimized in favour of group formation.

In this framework, the understanding of larger social units as cities, or megacities (a Western urban concept, actually) today, is more easily explained. In Western society, the individual is key, and his or her participation in (more than one, many at a time) social circles has been explained by Georg Simmel as the main attribute of modern metropolitan life. In Eastern societies, as in the case of Japan, individuality is based on group participation (family, company, neighbourhood etc.), each of them developing independence and closeness. This explains why the city itself is a chaotic and uncoordinated *foam-city*. And in the case of megacity-regions, it is a *desakota* region (Mc Gee 2014), in which urban and rural merge in a continuous flow. It is a collection of cells, of anthropogenic islands, as Peter Sloterdijk (2003) explained in his philosophy of space. He defines the contemporary changing urban space as the sum of diverse kinds of space organization. Among these, he defines *ergotope* as a space in which charge of tasks to be fulfilled is shared in a cooperative spirit. Its inhabitants, the ergotopians, are grouped in 'communities of effort'. The command to perform common tasks is produced through a 'family' form, informal and totalitarian, prompted by the

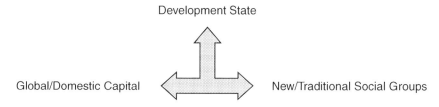

Figure 4.1 The Asian urban contract

120   *The Asian urban contract*

diktat of a tradition and later by 'rites of passage', professional needs and obligations and statutory bonds; later on these functional and command elements are absorbed into the *ergotope*. In this sense, the macro-interiors of megacities and the buildings of human assemblages that we observe in Tokyo or Shanghai are part of a more general organization of space. Its common nature is to 'frame' the social groups and to limit and reunite them against the external world, as Simmel (1908) argued in his space sociology. The frame, or border, has for the social group the same function as the frame for an artwork. In both cases, the frame delimits and closes within itself; the frame affirms that its world is regulated only by its norms; in the case of societies, the fact that a frame or border is not defined absolutely in a subjective way means that it can always be fixed by the subjectivity of agents. We can therefore interpret the general feature of urban modernity as the production of spaces of 'connected isolation' varying from West to East according to social structures, norms and cultures which remain distinctive.

Tokyo

A history of the shogun

Any attempt to interpret Tokyo, the 'capital of the East', with Western keys seems doomed to failure.[1] If the Japanese megacity-region of South Kanto (which includes Greater Tokyo), population 35 million, is compared to London, New York or Los Angeles in terms of size, density and diversity, its peculiarity is evident. It is much vaster and denser, but much less diverse (in terms of ethnic and social population diversity) than its Western counterparts. Greater Tokyo, governed by the Tokyo metropolitan government, has a surface of 2,188 square kilometres, including 23 districts, 26 municipalities and 13 million people, an extension of 90 kilometres from east to west and of 25 kilometres from north to south, and a density of 5,941 inhabitants per square kilometre. The foreign population accounts for only 500,000 people, mainly from other East Asian countries. Its magnetic force is distributed along a territory (the megacity of South Kanto) which is wider than a state: yet it isn't a city-state like Singapore. In terms of key economic functions, it is a global city like London or New York: yet the economy of the city is much less financial than that of London or New York, and much more diversified in terms of activities. The service economy employs 64% of the labour force, but industrial employment is still high at approximately 15% of the total, marking it out from other global cities.

It is also interesting and revealing that the recent major Western texts on world urbanization (Soja 2000; Storper 2013; Taylor 2013; Brenner 2014) devote relatively little or no attention to Tokyo. However, Tokyo is one of the three global cities studied by Saskia Sassen (1991). Until the end of the 16th century just a small village on a wide sea bay, Edo (mouth of the river) was the largest city in the world in the 17th century (when it counted more

The Asian urban contract   121

than 1 million inhabitants), and Tokyo is the largest in the 21st century. This calls for extraordinary analytical efforts on the part of urban theory. We should add that in the 20th century the city was destroyed twice. In 1923, the great earthquake destroyed 40% of the urban area, while in 1945, firebombing destroyed 28% of the urban area of Tokyo. And yet, increasing from a population of 4 million in 1947 to 35 million in 2014, Tokyo shows the most spectacular urban growth witnessed in the course of history. What key, if any, can most usefully be applied to analyze it?

Interpreting the urban form: The global village

A first answer comes not from the social sciences, but from Japanese literature. In 1930, Nobel Prize winner Kawabata Yasunari wrote a wonderful text, *The Scarlet Gang of Asakusa*, where the urban anthropology of a Tokyo neighbourhood is vividly illustrated. Haruko, a character in the novel, surveying the Tokyo roofs from a small tower, exclaims: 'But it is a small village! Tokyo looks like the sole of an old *geta* [the Japanese sandals], and these *getas* are also muddied. . . . it looks like an untidy village, doesn't it?' Asakusa, the site of a famous Buddhist temple, once a village, subsequently incorporated in the city, is described as a 'different place' with respect to the modern world: it is like an 'island', or an 'African village' with its village chiefs, embedded in a 'network of past social norms'.

A first analytical key emerges here: it is the social metabolism of a village underlying the metropolis. A village able to absorb and incorporate new population without any excessive change in its anthropological nature. Kawabata deals with the 'sociology of Asakusa' in explicit terms, the economic crisis of the 1930s extending over the entire country. Around 100,000 female workers have already lost their jobs. Where will they go? Maybe they will go back to their native villages, Kawabata answers, or they will fight against the capitalists who displaced their jobs . . . maybe the ambiguous Asakusa women will embrace those who have no other alternative.

Here the urban anthropology of Jinnai Hidenobu (1995) helps explain and generalize the findings. Tokyo today is still (or at least was in the 1990s) a megacity-region made of villages, and the way the people understand the urban space is not so different from two centuries ago. The rhetoric of modernity has in fact changed Tokyo along the lines of the Western models, yet many elements of tradition coexist and influence the change itself. No Haussmann-like urban transformation has taken place; the culture and symbolism of the city spaces were strong enough to avoid the mere redeployment of Western urban design principles (axes, grids, urban–rural continuity cut).

Jinnai, an urban historian, adopted an ethnographic method based on mapping and visiting the quarters of Tokyo to explain how natural and topographical features (hills, green spaces, rivers) were incorporated into the layout of the city. A variety of maps from the Tokugawa and Meiji periods, building floorplans, woodblock prints, photographs and so forth supplement his observations. The result is impressive. In the vicinity of the skyscrapers and beyond, a minor urban fabric survives, consisting of narrow streets, back alleys and lanes and rivers. Here visitors can see small temples and shrines, modest houses and shops: a new urban population is ready to adopt these spaces in a peculiar gentrification process. In 2010, I visited some of these urban villages with Jinnai: it is like deciphering the urban past in the present. In his book, Jinnai (1995) traces the historical roots of such urban structure along two main axes (see Figure 4.2):

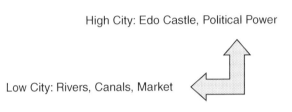

Figure 4.2 The Tokyo urban contract

The vertical axis refers to the political space of the shogunate: Edo is the city of power and its representatives. In the 'high city' were located not only the shogun's castle, but also the residential places of hundreds of feudal lords (*daimyo*), their families and servants. They were obliged to stay in residence in Tokyo for a while on a rotation base (*sankin kotai*). The result in terms of transfer of revenue from the lords to the shogun, and of the increasing population of direct and indirect employees of the feudal lord system, is of the utmost importance in explaining the Edo>Tokyo transition. In modern times, in fact, the political space is still there: the imperial palace Roland Barthes saw as the 'void centre' of Tokyo. It is the centre, symbolic in nature, of the 'endless Tokyo' studied by architects like Botond Bognar (1997).

The horizontal axis defines the 'low city' Jinnai studied following the natural cosmology of a city of water: of rivers, canals and waterfront. In the past, this was the axis of the economy: the markets were attracted by the communication functions of rivers and canals. Warehouses were located along the waterfront and the canals, as in Venice or Amsterdam. Fiscal revenue was reaped as a result of these functions of the market economy of a great consuming city. In the low city, the residential quarters were formed in the 1600s and 1700s: *nagaya* (long houses) for the lower classes, and *machiya* (urban houses) for the affluent merchants (Sacchi 2004).

A third minor axis was at the intersection of the first two. It was the place of temple and shrine entrances, markets, river banks and bridges developed as 'sacred' places. In Tokyo, places of religion do not have the same role as in Western cities. Western churches are places of civic functions and stand facing the political palace in the medieval square. In the 'capital of the East', religious (Shinto and Buddhist) places are distributed across the city and

The Asian urban contract   123

scattered around the natural background; later, they continued to exist as places of entertainment and pleasure on the fringes of urban society.

On observing the vaster Tokyo mega-region a fusion of history and ecology emerges. Actually, since the 1980s the rice fields and the landscape have become increasingly urbanized. Yet in cities like Hino in the Tokyo suburban area, a community is forming based on enhancement of the rural landscape of a 'water city'. The rural landscape has been inherited, water canals have been maintained and safety regulations have been imposed. There is still an abundance of environmental assets in the territory, with hidden potential for urban-rural integration: plateaus, springs and rivers, archaeological remains and ancient sites, villages, residential forests, farmland and trees (Jinnai 2015).

The political sociology of Max Weber (1922) explains the fundamental antithesis between urban development in Western and Eastern cities in terms of the presence (or absence), together with urban fortification and an economic market, of a peculiar body of legal procedural rights pertaining to citizens as such, and a court the citizens autonomously elect themselves. The lack of the city as a social group, hence the nature of 'citizen' as opposed to 'peasant', is what makes the difference. The plastic dualism between economy and polity which characterizes the Western city is not found in the Eastern city. Even when, as in Japan, civic administrative bodies (*machi-bugyo*) existed, citizens' rights were still lacking. The concepts of community, urban community and social class were unknown in a feudal world where only *samurai* and *kashi* (two kinds of feudal warriors) were opposed to peasants, artisans and merchants. Originally a military city, only later did Edo develop a mercantile world system. The social class of *chōnin* living in *chō* (city or a fraction of city smaller than *shi*, a modern concept emerging in the second half of the 19th century) is interesting. The ideogram can also be read as *machi* = city, in the sense of urban neighbourhood in urban proto-history. The *chōnin* are urban inhabitants differing from peasants in having obtained from the feudal lord some rights to conduct commerce in the city as from the 17th century (when the feudal system divided the population into three social classes: *samurai*, peasants and *chōnin*). Since then, an urban culture has developed with significant influence on the urban structure.

According to Arjun Appadurai (2013), Japan is a case of failure of the Weberian theory of modernization. Weber did not foresee – Appadurai affirms – the seductive aspects of the non-European capitalisms. Although a master in historical and regional comparison, Weber did not develop a connective association of great civilizations, their religions and their economies.

This is a really poor analysis of Weber's theory. Appadurai fails to make due distinction between Weber's theory of modernity and the subsequent modernization theories (self-defined Weberian), which he rightly criticizes. Weber's theory is always *tension* between different forces, polytheism of values and polymorphism of forms. Western rationality is not reducible to

124   *The Asian urban contract*

the iron cage, as Appadurai believes; it is diverse, and it is *not* reducible to a unifying principle. Weber's *Sociology of Religion* (particularly the 'Introduction' and 'Intermediate Reflections: Theory of the Stages and Directions of Religious Rejections of the World', both in *Collected Essays on the Sociology of Religion*) follows a line just the opposite of what Appadurai makes of it. India, China and Islam are constantly analyzed and contrasted in terms of 'salvation religions' and their relation to economic rationality. Different gods struggle with one another, as Weber points out in *Science as a Vocation*.

Italian ethnologist Fosco Maraini (2000) finds a deeper anthropological difference on examining the linguistic definition of the city. According to Maraini, in Japan, a single ideogram exists both for market (*ichi*) and for city (*shi*). Hence the city is not an organism, but rather the sum of practical, circumscribed solutions to problems of 'dwelling': it is an assemblage of buildings defined by necessity. If the Western city is a perennial, immovable entity, the Japanese city is a fluid, instable camp on the shore of Time.[2] Turning again to Chie Nakane, localism and tangibility are seen as constitutive aspects of Japanese society; social relations and social knowledge are limited to the group in which the individual is included and to a lesser extent to the group competed with, but no outward-looking relations and knowledge are developed. Tokyo's urban map is an expression of the strength of a constant faith shown to its origins: it is an irregular, radial map having its centre in the imperial palace and its nodes in satellite centres like Shinagawa (today a nodal railway station), Shibuya (one of Tokyo's main crossings), Shinjuku (the site of the metropolitan government and a major railway station) and Ueno (whose historic park is one of Tokyo's most important, second only to Yojogy and Shinjuku-gyoen).

Interpreting the contract form: Modernization and tradition

Traversing the endless Kanto region, which includes the urban region of Tokyo, from Yokohama in the south to Omiya and Takasaki in the north, is an experience that raises doubt about the term usually associated with city-region. This term, *city-region*, was in fact meant to define an urban amalgam with its boundaries, albeit only to enlarge them again: these boundaries are imagined, if not administered, by a population which is itself definable through its belonging to a territory. Is Tokyo, therefore, the Asian counterpart of Gottman's American megalopolis, whose citizens are not even conscious of being part of it? Again, the comparative effort can be misleading. Max Weber's concepts of citizenship, autonomy and autocephaly are, in any case, useful, helping to maintain the cardinal points of the discourse.

The Tokyo model of apparently 'deregulated' growth seems driven by one major function: mobility. Served by an astonishing capillary network of widespread railway services perfectly synchronized, the population traverses the megacity-region in perennial movement. An estimated 80% of Tokyo's population relies on public services to get around (the figure is 34%

in London, 10% in Los Angeles). In the wider Kanto region, the average daily commuting time is 44 minutes, which shows – given the enormous dimensions of the territory – pretty good performance on the part of the public transport network. The main nodes (Ueno, Shinjuku, Shinagawa etc.) are the agglomerating substance of many networks which run in every direction. The superposition, the ordered disorder of layers or urban artefacts, has apparently substituted for any idea of centre, border, zone. Can these residual categories of Western urbanity explain the Asiatic megalopolis? Again in Weberian terms: the *castra*, *oppida*, towns and burghs scattered around urban Europe have not developed here for the reasons explained by Weber (autonomous formation of free citizenship, itself a product of the usurpation of imperial power favoured by an entrepreneurial capitalistic vocation).

The Japanese Empire entered into modernity in the Meiji period (1868–1912), leaving little or no space for urban elites built on autonomy and conflict with monopolies embedded in the monarchy. Here I define modernity, following Peter Wagner (2012, p. xiii), as a plural and unstable set of processes aimed at 'understanding of the peculiar situation of the present in which a globally diffused capitalism seems to be aligned with unstoppable processes of "democratization", but in which both political and economic institutions are highly crisis ridden'.

The first element of Tokyo's 'modernity' was the abolition, in 1871, of the rigid distinction between the areas reserved to the *samurai* (68% of the total area, excluding the Castle, canals, streets and public spaces), the areas reserved to *chōnin* (urban artisans and merchants) and the areas devoted to temples (De Maio 2013). This triadic distinction between military, commercial and religious spaces is also useful in comparison of Japanese 'modernization' with Western urban traditions.

A second 'modernization' factor in the Meiji period lay in the introduction of centrally controlled urban planning (like the Bockmann plan for the imperial capital government district including boulevards and a new Tokyo station), civil engineering and the creation of infrastructures like the Yokohama–Tokyo railway in 1872, the Tokyo railway station in 1914, streets and tramways. In this respect, Western influence was of the utmost importance.

A third 'modernization' factor arose late in the imperial capital reconstruction project of Tokyo after the great earthquake of 1923 and implemented through 1930. The recreation of 3,600 hectares divided into 65 project areas, the street surface area growing from 14% to 26%, and the creation of 11 canals and 424 bridges: here we have some of the key figures. During the seven years of reconstruction, 6,000 bureaucrats and technical experts were employed: after that period they were distributed and absorbed in the wider metropolitan area.

The fourth 'modernization' factor lay in the post-war reconstruction of Japan's cities, and of Tokyo in particular. It was led by a Japanese civil

126   *The Asian urban contract*

engineer, Ishikawa Hideaki, influenced by the Western Garden City movement and the Japanese urban beauty movement: he designed a central Tokyo with a population of 3.5 million and satellite cities with 100,000–200,000 inhabitants (like Yokosuka, Hiratsuka, Machida, Hachioji, Tachikawa, Kawagoe, Omiya, Mito, Utsunomyia, Maebashi, Numazu, Odawara). However, by 1947, the central city population growth had already exceeded the assigned limit, at the expense of the project's effectiveness.

The fifth 'modernization' process saw the creation of a highway and expressway system starting from the 1950s and continuing up to the 1964 Olympic Games in Tokyo, as well as a fast train system (*shinkanzen*).

To sum up, as from the Meiji period Tokyo was destined to become a capital city inspired by European standards, like Paris and London. However, the key factors were the city destruction and reconstruction after 1923 and 1945. In both cases, the initial 'modernist' aim was to leave aside the past and to radically rebuild the city. However, in both cases, a more complex and articulated process took place with compromise between modernity and tradition. Extreme technical modernity was employed to build a new transport system, and to partially destroy the traditional river and canal system of Tokyo (utilizing the war ruins), as well as parks and green spaces. Implementing the new planning system led to development which destroyed agricultural land through 'one tan development' able to circumvent development control. Urban planning 'deregulation' led to the bubble economy of the 1980s–1990s. 'Every city in this region spreads out far and wide around its original nucleus; it grows amidst an irregularly colloidal mixture of rural and suburban landscapes' (Sorensen 2002, p. 176). Tradition was reserved to maintain habitat and habitus (urban structure and civic urbanity) in some neighbourhoods.

To some extent the result was the destruction of Tokyo's urban environment and indeed of the very idea of a public good including the urban heritage. The democratization process through which the feudal system was abandoned and citizens' individual autonomy was finally conceived produced, according to some (Nakajima Naoto 2013), the (unexpected?) result of dissolving the traditional links among individuals and the city as a community. However, this negative interpretation is partially balanced by the paradox that to some extent the destruction caused by the war made it possible to rediscover the permanence of traditional urban traits, as in the case of the Metabolism movement of Japanese architects in the post-war period. This amounted to an attempt to combine technical advance and biological processes in the growth of the city.

Tange Kenzo presented his plan for Tokyo Bay in 1961. The design was based on a 'linear city' concept: a civic axis from Ikebukuro, a northern Tokyo node, to Kisarazu in the south. Three levels of highways were designed to create the transport system needed by a megacity with a population of 10 million. The project was never implemented. However, new plans and projects followed, like Tange's Tokaido Megalopolis Plan (1964) and

Tokyo Plan (1986) and Kurokawa's (a colleague of Tange's) New Tokyo Plan 2025. The extreme interest in technical advance and respect for tradition is clearly at the heart of the Metabolism movement: cities can be regenerated like the famous Ise Shrine, which is dismantled and rebuilt every 20 years to be home of the sacred mirror *Yata no kagami*. Yet reinforced concrete and heavy technical structures predominate in Tange's works, a compromise between the Western and Japanese worlds.

In general terms, we can now try to define the Tokyo urban contract as an extreme attempt to reconcile modernity and tradition in a way that differs from Western urban renewal (starting from Haussmann's Paris). As from the Meiji period and up to the 1960s–1970s post-war boom period, the urban contract was directly led by the central state, its bureaucracy and the prefecture system. The developmental state created a strong triangle of interests with the economic elite involved in the process of urban growth. The old system of city planning (*toshi keikaku*) made centralized control possible and local participation impossible or irrelevant. The unit of analysis was the large area (the whole city including different municipalities), its regional infrastructures and extensive development.

Starting from the 1950s and 1960s, a different idea of the urban contract emerged (Watanabe 2007). Here the contract is jointly defined by agents of urban government and growing civil society. Voluntary forms of participation and even protest by citizens' associations are now permitted. Local rights finally emerge as part of the democratization process and modify the collective perception of the urban environment through direct bottom-up promotion.

Although it started in the 1950s and 1960s with limited impact, a more recent, peculiar form of this new civil society urban approach is seen in an institutional innovation called *machizukuri*. The term is complex, and also ambiguous. It is composed of two words: *machi* (community, local area as opposed to large area, hence neighbourhood, city, not only in its physical dimension, but also in its non-physical aspect of 'viewpoint' of local residents) and *zukuri* (making, building, growing through a process of participation). It is literally to sum up and simplify, 'the management of a community' (Kanai Ken 2013) – an activity based on the principle of civil society as distinct and even opposed to the principles of government and market (Watanabe 2007). A new triangle is designed, in which the emerging polarity of civil society can cooperate with and exert pressure on the other two poles of government and market economy. In a more recent elaboration of the already established concept, it is a pact for urban projects jointly conducted by the local community, the public administration and technical personnel. It is a case of participative urbanism combining economic, social and cultural factors. Tokyo's neighbourhoods like Kanda, Hongo, Nezu, Kagurazaka and Yanaka close to high building developments have been maintained, thanks to this pact. In some cases, like in Kyoto, a centre has been created hosted by the local administration to 'make the city with the citizens'.

128   *The Asian urban contract*

The pact utilizes the 'building agreement' included in the law on standard norms for building (art. 69), local autonomy regulations and charts based on the constitution (art. 94). In 1980, the district planning system introduced the 'small area' into planning. The *machizukuri* was then included in the urban planning law (*toshi keikaku ho*) in 1992 and 1998, and a law for the maintenance and enhancement of the traditional urban environment was passed in 2008. In this recent development, the opposition between the old and the new planning systems has found a compromise.

The Tokyo urban contract tries to reconcile the interests of maintenance and improvement of the traditional urban setting and cultural heritage as perceived by the local residents with the pressures for demolition and reconstruction that have characterized post-war Japan. The new agreement-based approach seems a novelty in Japanese urban renewal, possibly showing similarity to the agreements and neighbourhood place-based initiatives taking place in European cities under the urban European joint programming umbrella.

The possibility to adopt the *machizukuri* approach on a wider and intersectoral scale is an open question in Japan. But what about the pressures coming from the urban developers' sector and the major real estate and financial enterprises interested in urban renewal? The other side of the story is in fact the competitive need of Tokyo as a 'global city' to attract new international business in the urban region. The effects will be to densify and gentrify central areas of the city yet further. The modernization process seen as a complex interplay between democratization and institutionalization of capitalism development finds its roots here, and also its trade-off.

Another kind of urban contract is ongoing in Tokyo, this time between government and global enterprises: it follows the 'private city' logic. To bolster Tokyo's competitive profile in Asia, the metropolitan government has launched the Special Zone for Asian Headquarters project to persuade more than 500 foreign companies to set up shop in Tokyo by 2016. The Tokyo government wants to entice foreign companies doing business abroad to establish their Asian headquarters in Tokyo, rather than Hong Kong or Singapore, by offering such benefits as preferential tax treatment and financial aid. Five areas make up the special zone: the northern portion of Tokyo Bay stretching from Roppongi to Odaiba, Shinjuku, Shibuya, the district shared by the Shinagawa and Tamachi stations, and a vacant site formerly used by Haneda Airport. The goal is to shore up Tokyo's status in Asia, threatened as foreign companies increasingly move to other Asian cities. From 2005 to 2010, the number of foreign companies in Tokyo slumped from 2,645 to 2,330: a decline due to the rise of other Asian business centres, including Singapore and Seoul, which provide subsidies and other incentives to lure foreign firms. Tokyo launched the Special Zone for Asian Headquarters project taking advantage of the central government's Comprehensive Special Zones for International Competitiveness system. In 2010, the central government created a system of two special zones as part of its economic growth strategy. One of the zones is meant to boost Japan's international competitiveness, the other to revitalize the local economies. Tokyo applied to be designated as part of the international competitiveness zone in 2011. Other regions designated include Chubu, which is trying to become the centre of Asia's aerospace industry. Foreign firms that set up regional headquarters or research and development centres within the zone will see their corporate tax rate drop from 38.% to 26.9% (the corporate tax rates of Hong Kong and Singapore are 16.5% and 17%, respectively). The companies are also eligible for subsidies to cover fees and costs entailed in hiring staff and obtaining residency status for their employees. Foreign companies can take advantage of the Business Development Center Tokyo, a special organization set up specifically for the zone participants, offering assistance in English to ease transition to working in Japan. The metropolitan government is placing priority on information technology, chemicals, precision instruments and aviation. The medical field has potential, as Japan (with its ageing population) is the second-largest market after the United States. The field of content creation, such as animation and game software, is another possibility. By 2016, Tokyo wants to bring in more than 500 foreign firms, including at least 50 setting up Asian headquarters or R&D centres in the designated areas. Tokyo is shooting for ¥14.6 trillion in economic effects and 930,000 jobs.

Will the 2020 Olympic Games be the next occasion for a new wave of 'modernization'? Will symbolic places in the city, like the Tsukiji fish market and rare areas of parkland near the Meiji shrine, be demolished in preparation for the Games?[3] If modernist Tange Kenzo was the architect of the 1964 Olympic Games, will Kengo Kuma, with his organic architecture of fluidity and natural elements, inspire a civil society movement led by the idea that 'buildings should not overwhelm people'?[4]

Mumbai

A history of colonial and postcolonial power

The origin of the current megacity of Mumbai (12 million population in the greater Mumbai peninsula, projected to grow to 15 million by 2034, plus 9 million on the mainland in 2011) lay in the Portuguese Bom Bahia ('Good Bay'), hence Bombay, an archipelago of seven separate islands (Colaba, Little Colaba, Bombay, Mazagoan, Worli, Parel, Mahim) which later become a port, thanks to British investment, attracting people from all over India. The fort and the British East India Company were the symbolic buildings of the colonial age. It was a multi-ethnic Tower of Babel, according to Western visitors, yet a divided city – divided at least since 1772, when an ordinance decreed the central east–west artery, Churchgate Street, as the line of demarcation: Europeans lived south of Churchgate; non-Europeans

130 *The Asian urban contract*

lived to the north. This is still the main divide of contemporary Mumbai (Brook 2013).

The city boomed during the mid-19th century, thanks to growing export of cotton (replacing British import from America during the Civil War) and later to the Suez Canal, making Bombay the perfect port city between Asia and Europe. All urban innovations, from railways to telegraph, from stock exchange to university, were introduced early in this period. The population doubled to 800,000 inhabitants in the same period.

At the turn of the 20th century, the urbanization process created the *chawl*, 'a wide, squat five- to seven-story building with a central courtyard hosting three to four hundred cell-like eight-foot-by-eight-foot cubicles lined up along breezeways. A 1911 report found that 80 percent of the city's population lived in such single-room tenements' (Brook 2013, p. 204).

The mortality rate, the plight of people living in the street and urban decline all called for response. It came from the British-led Bombay City Improvement Trust through the creation of new, less dense *chawls* and the construction of large boulevards connecting different neighbourhoods. A Hausmannian response coupled the creation of new substandard living spaces, and, ironically, the technical-modernizing connection of disparate parts of the city in a multicultural metropolis prepared the ground for the Indians' unified reaction to British rule. The creation of a new, disorderly, hybrid urbanism unique to Bombay (Brook 2013) was, then, the unintended consequence of the work of the British-led Trust. We find here, and not in the illegal behaviour of urbanized masses, the origins of the encroaching nature of the Indian city, advancing beyond any proper or former limit. The 'construction of the poor' as encroachers has been rightly criticized (Roy 2011). And here, too, is the origin of the long-lasting resistance of 'the poor' to being moved away and rehoused in urban 'improvement' schemes (elaborated by the British in the past, by McKinsey in the present). The growth of the city in the 1930s (+30%) was accompanied by the 'anti-urban' Gandhian movement which took India to independence, based on an idea of modernity (attached to tradition and rural India) very different from the approach British imperialism had imported in Bombay. Yet the development of a diversified entrepreneurial class over time has been a distinctive feature of the city.

After independence in 1947, Mumbai become the capital of Maharashtra State, and the population tripled in the following decades. The mix of Nehru's state socialism, urban plans to decentralize industries in the mainland and the growth of new media industries like Bollywood were signs of a transition towards an increasingly divided city.

Urban development also followed a divided scheme, with new towns featuring strong infrastructure for the middle class like Navi Mumbai on one side, and the north-west axis of mostly unplanned and 'illegal' expansion on the other side. The cohabitation of *pukka* (planned) and *kucha* (unplanned) cities is a permanent, ontological divide in Indian cities.

The Asian urban contract 131

Interpreting the urban form 1: Creating a low-density, middle-class new town

The urban densities of Mumbai are represented in Table 4.1:

Table 4.1 Urban densities in Mumbai

Municipal Corporations	Density (per km²)	Share of Population	Growth in Past Decade
Greater Mumbai	20,680	59%	4%
Navi Mumbai (including Panvel)	6,382	10%	88%
Thane	11,618	8%	52%
Kalyan-Dombivali	11,275	7%	30%
Vasai-Virar	11,631	6%	31%
Mira-Bhayandar	9,179	4%	57%
Bhiwandi-Nizampur	28,659	4%	36%
Ulhasnagar	18,407	2%	7%

Source: Census of India

The idea of creating a new city as a counter magnet to Mumbai was originally envisaged in the regional plan of Mumbai Metropolitan Region (MMR) in 1965. The actual planning process of this new city began in 1971 after the formation of CIDCO, a Government-owned company for the development of cities.

The initiative was spearheaded by renowned architect Charles Correa and a specialist team of planners, including Shirish B. Patel, Pravina Mehta and Chief Planner R. K. Jha. Their idea was to create a combination of 14 mini towns or nodes, each to be provided with connectivity through well-designed roads, and later on through railway networks. Recently, the metro system was added to the original master plan.

Infrastructure, including water supply, power, sewerage and rain water discharge, was meticulously designed. The concept of holding ponds helped prevent flooding of streets and buildings even during heavy monsoon rains. Thanks to this planned approach, the quality of infrastructure at Navi Mumbai today is much better than in most parts of Greater Mumbai.

Navi Mumbai was added as the last mega settlement zone of the MMR region in the seventies; other cities and conurbations already existed prior to the creation of this satellite city. Today, Navi Mumbai's success as a city is vouchsafed by its tremendous growth over time. In a span of four decades, it has not only caught up with the existing settlements but has also become the second-largest settlement city within MMR in terms of population share. In the last decade, Navi Mumbai has grown at an incredible rate of 88%, the highest in the region.

Despite its fast growth, Navi Mumbai continues to be defined by a spatial openness which cannot be found anywhere else in MMR. Again, despite

132   *The Asian urban contract*

its high growth rate and burgeoning population, the population density in Navi Mumbai – about one-third of the density of Greater Mumbai – is the lowest among all the cities in the MMR region. This is one of Navi Mumbai's defining aspects and biggest USP (unique selling proposition) as a real estate market – the quality of life available in this city.

Navi Mumbai also ranks high in terms of social indicators like literacy rate, which is over 95% among its predominantly middle-income population, as well as social and civic infrastructure.

The success of Navi Mumbai can be largely attributed to the efficient integration of economic activities and infrastructure. Even before the development of the city, there were two major industrial clusters here, namely TTC and Kalamboli. The new Plan envisaged growth of a new commercial district at CBD Belapur, an IT and Technology node at Mahape, wholesale and retail activity at Vashi, etc. All these economic nodes were later integrated with the residential nodes by way of road and railway networks, and a good public transport system.

As the human capital in the city grew, it started gathering strength in the Knowledge sector as well. Today, the city boasts of many additional economic anchors such as DAKC, Mind Space, Reliance Corporate Park and Siemens, to name but a few. The only disappointment was CBD (Central Business District) Belapur, which failed to attract the corporate sector from South Mumbai as initially envisaged. Today, CBD Belapur in fact faces huge competition from Bandra Kurla Complex (BKC) in Mumbai.

Navi Mumbai is now poised at the next stage of transition, which is likely to be by way of expansion of its services sector. The city already has most key ingredients – including good human capital, support infrastructure and land availability – to become a strong service sector hub. What it lacks is faster and smoother connectivity with the existing commercial hubs of Greater Mumbai, particularly the suburbs. Without such linkage, there are definitely pitfalls to a smooth transition for Navi Mumbai's economy.

There are two new major economic drivers planned for Navi Mumbai – the proposed SEZs (Special Economic Zone) at Dronagiri, Ulwe and Kalamboli and the proposed international airport at Panvel. Both of these factors are expected to generate a massive amount of employment, providing a further impetus to the demand for commercial and residential developments.

The successive regional plans of MMR have laid emphasis on further decongestion of Greater Mumbai. It is the high congestion premium that makes Greater Mumbai unaffordable, and its infrastructure is also under crushing pressure, victim to irreversible damage to its environment and overall degradation of quality of life.

The way forward for a more sustainable future for Greater Mumbai is to initiate a planning process that integrates it more closely and intensely with surrounding cities like Navi Mumbai. Only such measures will provide a vent for the crunched-up population out of the city.

The Asian urban contract 133

Unfortunately, the recently scrapped Development Plan of Greater Mumbai (DP 2034) actually proposes reversal of this concept. By increasing the FSI (floor space index) and diverting environment sensitive zones into 'urbanizable' zones, the message being sent is that decongestion of the city is no longer a priority. For the larger benefit of the region, all DPs should be in line with the philosophy of the Regional Plan. The survival of Greater Mumbai will be greatly dependent on the success of cities like Navi Mumbai.

(Source: Subhankar Mitra, *Indiainfoline*, May 22, 2015)

The complexity of such divisions is well explained in the 2005 Appadurai-sketched analysis we have already quoted. Internal (class, caste and religious) division, national (with the regional mainland) and geopolitical division (sea against land) all sum up and coalesce in a complex puzzle. Real estate boomed after the 1991 reforms introducing liberalization: hundreds of developments led by private interests were launched, without public intervention in providing services or social housing. 'Reforms to unleash the real estate market have so empowered developers that comprehensive planning has become all but illegal' (Brook 2013, p. 334). Privatization has led to real estate deals to build Los Angeles–like urban gated communities for cosmopolitan elites of 'global Indians', close to slums where their maids, gardeners or drivers live. Poverty and street children are the other side of the boom.

The informal economy of the cities also has to be taken into account to understand the urban phenomenon. In 2005–6, the number of persons engaged in organized manufacturing was about 697,000 in Gujarat, compared to 1.3 million in the unorganized sector. In Maharashtra (Mumbai's state), the figure is 1.03 million, against 2.5 million. As for services, the numbers are 870,000 in the organized sector compared to 1.7 million in the unorganized sector. To sum up, two out of three workers (in both the private and public spheres) are in the informal sector.

The lack of investments in infrastructures (both physical and social) is the dark side of the city's growth (Zérah 2011). In transport, sanitation, water and electricity, the crisis is permanent – with emergency peaks like the 2005 flooding causing 1,000 victims. The constant competition between the state-led Mumbai Metropolitan Region Development Authority (MMRDA) and the urban collectivity–led Metropolitan Corporation of Greater Mumbai (MCGM) is part of the fragmentation and resource control competition of the political and administrative structure in charge of the infrastructural and housing development. The other political factor behind the permanent infrastructural crisis is the distributive and micro-negotiation role of both the local political system and low-level porous bureaucracy, as opposed to any universalistic technical-bureaucratic ideal. A significant outcome is the contractual structure of infrastructure construction and management, subcontracted to small local firms based on proximity linkages, informal labour and without any innovative potentials, and excluding national and international players in the field of public utilities. On the other side, in the

134 *The Asian urban contract*

cases of big infrastructural projects (like the Mumbai Trans-harbour Link connecting Mumbai and Navi Mumbai), big oligopolistic players (like the two Ambani conflicting groups) and the state play a dangerous game, in the absence of strong modern urban enterprises.

According to Brook (2013), in Mumbai, democracy 'means that no one can ever be moved' (but where are the poor supposed to go?), and 'the legacy of the caste system means that living next to a slum doesn't necessarily diminish the status of the wealthy any more than living next to a luxury tower raises the status of the poor' (p. 344). A paradoxical compromise would emerge: on one side poverty and its claims to stay (in exchange for votes and 'loyalty' to the power), on the other side the wealthy and their concession to stay (as a mean to reduce both 'voice' and 'exit' choices of the useful urban poor). We should, however, remember that the side-by-side cohabitation of golden neighbourhoods and slums is not exclusive to India; it is part of metropolitan history as early as Zorbaugh's 1929 urban sociology study of Chicago: *The Gold Coast and the Slum*.

Is the Mumbai urban contract based on the reciprocal interdependence/ coexistence of wealthy and poor without any possible changes, and 'blockade' (Roy 2011) the inevitable consequence? Two competing, opposite visions have been advanced against the status quo. The first identifies the 'global city' alternative as a matter of fact on behalf of the Mumbai economic elites; the second elaborates a different response based on the capacity to aspire to and negotiate substantial improvement in their condition on the part of the Mumbai poor.

Interpreting the urban form 2: Vision Mumbai

Vision Mumbai. Transforming Mumbai into a world-class city was drawn up by Bombay First and McKinsey in 2003. The style is of a standard consultancy product consisting of interviews with key officers, stakeholders and interest representatives and statistical data assembled in a simplifying scenario. The report's recipient is a lobby, Bombay First; the author of the report is a well-known international consultancy agency ready to produce the same recipe for development all round the world for local governments inclined to be influenced by its consultancy service.

The first 'choice' made by the report is to benchmark Mumbai with 10 cities (London, New York, Singapore, Hong Kong, São Paolo, Sydney, Shanghai, Bangkok, Rio de Janeiro and Toronto) with very different backgrounds. This is particularly absurd as far as housing is concerned: slums in Mumbai account for 50–60% of the housing of the total population (which means at least 6 million people) whereas the benchmark is 4%! This means that no comparison can be made: the dimension of the phenomenon is so peculiar and structural that no benchmarking to reach the 'average' policy can be advocated. This is also the case with public toilets: the Mumbai value is 17 toilets per million people against the benchmark value of 140. It is

The Asian urban contract   135

evident to everybody that no comparison can be made, and a very different approach is needed if changes are to be made in Mumbai.

The report's proposed approach is to create 800,000 low-income houses to rehabilitate existing slum-dwellers by redesigning the Slum Rehabilitation Authority (SRA) process. It is commercially unviable to rehabilitate almost 60% of the existing slum land because of current market prices, the incentive ratios provided under the SRA and the generosity of the current scheme (with its promise of 'free housing'). Therefore, the SRA scheme, as currently designed, is unlikely to succeed. Hence, the report suggests that the government reform the SRA process such that slum dwellers get free land, but contribute towards the cost of construction. Under this scheme, they will be asked to pay either a lump sum or Rs. 750–1,500 per month towards their constructed homes as a 'user charge'. To facilitate this payment, they will be given secure land tenure/apartment ownership rights once their redevelopment has been approved to use as collateral to obtain housing loans from private/public sources. Moving to a limited user charge model will make rehabilitation of all slum areas economically viable – thus jump-starting slum clearance. It will also reduce the incentive for new slum dwellers to squat.

The government approach is much weaker and more inclined to compromise with the inhabitants. Although the slums in existence prior to January 1, 1995, have already been regularized, in many cases, the original inhabitants have moved out. Former Maharashtra Chief Minister Prithviraj Chavan recently announced in the Legislative Assembly that the government had decided to make the current residents (even those who occupied the dwelling after 1995) eligible for SRA schemes. Necessary changes will be made in the Development Control Rules (DCR) and Maharashtra Slum Areas (Improvement, Clearance and Redevelopment) Act, 1971. Section 33 (10) of the DCR would be amended. Explaining the rationale, Chavan said that as in many cases the original inhabitants had moved out, 'this was creating problems in expediting several development projects'. The decision is expected to help long-pending projects such as Dharavi (the main Mumbai slum) redevelopment and the Mumbai airport expansion plan.

A striking critical overview of slum formation has been presented in the essay 'Becoming a Slum: From Municipal Colony to Illegal Settlement in Liberalization-Era Mumbai' (Bjorkman 2014). The study demonstrates that the often assumed equation slum = unplanned settlement product of poor as encroachers (through unauthorized occupation of land or violation of zoning laws) is not correct. The grid pattern of Shivajinagar-Bainganwadi, the neighbourhood Bjorkman analyzed, is explained by the fact that it was laid out in the 1970s as a municipal housing colony. Only later did the neighbourhood *become* a slum, due to (or at least facilitated by) politically mediated deterioration and criminalization of its water infrastructure. The Maharashtra State Slum Act of 1971 was finalized to improve and offer services to substandard settlements, while slum formation was the result of

136 *The Asian urban contract*

demolition-rebuilding-negotiation processes (including the possibility of regularization of encroached land). The 1970s in Mumbai were years of assessment of 1,680 neighbourhoods authorities deemed to violate the zoning or density norms laid down in the 1967 Development Plan and Control Rules. People were photographed in front of their dwellings and given a pass. Demolitions in areas destined for development took place, with relocation of people in municipal colonies like Shivajinagar-Bainganwadi. As Bjorkman accurately explains: 'The area was laid out in two phases – Shivajinagar 1 and Shivajinagar 2 (now known as Shivajinagar and Bainganwadi) – with 14 roads and at least 94 blocks (or plots), each with 8 lanes (or *chawls*). *Chawls* were designed to be allotted to 16 families (8 on either side of the lane), each with a toilet block and four shared water taps (or standpipes) – two at either end of the toilet block.' This is apparently a social housing programme: how did it turn into a slum? Simply because the municipality failed to build houses: people had to build their own houses and pay a small fee to occupy land. The people came from (or were expected to come from) displacement and relocation. But given the very poor conditions of the place (practically a dump) many were ready to leave, 'selling, renting or simply abandoning their plots of land and going to live with relatives in more salubrious parts of the city, or returning to areas of the city where they had lived for generations, where they had access to jobs, relatives, schools and hospitals.' A further step toward the slum creation was the drying of the water pipes due to the use of new water for other-than-residential purposes (e.g. industry). On top of this came the settlement of new rural-urban migrants beyond the planned gridded area and not in the abandoned plots of the gridded area, due to its poor condition (no housing, no water) and the risk of eviction. A 'war for water' among the different neighbourhoods was the ultimate result. The 1995 promises to give free housing to slum-dwellers (through removal of the 25% profit cap on slum redevelopment and extension of the cut-off date to bring all existing slums under the ambit of redevelopment) opened the new phase of slum redevelopment. It is now based on a legal-illegal combination, as post-1995 dwellers are excluded from redevelopment. This opened a political market for entitlements: negotiations to obtain the documents for eligibility to redevelopment schemes and public water supply were political (including vote banking and corruption) in nature. A vicious circle arises: people increasingly leave the neighbourhood, and it becomes an uninhabitable slum.

Not all slum redevelopment projects are the same: in Mumbai itself, a scheme with independent plots on which residents built their *pukka* houses with loans repaid after 20 years can be contrasted with a high-rise apartment scheme which failed to come up with the desired results. The same is true elsewhere in Indian cities.

Bangalore, 6 million inhabitants (11 million in its greater metropolitan area), the capital of Karnataka and the 'knowledge city' of India, is for this reason included among the global cities in the 2014 Princeton University *Atlas of Cities*. Its global reach is witnessed by the famous, well-documented linkages with Silicon Valley firms given the value of its technically qualified and educated labour force. Bangalore as growing, thriving (although socially divided) city is part of the wider north–south divide among Indian states and cities carefully documented by Paul and Sridhar (2015).

The high-tech development areas of Bangalore are mixed with 'vast territories of small plots strung together into what is known locally as 'revenue and *gramthana* (or village) layouts' (Benjamin 2014b). Many settlements, now considered encroachments or slums, actually pre-date urban planning and are therefore the result of 'negotiating urbanization' in which public and private actors were part of the game.

In Delhi, the process of liberalization as from 1991 has resulted in an 'apartheid city', according to urban scholars, with the affluent in the centre and resettled slums in the periphery. The mobilization of the urban middle class and the courts, imposing zoning rules, have made this exclusionary policy possible. In Mumbai, the municipality launched the Advanced Locality Management Programme in 1997 to create community committees (648 have been recorded, 150 are active) for waste disposal in middle-class residential quarters. This is a participative tool enabling cooperation between city users and technical administration. Moreover, a larger network of civic associations in the fields of urban planning, environmental issues and heritage conservation has been created on this same ground. Cleaning up the streets and modernizing the city amount, at the same time, to action against and expulsion of street vendors, and elimination of the poor habitat. In this way the middle-class taxpayers' mobilization tends towards exclusionary policies. Of course, the Indian scholars rightly underline the specificity of postcolonial India, but let us not forget that the term 'apartheid city' was used by French Prime Minister Valls after the January 7, 2015, terrorist attack in Paris, with reference to the current exclusionary condition of Parisian *banlieues*. Right, or more probably wrong, Valls' view shows the interconnected nature of the urban problems as they are perceived around the world.

The alternative vision of the alliance formed by three civic organizations in Mumbai to address poverty – the Society for the Protection of Area Resources (SPARC) NGO, the National Slum Dwellers' Federation and Mahila Milan – was authoritatively presented by Appadurai (2001). This is a case of direct involvement of a network of NGOs like SPARC, a national federation of slum-dwellers and a committee of slum women in the resettlement policy of slum-dwellers linked to new urban transport projects implying the eviction of many thousands of families.

The contractual structure is based on the subcontracting of implementation phases by the municipality to the NGO, hence the risk for the alliance of becoming institutionally encapsulated in the scheme that needs to be

138 *The Asian urban contract*

implemented. The complex scheme of socio-contractual and urban governance relations can be represented thus in Figure 4.3:

Figure 4.3 The Mumbai slum interplay

Moreover, the mechanism of community participation is closely related to political intermediaries and political patronage based on affiliation and distribution of both human and financial resources (Zérah 2011). The criticism Roy (2011, p. 267) raises is more ideological ('SPARC maintains the dominant narrative of the poor as encroachers') than politically effective in censuring the approach followed by the alliance. Appadurai (2001) makes clear that the three civic organizations taking part in the alliance are 'committed to a partnership based on a shared ideology of risk, trust, negotiation and learning among their key participants'. Their approach is critical towards the project logic and timing, and favours patience, long-lasting engagement and empowerment of the poor. However, on this ground Appadurai points out that 'the most recent such episode is a massive demolition of shacks near the railroad tracks, which has produced an intense struggle for survival and political mobilization in virtually impossible circumstances in the period since April 2000, a crisis still unresolved at the time of writing'. This means that subsequent to the facts underlined by Appadurai, the alliance decided to take part in the resettlement project – which is hard to accept in Appadurai's logic. Becoming part of the resettlement game is probably an inevitable development in alliance politics, but it also means sharing the project's logic and timing criticized by Appadurai.

We should also note that the urban phenomenon of 'illegal' building, political cronyism and the local 'mafia' network regulating the slums, which we recognize in India, is widespread in Western cities as well. In Rome, 40% of the population lives in areas not recognized as residential, having been first illegally built by developers and small landowners and only later regularized by the municipality. Also the phenomenon of the 'formerly social housing, then slum' process that we find in India is all too familiar in Western cities. In Naples neighbourhoods like Ponticelli, once an old village, now a densely populated area with 80,000 inhabitants in the eastern part of the city, were characterized by social housing during Naples' disastrous urbanization in the 1950s–1960s and by in-migration of displaced population in the years following the Naples earthquake (1980s). Now, the *camorra* controls the streets and gunfights between rival gangs are the order of the day (2015).

Interpreting the contract form: The opaque compromise

In a very important paper on urban India (Sivaramakrishnan 2006), the author, a leading urban expert (who died in 2015), denouncing inequities in distribution of water, the sewage system, infrastructure, road systems and transport in Indian cities, asks: is urban planning abandoned? His answer is: 'Over the past five decades of "planning", India has managed to confound the very meaning of the term. At one end of the spectrum at the national level is the nearly philosophical discourse on planning for economic development. At the other end, at the municipal level, "plan" only means a statutory land use master plan. Eventually this is further reduced to the exercise of passing building plans, usually by deceit and corruption rather than any simple and transparent system. Between these two extremes, planning as practiced by most government departments and agencies only means a collection of schemes and projects, a largely opaque process of sanction and funding, and a spotty record of implementation' (Sivaramakrishnan 2006, p. 6).

'Cities are born out of complex processes "beyond the plan", where spaces (political, institutional, legal) are shaped by the complexity of politics on the ground and constituted by everyday practices' (Benjamin 2014b). In this account of the Indian urban contract, many social roles need to be more precisely defined (see Figure 4.4). Urban transformation and land use are constant matters of contested terrain. Increasing the Floor Space Index (FSI) is a major stake in central and peripheral urban areas (Sridhar 2010; Brueckner and Sridhar 2012). According to Kundu (2007), 'the shift from centralised planning to free-market development may, in fact, reduce rather

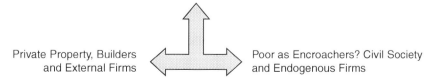

Figure 4.4 The Mumbai urban contract

140   *The Asian urban contract*

than fuel urban growth in India, even in the larger cities which are successfully attracting new infrastructure and investment. This process, however, is likely to institutionalise disparity and strengthen the process of segmenting cities into rich and poor areas.'

The 1992 legislation introducing the 73rd and 74th constitutional amendments decentralized more functions[5] formerly held by national and state governments to cities and their urban municipal corporations. However, a failure in effective decentralization emerges from the research conducted by independent urban research experts. In particular, devolution to municipalities and lower-level units (*wards*) is limited by the states' determination to maintain their powers. 'An extensive review of the creation and functioning of the Wards Committees in the States of West Bengal, Maharashtra, Karnataka and Kerala carried out by the Institute of Social Sciences brings out clearly the patent reluctance of the State governments to accept wards committees as an important forum of public participation at the local level. Most of the State governments and the city administrations prefer a loose and informal arrangement for public participation rather than formal systems of empowerment and public accountability' (Sivaramakrishnan 2006, p. 20).

This clear analysis is confirmed by recent research on political accountability over housing issues in Mumbai. Given the enormous pressure deriving from slum development and rehabilitation, one would expect these major issues to be debated and deliberated in local democratic institutions. Land, housing and urban development being matters assigned to the states, the Maharashtra State Legislative Assembly should be the right place for that. On the contrary, of 40,520 questions asked in the Legislative Assembly over a period of five years (2009–14), only 5,970 were on the subject of housing and related issues, and only 566 (1.3% of the total) related to slum development and rehabilitation (Praja Org 2014). This is an astonishing finding of a project engaging with the citizens, the elected representatives and the government on issues which concern the citizens of Mumbai (affordable housing, education, health, crime, civic issues and working of the elected representatives). The research project neatly confirms the opaque nature of the urban contract in Mumbai. Ways other than democratic assemblies are clearly followed in raising the urban question and obtaining answers.

This is a major difference that emerges when comparing Indian cities to their Western and Eastern counterparts. Effective power of the local community in the building process is seen in Japan and China, as well as the United States and Europe (see infra). In Europe, 60% of the public expenditure is in the hands of local and mostly urban administrations.

Another major issue is the municipal and urban development authorities' (UDA) competition over land; the conflict is a key factor in making urban strategies and policy-making opaque and far from showing accountability. Sridhar and Venugopala (2010) have explored the potential of land as a financial tool for cities, yet the fragmented institutional arrangements between municipal authorities and parastatal entities regarding the asset clearly emerge.

The Asian urban contract 141

A third major issue concerns municipal and parastatals' (agencies debt-financed for special purposes) competition over functional governmentality and the increasing role of special task force governance as, in Bangalore, BATF-Bangalore Agenda Task Force and ABIDe-Agenda for Benagaluru Infrastructure Development (see Goldman 2011). This kind of agencification boils down to an attempt to reduce or annihilate the people's control over city development. As in the case of the United Kingdom, this process can lead to oversimplification and reduction of democratic control over bureaucracies, as well as to an increase in opaque, fragmented initiatives.

In many cases, land rights are contested, legal *status-quo ante* is a matter of reciprocal claims and urban planning comes later to define the legal use of land. Civil society often plays the role of a lobby to promote 'proper' use of public commons (as in the case of wetlands in Bangalore) to privatize the city, hegemonically subsuming the subaltern groups. This seems to be another Indian peculiarity: the middle class is less of a progressive force than in its Western counterparts, and its drive for modernization more exclusionary and aggressive. The poor are seen as encroachers, but often their presence on the land is based on older rights or arrangements, the weak messianic force of tradition and religious past, or simply the extremely strong urban practice of informal economic activities. Politics plays an opaque role in collecting votes[6] and exchanging its political capital in the political process of land use, sometimes favouring but often blocking or delaying the capitalist imperative of urban renewal. The bureaucracy plays its role of arranging decision-making according to its own interests. Market forces play the role of transformative agents, but often lack legitimacy and resources. The final possible outcome is a zero-sum game in which all parts lose ground and anomic powers dominate Indian urbanity.

Indian urbanity derives from dramatic growth (only partially due to migration from rural to urban, mostly to natural population increase[7]) and intense demand for land. But the dimensions of the urban phenomenon are not clearly known: for example, the cadastral mapping is unusable and alternative ways of mapping (satellite technologies) are ongoing. Moreover, the urban land regime is very peculiar. Laws have fixed urban ceilings,[8] resulting in situations of absurdity. Zoning regulations in India create conflict between the courts and the government – the former declaring that zoning must be enforced, the latter holding it to be impossible as 60% of the buildings are in violation of the zoning law. According to Indian urban scholars,[9] 80% of the sanctioned urban plans are violated, and if Indian cities are still liveable, it is also because of such violations. It is in fact the legal land use system which forces the majority of the population into a position of 'technical' (not 'intentional') illegality. Urban planning is a tool often based on exclusionary logic. There is no tradition of local self-governance, and the 'city' as a concept is too recent a phenomenon in India compared to other countries (but not so different from China, as we will see). The price of land in cities like Bangalore is prohibitive, and most of the urban

142   *The Asian urban contract*

population lacks the sanction of legal regimes of tenure. Negotiations over zoning regulations occur on a daily basis within the Bangalore Municipal Agency and the corporation office, but this is not a public process. The poor have survived because of the failure of enforcement, and increased efficiency would result in social disaster. The slum itself is not a drain on resources, but a self-sustaining economic unit of the city. According to a survey conducted in the Dharavi slum in Mumbai, only 5% of heads of households state that they are unemployed, 50% of those who live in Dharavi also work there, and more than 90% say they have no plans to leave (Knox 2014). The informal economy of the slum is made of self-organized 'manufacturing' districts: plastics produced through garbage collection and selection, leather produced with on-site tanning of animal hides and skin, earthenware produced with rubbish-burning furnaces. There are no alternatives, nor are any exit strategies possible. However, other scholars point out that the big building firms also benefit from illegality, as Adiga's urban novel shows. And, finally, also the Special Economic Zones (SEZ) policy has led to large-scale capture of land outside the scope of urban planning.

According to Benjamin (2014a), in such a framework of occupancy urbanism, the practice of occupying land by the poor is not only a 'voice' strategy, but a 'legitimate' substantial answer and triggers multiple crises for global capital. Locally embedded institutions subvert high-end infrastructure and mega projects. Occupancy urbanism helps poor groups appropriate real estate surpluses via reconstituted land tenure to fuel small businesses whose commodities jeopardize branded chains (note that in India only 9% of the food is sold in supermarkets, against 91% in the United States sold in grocery stores, including supermarkets, according to the USDA-U.S. Department of Agriculture). Finally, it involves a political consciousness that refuses to be disciplined by NGOs and well-meaning progressive activists and the rhetoric of 'participatory planning', which is often the monopoly of wealthy urban middle classes looking for American-style models of consumption. This is also a policy that rejects a certain connotation of development: 'developmentalism', where 'poverty' is ghettoized via programmes for 'basic needs', allowing the elite's 'globally competitive economic development': Mumbai like Shanghai, Bangalore like Singapore, and so on.

The urban social contract is, then, fragile. It seems that the right to the city, in the sense expressed by Lefebvre (1996, pp. 194–5) – 'the rights of citizens and city dwellers, and of groups they constitute, to appear on all the networks and circuits of communication, information and exchange' – as a concept is quite unusable in India. As a matter of fact, the poor survive by staying 'off the radar', in the informal sector and through 'illegal' housing.

In the case of India, we have not yet found a 'community building' movement already established, as in Japan and China, on the basis of local pressures (Japan's *machizukuri*) and/or central initiative regarding the powerful dynamics of urbanization (China's *shequ* construction). To be sure, ward committees, citizens' committees and city advisory committees have been founded in Indian cities to institutionalize community participation in

The Asian urban contract   143

the planning, monitoring and implementation of municipal activities, as in the Karnataka cities (Paul et al. 2012). But other research has shown that no ward committees have been empowered by Indian state governments. The reasons are certainly complex and probably beyond the scope of this chapter. What I find interesting is to start digging into the process of 'Producing India' (Goswami 2004) as the creation of a postcolonial national space, seeking some trace of local community building.

The *swaray* has constituted the main solution available in the Indian transition to postcolonial modernity. Gandhi wrote that *swaray* is a sacred word, a Vedic word, meaning self-rule and self-restraint, and not freedom from all restraint. Which 'independence' often means. But *swaray* is the creation of an imagined community, Mother India, in which state-building nationalism has been the dominant feature. This has been true not only in the past (late 19th century), but also today:

> The contemporary neoliberal state/capital configuration has not signaled the retreat or withdrawal of the state. It has rather taken the form of a selective privileging of particular urban-regional nodes (Hyderabad, Bangalore), spheres (most strikingly, information technology), and class constellations (Hindu, urban, middle class, and avidly consumerist) as the economic motors of national development. Contemporary processes of political and economic restructuring have not only reinforced territorially grounded assertions of nationalism tied to an exclusionary and violent Hindutva ideology but generated new forms of sociospatial and economic unevenness.
>
> (Goswami 2004, p. 289)

The lack of community building in India, as an expression of a fully developed civil society (in the sense of Western urbanity since the 17th century analyzed by Habermas 1989) and of a growing urban constellation of society (as in Japan or China today), probably has something to do with the peculiar formation of the Indian nation-state in the postcolonial era. The religious-political cohesion forming Indian nationalism does not leave room for urban social movements as expression of 'the city'. Yet there are in India 'social movements that oppose transnational capital and self-consciously invoke the inherited vision of a popular and sovereign national economic collective' (Goswami, ibid.).

Hong Kong and Shenzhen

A history of diverse trajectories of modernity

Unusual as it may seem, our analysis of the Chinese urban contract starts from the unparalleled comparative sociology of religions Max Weber developed in his last years, in his texts on 'The Religion in China' written between 1916 and 1919 and on 'Economy and Society'. In his analysis, he

144   *The Asian urban contract*

wrote that 'the unity of Chinese culture is essentially the unity of that status group which is the bearer of the bureaucratic classic-literary education and of Confucian ethic with its ideal of gentility' (Weber 1978, p. 1050). And, he added, 'the bureaucratic structure of Chinese politics and their carriers has given to the whole literary tradition of China its characteristic stamp. For more than 2000 years the literati have definitely been the ruling stratum in China' (Weber 1964, pp. 107–8).

Scholars criticizing Western Orientalism as a construction of functionalist thought (Ruskola 2002) note that 'Weber, in particular, defines China in relentlessly negative terms, by what it is not. He attributes China's "failure" to develop a rational bourgeois capitalism to the "absence" of a dynamic religious ethic of the Protestant variety.' They quote Weber's 'Protestant Ethic': 'Chinese intellectual life remained completely static, and despite seemingly favorable conditions modern capitalism simply did not appear.' And they conclude: 'While Weber has many fascinating local insights into Chinese law, his global view suffers from the essentially negative nature of his general approach.'

This is a limited account of Weberian thinking. His oeuvre is dedicated to understanding the influences and causal chains accounting for complex social phenomena like capitalism. Economic rationalism, for Weber, is not only a product of rational technology and rational law, but also of human attitudes and practical disposition towards rational economic behaviour. In this respect, explaining the non-development of capitalism is not a negative scholarly approach, but an exercise in critical thinking about human history.

The need would, rather, be to offer an alternative view of the Eastern path of historical development (Isin 2002). Weber took into consideration the state of current research on Asia and often made clear the need for further investigation, leading to analysis in greater depth. Among the traces of such efforts, there is the possible role of Confucianism as a seedbed for the development of a future capitalist ethos. Traditionalism is also part of Confucianism, hence the complex dynamic interplay of historical factors in accounting for the specific phenomenon of capitalist development.

Postcolonial critics of Weber are probably keen to discuss the rationalization thesis. Rationalization 'can thus include pervasive features of modern life such as standardization, commodification, measurement in terms of efficiency, cost-benefit analysis, legalistic administrative procedures, and bureaucratic coordination and rule' (Scaff 2000). However, in many postcolonial essays, such aspects are not taken into consideration. We can assume that multiple rationalization models are admitted, including the possibility that 'States and governments capitalize on the global circulation of ideas, objects, codes, and standards to engage in a spectrum of experiments that reinvent notions of urban modernity' (Ong 2011).

Given this background, it is unthinkable not to consider the state as the dominant actor, the unquestionable dominant partner of any social contract taking place in China, including the urban context. Chinese communism has inherited a millennial bureaucratic state tradition and used it to create the peculiar state-driven modernization we have seen in the past 30 years. State-driven means: decided and asserted by an actor (the Party-state) which is the only legitimate one. This is in sharp contrast with Western modernization based on a plurality of legitimate agents (state, civil society, intermediate bodies, democratic party system). Yet the creation of a seedbed for civil society is probably an ongoing by-product of China's current urbanization. Recent surveys conducted on Chinese youth show that a dramatic generational conflict is emerging: the youth population is ready to refuse both its parents' tradition and values and the Party-state's guardian attitude.

If we now go on to consider the urban field, we find in the same Weberian vein that 'in China the state was already unified at an early date and controlled large areas of territory before cities had advanced much beyond villages. Thus, even when urban growth occurred, Chinese cities did not function as corporate bodies, were never self-governing, and in consequence did not produce charters and other legal protections to guarantee the rights and liberties of their citizens' (Love 2000, p. 175).[10]

This is the point still taken up by Tang (2014a, 2014b) to criticize the Western use of 'city' (or 'city-region') concepts, clearly unable to interpret the peculiarities of current Chinese urbanization.

Current urbanization in China, with mass migration from the countryside to new urban agglomerations (48 metropolitan areas both coastal and inland), is therefore the first and foremost change of rural/urban millennial equilibrium. For the first time, population increase (according to Weber, a mistaken condition for capitalism growth since it can increase different social strata) goes in the very same direction as in the West. It is now urban and oriented to the economy. In Imperial China, cities were administrative nuclei of state centralization; however, in the model proposed by G. William Skinner (1977), two urban systems actually coalesced: one bottom-up, one top-down. The bottom-up hierarchy is created 'spontaneously' by the markets; the top-down hierarchy is created 'intentionally' by imperial agents for purposes of conquest and control (see also Tilly 1984). Religion, in almost Weberian terms, played a political role too. Confucian school-temple and City God temple were part of the administrative hierarchical structure of the city associated with the *yamen* (local bureaucrat's or *mandarin*'s office and residence in the Chinese Empire), and the customary law of contract and agency. The formal *yamen* courts rarely entered upon regulating claims regarding merchants' activities and other interpersonal disputes. Hence business guilds and religious institutions were self-governing bodies, but never in the Western sense of autonomous governments with respect to the imperial power.

On the other hand, dispersion of commercial activities in the late Imperial Chinese city made a difference with respect to the standard Western city 'central business district' model. The 'centre' was not the place of the market, and the main concentrations of merchants' activities were spatially

146 *The Asian urban contract*

variable, sometimes outside the city walls or in suburbs near the rivers. Also the class-space division is different: in the traditional Chinese city, it is rare to find a divide between a rich and a poor quarter, a fashionable and a slum quarter, as in the Western city. Essentially similar, internally differentiated 'neighbourhood units' (each replete with rich and poor dwellings and inhabitants and market and religious structures) were the standard units of analysis of the traditional Chinese city.

In the subsequent colonial urbanization, cities followed strictly Western models of marketplace islands of modernization. After the 1842 Treaty of Nanking, in treaty port cities (like Shanghai) spatial fragmentation emerged due to different building regulations in foreign (French, British, American) and Chinese settlements (Wu 2015). Western principles of urban planning, from city civic centre to 'organic decentralization', failed to find application to the underdeveloped, pre-industrial Chinese cities of the first half of the 20th century. However, Western urban concepts like the New Satellite Towns, city decentralization and green belts influenced modern and contemporary Chinese urban patterns, as in Shanghai (Wu 2015). Beijing's impressive regime architecture of the 1950s (the monumental Civic Center) is an example of how urban Westernization *and* Soviet Union influences have been turned into political instruments under communism (Chipperfield et al. 2012). In fact, satellite cities, a Soviet urban tool later applied to socialist China, were originally a modernist urban planning tool in the West during the 1920s–1930s. City planning in China was not applied until the recent urbanization boom, when regulating urban rent extraction became essential for the Chinese government.

After the socialist phase based on industrialization supported by urbanization – favouring rural locations and villages for industrial workers, maintaining 'compact' cities, and leading to deterioration in housing due to lack of property rights incentives – a phase of land development was launched in the 1980s–1990s. The state essentially leases land to developers; the pressure for growth on urban plans is strong, the rural and peri-urban land developments are based on informality between government and developer, and political negotiations over land uses are the rule (Wu 2015). Local urban entrepreneurialism and inter-city competition emerge, as well as growth coalitions between government and developers. Interestingly, the more innovative forms of land planning (zoning ordinances) have been tried in Hong Kong and later in Shenzhen. The land market is now a major resource for local government, whose incentives to fuel the development project mechanisms are of the utmost importance.

In the diamond of factors shown in Figure 4.5, the value-creating mechanism is explained, but the terms Chinese scholars use (Wu 2015) are clearly indebted to Western theories. A more critical account of the use of such terms as *growth coalition*, *entrepreneurial state* or others is recommended.

'Growth coalition' in Western terms is an alliance or interests group led by urban managers and urban developers to increase the rent extracted through

The Asian urban contract 147

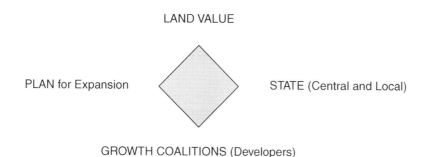

Figure 4.5 The Shenzhen value diamond

development or redevelopment of urban land. Processes of gentrification, exclusion or relocation of lower social groups and so forth have been the consequence, well explained and criticized by (among others) Jane Jacobs with reference to North American cities. The case of China is clearly different. As explained by Wu (2015) and in different terms by Tang (2014), the main game here is extending urban land through expansion and urbanization of formerly rural land. We should return to Marx's first volume of *Das Kapital* to understand the primitive accumulation of capital taking place in rural-urban China.[11] But the coalition between the government and developers is not the same as in the West. The social groups involved here are farmers as 'informal developers', urban villagers and urban fringe or peri-urban inhabitants and local governments in alliance or negotiation with urban development corporations. Limited property rights of housing in China do not prevent local governments (holding a compulsory purchase power, according to the Land Administration Act) from buying land from farmers at a low price and then selling it at a higher market price (Wu 2015, p. 80). The power of the central state to determine land development quotas is also to be noted. Negotiations on land quotas and land use for urban and industrial development are recurrent topics in the literature, including the removal of rural villagers and the resettlement of farmers (Wu 2015, p. 100). The picture is clearly different from that of Western countries, and we know less about the effective process of coalition-building in the Chinese city.

In the Special Administrative Region of Hong Kong, a 'high-density' development model has been followed by local government at a very intensive rate.[12] This has led to urban growth without suburbanization and also to land-related revenue accounting for 20–40% of GDP. The urban redevelopment agency of local government has led the process through intensification, high-rise density and building of new public housing estates. The trend has been towards increasing homeownership for the sake of social peace and harmony. Since the 1950s, when immigrants from Mainland China started to arrive in Hong Kong, and on to the current local government

148 *The Asian urban contract*

policy to foster the market in attracting foreign investments and creating a new private market, there has been a strategic continuity in this direction.

Today local government in Hong Kong aims to increase homeownership (rising from 70% to 80% and more), but the prices are too high even for the middle class, and are still increasing. A certain degree of social conflict between an elite buying homes to sell in high market phases and people willing to buy their homes expecting stable prices is destined to grow. This does not mean that the government is adopting a neoliberal strategy, because the role of market is always supervised by local government and the state ownership of land is not under discussion.

Moreover, the Hong Kong local government is renowned for its public housing programme, including 50% of the population in public housing, whether as tenants or owners. This is the highest percentage known of public housing in a world city today (see Chapter 6 for comparison among the 10 cities included in this book). A recent case is seen in the Kai Ching Estate, built in 2013 on the former site of Hong Kong Airport as part of a huge redevelopment project. More than 5,200 families and 13,300 persons live in high-density towers, sharing facilities like schools, shops and playgrounds. The monthly rent is 2,400 HKD (300 USD) for a 25-square-metre apartment. There are long waiting lists (up to six years) for eligible families based on earning criteria. The maximum family earning permitted for eligibility is 16,000 HKD (2,000 USD) for two persons. The district council in the Estate is elected by residents and plays the role of collective supervisor. Walking through the Estate, you can see posters warning that illegal use and trafficking of housing is prohibited. Additional investments by tenants to make the flats more comfortable are permitted. A visit to the Estate leaves a distinct impression of a lower middle-class lifestyle.

What is clear is that a new, ambivalent 'autonomy' of local governments is under construction in Mainland China, thanks to their capacity to play the role of landlords (buying and selling land). Their game is associated with the capacity of villages, and their clans, to shift from cultivating crops to cultivating real estate (as Helen Siu 2011 has put it). Whether this will lead Chinese cities to become more 'autonomous' towards the state remains to be seen. Moreover, in other cases, like that of Taiwan, the local government and the central government compete over public land use.

It is also interesting to see that, in order to explain current urbanization in China, it is necessary to refer to Western concepts like city-region, urban clusters, mega-region, new state spaces and so forth formulated for other kind of cities, states and political systems. There is an urgent need for urban theory today to make clear that a postcolonial urbanism (Roy 2011) starts from dismissing colonial conceptual apparatuses and elaborating original conceptual tools embedded in postcolonial societies. As Roy clearly stated, the symbol of Shenzhen (according to local young reporters met by the scholar) is not high-rise central city development or high-speed rail to Hong Kong: it is the migrant worker. And this is correct: in 2000, the migrant population accounted for 82% of the total population (Wu 2015, p. 112), an astonishing phenomenon clearly unthinkable in Western cities, but widespread in Chinese cities. The new towns in Shanghai are characterized by migrant populations with percentages ranging from 46.8% in Nanqiao to 78.8% in Jiading and Linggang (Wu 2015). We should start from here to try to understand the Chinese urban contract, instead of repeating Western concepts.

An urgent field of application is Chinese rural migration. Chinese sociologists have carried out careful fieldwork, and we will take into consideration the research conducted in Guangzhou by Zouh and Cai (2008). The massive immigration of rural workers to the new industrial district of Guangzhou accounts for 85% of the workforce. How *waidi-ren*, migrants from outside, that is, without Guangzhou *hukou* (registration), and *bendi-ren* (local workers with Guangzhou *hukou*) cohabitate is well described. In fact, they live in separate settlements outside the factory: the locals in the city, the migrants in factory dormitories, union housing or peasant-owned rental housing. The phenomenon of a 'black market' in Mainland China tenements is well-known to local observers. Each case is well investigated, and the resulting social segregation is clearly denounced. It is said that such social marginalization is both intentional and unintentional; further elaboration on these fundamental interpretative categories is now being conducted. What is lacking is a sociological interpretation based on Chinese realities: when it comes to generalization or theorization, the researchers are indebted to Louis Wirth's classical statement regarding the main urban characteristics of density, heterogeneity and social disorganization. Thus we really need a new Louis Wirth, so to say, able to write a new 'The Ghetto' founding a grounded theory of Chinese migration – and possibly a generalization about Chinese urbanization, as Wirth did on US urbanization in his 1938 seminal work, whose influence has been enormous in the 20th century; it has only recently been revised.

What is striking in Chinese massive migration is that it is a *domestic* flow, whereas Western migration has been (as in the United States in the 19th–20th centuries) and still is (as in the case of undocumented Mexican immigrants) mainly an *international* flow. Thus any comparative work is rather more complex than suggested in Wu and Rosenbaum (2008). Comparing China's internal migrants with US foreign immigration is therefore misleading, as is comparing American citizenship with Chinese citizenship. The concept of citizenship is not simply a matter of legal status and related rights (which can be compared), but also of political and cultural identity (much more difficult to compare).[13] 'One country, two systems' is a notion appropriate to analyze the contemporary People's Republic of China. However 'in many ways, the Chinese economy is not just a dual economy of rural and urban sectors but more a collection of several regional economies that are at various stages of development, with hugely different degrees of economic prosperity, separated chiefly by the PRC *hukou* system' (Wang 2005).

150 *The Asian urban contract*

We should also note that China's urbanization, and more generally emergent world urbanization, are producing a reduction in poverty and better living conditions, again showing a considerable difference from Western urban history. In the 19th century, European cities had higher death rates and lower life expectancy than the countryside. In China, India and elsewhere today, it is exactly the opposite (Therborn 2011). In this respect, Chinese urbanization is a success story. In 2015, with a 54% urbanization rate, urban China had 700 million inhabitants, 250 million without urban *hukou*. The ongoing *hukou* reform (2015) will relax *hukou* registration for migrants in small and medium-sized cities, but will maintain tight control for migrants in great cities. However, agglomeration effects will increase the attractiveness of larger Chinese urban regions.

One line of reform would be to separate *hukou* registration and the social services related to it through a full reform of social welfare policies. The striking differences across regional welfare regimes are documented by Wang (2005): for example the welfare pay for people below the poverty line varies from 135 RMB to 180 RMB/month in Shanghai to 35RMB to 40 RMB/month in a small city or township. Some social services, like pension and medical services, are already linked to the occupational contract, but others, like housing and schooling, are normally not (except factory dormitories). The average cost of one *hukou* is estimated at 30,000 USD for the state government. Investment in education for rural migrants and their children is also needed. But local government has no incentive to invest in this direction given certain externalities (trained migrants will not necessarily remain in the same locality), unless land reform and fiscal reform are designed to this end.

Today, China's urbanization is growing fast, and social inequalities with it (see Figure 4.6). According to Chinese scholars,[14] Chinese cities have witnessed the largest housing boom in history, and also unprecedented housing privatization. Since 1988, a housing reform has enabled direct transition from rent to private ownership of houses, and 80% of new home buyers are private owners. In many cases, it is a matter of enclosed residential quarters, but the comparison with Western-style gated communities is probably misleading: they represent a continuity of neighbourhood enclosure in the past, when

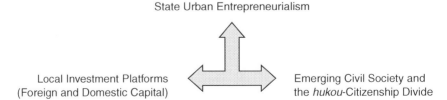

Figure 4.6 The Chinese urban contract

most streets were gated during the night. Walls and gates continue to be the preferred planning tools to promote collectivist living, according to Huang and Low (2008). In any case, a new, huge market for finance operators and banks, property management companies and real estate developers has been created. China now is a country of homeowners, with more than 70% of urban residents owning homes, higher than many developed countries and close to Western countries' standards (and the price of a new Chinese home fell by 5% on average in 2015). This success is not shared by all social groups, with rapidly rising housing inequality, and residential segregation increasingly prevalent in previously homogeneous Chinese cities. Although no Indian-like slums exist in today's China, two extremes of the residential landscape are seen: low-income households living in shacks in 'urban villages', and the nouveaux riches who live in exclusive, gated villa communities.

Urban elites, entrepreneurs and intellectuals are growing fast as well. The inevitably 'modernizing' effects on society are expected. Although neoliberalism is far from the driving force behind contemporary Chinese capitalism, a Weberian concept, rational prophecy, can help us understand Deng Xiaoping's reform. In China, Weber observed, an autochthonous prophecy never emerged; it came from outside, as in the case of Lao-tzu and Daoism. This goes together with *non-rational capitalism* in India and China to finance wars or to outsource taxes, as opposed to rational capitalism oriented to market opportunities. But such rational prophecy is now possibly emerging in the form of market-oriented 'radical pragmatism', a term used to define current economic reform no longer opposed to capital.

A final 'Weberian' surprise comes with the current growth of Christians, mostly evangelical Protestants, and mostly among the urban population: more than 60 million in 2011, according to experts' estimates, more than 100 million in 2020, according to forecasts. In other words, there are possibly more Christians than Communist Party members in China today! Their ethical contribution to civil society building and their biblical approaches to making money are the surprising result.[15] In the same direction go the New Confucians. In the wider sense of the conflict-driven civil society, we can then evaluate the creation of a political movement towards civil rights and democratic elections among the educated, young, urban population in the financial capital of China, Hong Kong, during 2014.

The Chinese urban contract: 'New towns' or 'desakota'?

Modern Hong Kong's urbanization, geographically comprising Hong Kong Island, Kowloon Peninsula and the New Territories, started at Victoria City in 1842 under British colonial rule, and later spread to the Peninsula and New Territories. In 1911, 70% of the population of the New Territories was still engaged in agriculture.

The first urban development followed the 1949 Chinese Revolution, with large-scale migration of capitalists and workers from continental China

152 *The Asian urban contract*

(and later from Vietnam) to the British colony of Hong Kong. Urbanization encroached on the urban fringe and transformed the New Territories from agricultural to urban, also due to the new town programme of the 1970s. A programme of seven new towns for 2.5 million people was launched. In this respect, we can try to compare Hong Kong to its Western counterparts, London and Paris, which adopted the same model in post-war growth. How the Western model was adapted and implemented in the East is a matter of research. According to Hall (1984a, 2002), the new towns were built so big, high and dense there is no conceivable resemblance to Ebenezer Howard's original model. Yet thanks to this revised model and to the integration of the reshaped public transport system, a planned polycentric agglomeration was created in Hong Kong, thus constituting a dramatic realization of Howard's Social City vision, probably the last of the 20th century. This is also a matter of high-quality public housing and transportation systems. Visiting the current Kai Tak Development Project for 86,000 new residents (three classes of residential zoning: A. subsidized high-density public housing with 13,000 new flats for 33,000 residents; B. middle-density for middle class; and C. low density for affluent families), one can perceive the nature of market-led development in Hong Kong and, at the same time, the socially oriented nature of such programmes (including a network of parks and gardens, new fast transport services and sport facilities).

A second phase of urban development started in the 1980s both in the 'inner city' and on the 'edge city', due to the growing importance of the former colony, destined to become the Chinese gateway to the West after 1997. In more recent years, Hong Kong has shown complicated patterns of growth due to the competitive pressure of the mainland's booming cities (like Shanghai) on the old colony. Yet the peculiar growth of a middle class in Hong Kong and the political demands it cultivates in terms of civil society expressions are good reasons to assert that Hong Kong will be crucial in determining a mixed, truly original response to Western/Eastern urban-contractual models and relations.

What is clear from long-lasting patterns of history of both China and Hong Kong is that 'the Market' has *not* been the main partner of the urban contract as it was in the Western world. Town and country, city (*cheng*) and county (*xian*) were constantly enmeshed without a clear-cut border, in both administrative and social terms. The division, the *nomòs*, of the Western city towards the country, and hence its political nature and its autonomous capabilities, were simply not made in China: here *non-duality* is the heuristic principle (Tang 2014b). The *inability to develop independent industrial and commercial activities* is the most important consequence. Whereas in the West autonomous city and urban markets grew together (city as economic capital, state as political coercion), in the East, or at least in China, imperial coercion was exercised over a multitude of landlords, tenants and peasants. There was no autonomy for the urban bourgeoisie and, after colonization the merchants were only British (Tang 2014b).

The Asian urban contract   153

In Hong Kong (as in the coterminous regions), the land property system was very complex and articulated: a double system between topsoil (*dipi*) and subsoil (*digu*) enabled different landholders to utilize it and pay the relevant taxes. The topsoil was permanently inherited (and given in lease or even sublease for cultivation) and represented fiscal revenue for the emperor, whereas the subsoil was the native place for its inhabitants. Many different persons had rights over the same land. The result was an inability to develop Western capital accumulation processes (the British model of enclosures) and maintenance of strong bonds with the land.

The duality of the land system in Hong Kong re-emerged under British colonization: whereas the land on the Island (the urban centre) was declared property of the Crown, the Peninsula and the New Territories (the urban fringe) were urbanized without land dispossession through relocation and payment of rents to the owners.

The result was the urban–rural continuum (to use a classic sociological term). In the central permanently ceded territories, commercial activities and capitalist extraction of urban rent were the rule, whereas in the New Territories borrowed by the British for 99 years (1898–1997), a peculiar mix of British common law and Chinese traditional land rules coalesced. The 'primordial inhabitants' were entitled to Chinese traditional rights, whereas the outsiders (post-1898 settlers) had to rent land for housing and pay building licences and taxes. The urbanization process went ahead in the fringe.

The arrival of immigrants from China after the revolution (1950s) led to cultivation of land rented from landlords, and hence new development of agriculture and rural activities in the surrounding areas. In the 1970s, the new towns were created in the New Territories and new flows of immigrants made urban expansion inevitable. Hence a new urban–rural continuity emerged, and the *desakota* model came into place (Mc Gee 2014).

The *desakota* (village-town) model is based on the interrelation of urban and rural in three possible ways: 1) rural decline subsidized or protected + growth of non-agricultural activities; 2) productivity gains in both agriculture and industry + strong development of the urban cores; 3) slow growth of both agriculture and non-agricultural activities + secondary urban centre development. The case of Hong Kong is clearly included in the second type. The model can help explain the creation of favourable conditions for big investments by foreign or national companies.

'The desakota zones are generally characterized by extreme fluidity and mobility of the population. The availability of relatively cheap transport such as two-stroke motorbikes, buses and trucks (explains why) these zones are characterized not only by commuting to the larger urban centers but also by intense movement of people and goods within the zone. . . . The desakota zones are characterized by an intense mixture of land use with agriculture, cottage industry, industrial estates, suburban developments and other uses existing side by side' (Mc Gee 2014, p. 131). These zones sum up some characteristics of the Western flexible specialization literature of

154   *The Asian urban contract*

the 1980s (decentralized flexible production, SMEs networks and industrial local subcontracting districts, some integration with specialized agriculture) and the Eastern local tradition of urban–rural continuity and labour informality. Cheap labour and subcontracting in the region, good infrastructures and avoidance of urban core diseconomies led state-driven and private companies to invest in new production platforms in the enlarged area (see next section).

The Hong Kong policy side of this story was written by government in 1972 creating a small house policy entitling each of the primordial inhabitants of the New Territories to build for himself one small house in his village during his lifetime (Tang 2014b). Each village created an 'expansion area' for this purpose.

This is an astonishing creation of 'diffused small property of homes' similar to urban and rural middle-class policies in countries like Italy and France in the post-war period (Berger and Piore 1980). In both cases, such policies favour a stabilizing and consensus-building middle class as opposed both to landowner policies of former communist regimes in the East and to industrial policies favouring mass industrialization in the West. In the case of Hong Kong, such a pro-rural housing policy has a major urban consequence consisting in the inner city's further densification by raising the already high-density development to ever new heights. As the primordial inhabitants prefer to maintain their ancestral houses (*wu zu*) as a symbol of lineage, the result is a mix of high-rise development and the maintenance of traditional *wu zu* – a truly impressive example of *desakota*.

The Chinese urban contract: SEZ and local investment platforms

Has the model of reference to understand recent economic and urban development of Asia been traced by the Singapore and Hong Kong creation of free port zones in the 19th century, as the World Bank suggests? 'City-wide free zones with goals and methods not too different from those employed in modern zones were in place in Gibraltar and Singapore as early as 1704 and 1819, respectively' (FIAS 2008, p. 2). The Hong Kong *entrepot* trade started in 1842 as a free-port model. Its diffusion through the Special Economic Zones (SEZ) model is again a matter of discussion. Has Hong Kong proved an original seed for elaborating and adopting the 'Urban Enterprise Zones' envisaged by British urban planner Peter Hall since the 1970s? Is it an endogenous or exogenous model?

According to global players like the World Bank (FIAS 2008), SEZs are experimental laboratories for the application of new policies and approaches: China's free ports are seen as classic examples of this category. In other words, it is a policy tool to prepare financial, legal, labour and other related innovations to be diffused later throughout the economic system. In some cases, like Suzhou in Jangsu Province, it was a project launched through the leasing and managing of industrial estates by the Singapore government's regional industrial park programme: and it was a failure. An agreement between China's vice premier and Singapore's senior minister was signed in 1992 to jointly develop the Suzhou Industrial Park: it was a commercial joint venture to attract foreign direct investments (Pereira 2002). Multinational industrial investors then located in the Park (42% from Europe and the Americas, 22% from Hong Kong/Macau/Taiwan and 18% from Singapore) and the Singapore Economic Development Board gave financial grants to the Singapore firms to locate, but in 2001, the Singapore government decided on a disengagement strategy. Interestingly, the main reason was a matter of governance: the lack of relations between the Singapore government and the Suzhou Municipal Authority, and the lack of familiarity with China's business and political structures.

And yet a learning process got under way as the Chinese government adopted the Singapore regional economy model in its labour mobility and fund schemes implications. However, effective knowledge transfer from Singapore to China proved more difficult to achieve. Software transfer referring to the sharing of Singapore's public management experience with the Chinese authorities, in order to diffuse it across China, was a primary objective. The Singapore leadership was convinced it had something which was valuable to any Chinese city: the ability to integrate development. Fields like master planning and urban management were of interest here. But Singapore's expatriates did not really teach their Chinese subordinates, and tacit knowledge was not transferred. A lack of trust regarding the venture contract (responsibility for the costs, totally different business culture) made it difficult to elaborate norms of equity and reciprocity between the Singapore and China. As a Singapore leader made clear: 'Singaporeans take for granted the sanctity of contracts. (. . .) For the Suzhou authorities, a signed agreement is an expression of serious and sincere intent, but one that is not necessarily comprehensive and can be altered or reinterpreted with changing circumstances. We depended on law and systems. They were guided by official directives' (quoted in Inkpen and Pien 2006, p. 802). This clearly means that the adoption of contract models, from Western or Eastern counterparts, does not fit well in the Chinese system. There were many reasons for China's choice of Singapore as an industrial model (Wong and Goldblum 2000), including ideology and the need to move on from low-cost production (1.7 million jobs provided by Hong Kong investors who had close family ties in Guangdong Province) to more advanced technological industries. Yet this does not mean that the different contract culture and the lack of social capital – at least according to Western or Singaporean standards – are uninfluential.

A different approach is followed by scholars (like Wu 2015) under the label of Chinese state entrepreneurialism. This can be seen as the instrument for the diffusion of the same principle: with this system, the local state driven by its fiscal incentive aims at setting up development corporations

156   *The Asian urban contract*

known as the local financing and investment platforms. These platforms carry out land acquisition through the monopolistic power of the state in the land market, and borrow capital from the banking system using land as collateral. Using land development, this state entrepreneurialism generates the revenues to finance local development. Further, a policy of a new type of urbanization has been advanced by the new Chinese leadership with the hope of creating a new scope of growth relying more on domestic consumption in the aftermath of the global financial crisis. All these require greater involvement of the state in urban development and urbanization. More generally, such authors believe that 'strategic spatial plans' and 'urban cluster plans' have emerged and stimulated rapid urban expansion and transformed compact Chinese cities into dispersed metropolises (Wu 2015). This is a classic case of applying Western planning tools to non-Western contexts.

The Chinese urban contract: Shequ jianshe *(community construction) and negotiating urbanization*

'The advancement of Shequ Construction is an important element in the nation's economic and social development. Insisting on bringing together government guidance and society participation, [we shall] construct a shequ management and operational structure appropriate to the market socialism of our economy' (National People's Congress 2001).

Visiting Chinese urban spaces, Westerners are surprised by the intensive use of the public space: each square metre is utilized.[16] At every street corner men play cards or *majong*, the elders sit in groups or take care of their grandchildren, and street food vendors sell their goods all over the place. For each housing complex a common zone exists where young and old alike practise gymnastics and other sports. The local administration organizes free dance lessons every night for dozens of people, usually held informally in open spaces at street corners. In the housing courtyards, elders, families, *taichi* masters meet in the evenings. This communal life in the open air may be due to the very confined apartment spaces. Not to mention the small shopkeepers: you can meet the tailor with his sewing machine, the barber, the farmer selling fruits, the handyman ready to sell any personal service. Such vital, intense community life is peculiar to China, even in comparison with India or Malaysia.

Village and urban life have seen extraordinary changes over the past 30 years. The massive urbanization and creation of new towns and conurbations has led to large-scale inurbation of floating people, and the related social phenomena (housing, welfare and employment) have had explosive impacts mitigated only by a strong, state-led urban policy. It is difficult to understand – by Western standards at least – how the massive urbanization of China has not led to the creation of slums, as in the other emerging countries of the world.

Shequ jianshe, or community construction, is a key concept for a better understanding of the transition. Community is not a recent phenomenon in China: Imperial China developed historical interest in the community as local social fabric, especially rural but also urban. However, the centralized powers have always strictly controlled local communities. This was true also under the post-1949 Communist government. Community in China is more a matter of territorial geography than a collective political dimension of citizenship.[17] It was only as from the 1990s that the urban community-building strategy emerged, first as a matter of experiments in a number of cities like Shanghai in 1996, and subsequently (starting from Document 23 in November 2000) as a top-down policy.

It is the central state *shequ* reform that in many ways serves the purpose of maintaining order in the face of growing threats to social stability (Shieh 2011). According to one interpretation, *shequ* strengthens the Party's governing capacity and does not create any community 'autonomy'. '*Community* in China does not mean natural social groupings but refers to a spatially defined, officially administered urban unit' (Nguyen 2013). *Zizhi* (autonomy) is considered an integral part of the state's discourse. Yet, given the scale of China (a population of 1.3 billion, many cities with 5–20 million inhabitants), a problem of governance and autonomy arises: it is suggested that there are 32,000 people to one official in China, far fewer than any Western counterpart (Keith et al. 2014). Officials are also incentivized to change rapidly from one district to another.

Shequ can also be seen as a way for local (district) government to obtain more autonomous influence and develop local bureaucracies. It is therefore a two-tier process. Some label it as 'developmental local state' or 'local state capitalism', given the incentives to sell land and extract property taxes. Districts compete in setting up local government investment vehicles (LGIV) to finance investment in infrastructures and urban transformation projects.

Shequ (*she* = society, *qu* = territorially defined area) originally meant the 'spirit of the earth' of the district, but the reform which introduced it places the small groups of residents and *shequ* staff under the control of the Party secretary, representative council and residents' committee. According to the Ministry of Civil Affairs introducing the *shequ* building campaign, a *shequ* is 'a social collective formed by people who reside within a defined and bounded district'. Hence, in contrast to the emphasis on interpersonal communitarian relations, it is more a matter of a controlled territorial entity (Huang and Low 2008). The services the *shequ* are in charge of in such areas include safety and security, family planning, environment and hygiene, culture and education, welfare services and complaints and mediation. A full range of – to put it in Western terms – welfare community services are produced. The number of social workers involved is huge: according to Shieh (2011), in Nanjing, one social worker supervises 400 households. They are selected from laid-off workers and graduates from vocational schools and technical colleges with good ideological education (*zhengzhi suzhi*), a high

158   *The Asian urban contract*

cultural level, good skills and commitment to social development. Again, it is a matter of both social control and welfare community, to a certain extent interlinked. In 2007, 80,000 *shequ* existed in China, lying in an intermediate dimension between the residents' or district committees and the local Chinese Communist Party branch. According to Shieh (2011), the *shequ* is small enough to retain the intimacy and sociability of the old residents' committee, yet large enough to support and make effective use of resources without making it part of the state bureaucracy. The *shequ*, in other words, is seen as the local neighbourhood ('agent') of the Party-led ('principal') system, but also as the social unit of local society.

Creating a local welfare system to support urban development is clearly of the utmost importance, given the high rate of Chinese urbanization. With the growing economic importance of large cities and of their fiscal revenue base, the municipal governments' power has been further fuelled by granting them governing authority over their surrounding counties (according to Party leaders, a rational economic network using large and medium-sized cities as the foundation). The role of *shequ*, being at the intersection of the urban and the rural, can be vital in terms of social integration. Socially, the resettled villagers, or land-loss farmers (*shidi nongmin*) as they are typically referred to in the city, are looked down on by their neighbours, who often regard them as 'uncivil' (*bu wenmin*) or 'uncultured' (*mei wenhua*) (Shieh 2011). According to local observers, however, *shequ* is important in Shenzhen only for gated communities.

Urban villages are a complex phenomenon of urban-rural mix of activities and land uses in an urban jurisdiction. Within the extended *desakota* region (Mc Gee 2014), urban villages can be categorized into three types: 1) villages that are now part of the urban core. These villages are without farmland, but the land-use rights remain with the villagers and the village committees; 2) urban villages located in the suburbs in the recently incorporated urban districts. These villages have some remaining farmland, but the majority of residents no longer work in agriculture as their main source of income; 3) urban villages one to two hours' commute from the urban core, there still being a large amount of farmland. Although some villagers engage in agriculture, their ways of life and livelihood are heavily impacted by their proximity to the city (Shieh 2011).

Different proportions of (permanent) residents and (temporary) migrant renters live in the urban villages, bringing problems of social integration and of coexistence of two culturally diverse populations. In some cases, urban villages with 2,000 residents host 50,000 immigrants. Anomic behaviours (crime, poverty, substandard conditions of life) and the dissolution of traditional social norms may be (in part already are) the outcome.

With wider administrative boundaries, local governments could acquire agricultural land and offer it at a higher price as industrial, commercial or residential land. Consequently, the exploitive attitude towards cities typical of the former phase of 'industrialization without urbanization' has been reversed and rural areas now play a role supporting urban development. However (as we have seen in the case of Hong Kong), the two dimensions of urban and rural are intermixed and not opposed to one another.

More generally, the role of agriculture in the Chinese development model is at stake here. The increase of Chinese productivity in agriculture is unparalleled in the world, and reduced the numbers in poverty (which is mostly rural) from 600 million in 1980 to 100 million in 2004. The increase in small farm unit production (1/3 hectare) involves 250 million farms. These productive units make the difference in terms of markets: in China, there are many different markets, and the distributive chains (production-consumption) are much shorter than in Western urban economies. The country-to-city migration process itself is not unilineal but cyclical: the typical migrant leaves the country for the city at the age of 18, then after marrying, his wife returns to the country when the first child is born; the husband finally returns himself (Ploeg 2013). But this is possible only if the village is not dissolved through the process of demolition, compensation and relocation of villagers, which is all too often the case. This is why 'often villagers prefer their rural registration status (*hukou*). Residents see little benefit to having the once-treasured urban *hukou* that had meant guaranteed employment, food provision, and access to social services. Their rise in income from rents and collective dividends and their proximity to the city have long afforded them an urban lifestyle. Rather than benefits, a change to urban status would mean giving up the rural advantages of early marriage with the possibility of having two children. Furthermore, they feel at a disadvantage to compete in the urban knowledge-based labour market' (Shieh 2011, p. 145).

To protect agricultural lands, the 1998 Land Management Law placed a mandatory cap on the amount of farmland that can be converted to construction land. Nevertheless, the urban district governments and cities are growing in importance: cities at and above the prefecture level are recognized as districts and are also referred to as 'cities with districts' (*she qu de shi*). District governments have expanded their bureaucracies and new bureaus have been created: whereas in the past the districts only handled the maintenance of urban infrastructure, most have by now established an urban construction bureau to undertake infrastructure planning and construction. With marketization, the regulations have allowed offices that manage infrastructure to incorporate (*gongsi*) and in the process become intermediary organizations between state agencies and private enterprises. For local governments, the sale of land leases and land-use rights is one of the major extra-budgetary sources of income to finance investments and services (Shieh 2011).

Marx in Shenzhen: Status and contract

The 'mobility regime' is a constellation of policies, cultural norms and networks that condition, constrain or facilitate migration (Xiang 2007).

160 The Asian urban contract

Migration from countryside to cities and the attraction of Chinese returnees from abroad are two opposite, yet complementary sides of this constellation.

A special field of application has been Shenzhen, Guangdong Province, since its choice as the first, privileged Chinese SEZ for attracting new industrial foreign and domestic capital in 1980. The choice was also due to its closeness to Hong Kong, creating a special twin-city regime: dual labour market, dual wage level and mobility to and from both cities. In 30 years, Shenzhen's population grew from 20,000 to 13.5 million. According to estimates, in 2011, the total population with Shenzhen *hukou* was 2,594,000, without Shenzhen *hukou* 9,017,000, making the official population 11,611,000.

Shenzhen's impressive central business district (CBD) has grown right in front of Hong Kong's New Territories border in the space of just a few years. The headquarters of major Chinese banks, enterprises (both Chinese and foreign) and public utilities are located there and a huge population of service-sector professionals crowds the streets. The gigantic poster commemorating Deng's visionary idea of creating Shenzhen's SEZ stands right in front of the Shenzhen Stock Exchange building, and hundreds of office towers are close witnesses of the vision endowed with concrete form. The corridor uniting the twin cities of Shenzhen and Hong Kong is already a reality: thousands of commuters and visitors cross the border daily and a new highway is under construction. Shenzhen has strong ties with Guangzhou, hence the corridor is destined to continue in the direction traced by these three poles of attraction. Hong Kong's capital investments in service firms, dispersed manufacturing and real estate have created the conditions for Shenzhen's growth. However, the effect of the alliance of these two cities is still to be ascertained.

Around the Shenzhen CBD a variety of districts can be observed, from rich to poor. Futian ('blessed fields' in Chinese), whose origin dates back to the Song dynasty, is now the leading district in the SEZ, with a population of 1.3 million and the highest density in Shenzhen. The local government approach is based on urban marketing, like the following declaration (on the Futian government website) bears witness: 'Many Futian residents are migrants from other parts of the Chinese mainland. A melting pot of diverse cultures, Futian is tolerant and open. "Encourage innovation, forgive failure, pursue excellence" is the city's motto.' But in the Hengtaiyu Industrial Park in Shenzhen, a disaster occurred in December 2015 due to mismanagement of the territory, destroying a total of 22 buildings, causing a gas pipeline explosion and harming many victims.

Regarding internal migration, a major aspect of *hukou* is the agricultural–non-agricultural divide. 'One's *hukou* status remained unchanged no matter where the individual moved, unless he/she went through a formal *hukou* conversion. For instance, a person with non-agricultural *hukou* status, regardless of the individual's physical location (or whether he or she resided in a town, small city, or large city, or even in the countryside), was automatically

The Asian urban contract 161

entitled to the basic benefits because they are distributed and funded by the government, making non-agricultural status highly desirable and sought throughout the country. Therefore, *hukou* type was very much a social status, and naturally an important consideration, for instance, in the marriage market. This remains largely unchanged today' (Chan 2009).

In addition, each person was assigned a *hukou* based on location. Hence a double process occurred: changing from agricultural to non-agricultural status, and then moving from one (rural) locality to a new (urban) one. Later on, 'what used to be a two-step process in *hukou* migration has now been simplified to a one-step procedure in a few places, such as Shenzhen, Guangzhou, and some city districts of Beijing' (Chan 2009).

Moreover, access to *hukou* urban status by the rural population is often conceded in exchange for their permanent loss of land-use rights. Such was the case in Shenzhen, where the local government first came up with the principle of 'separation of living areas from household', allowing rural populations to move towards urban areas. In 1995, a new system was created in Shenzhen for 'recruited and transferred cadres and workers blue chop *hukou*'. This permit created another category of citizens entitled to permanent residence in Shenzhen: this category pertained to highly skilled workers and investors in the city, as well as cadres employed by the Shenzhen government organs after a certain number of years of residence in the city. The second type of permit was the 'flat purchase blue chop *hukou*', which entailed entitlement to legal residence in the city upon purchase of real estate property.

Regarding the attraction of talented worldwide Chinese returnees, the provincial and municipal governments have adopted numerous policies. They offer high salaries, beneficial tax rates, special business loans, housing subsidies, grants for children's education and so on. The Guangzhou municipal government, for example, offers RMB 100,000 (USD 12,000) as a 'golden hello present' (*jianmainli*) to a returnee. Special industrial parks for returnees (*huiguo liuxuesheng chuangye yuanqu*) are another initiative. The returnees in the park are offered excellent facilities and beneficial policies, and are expected to turn their research innovation into commercial projects. The Beijing municipal government had set up 12 such parks in Beijing by July 2004, investing about RMB 24 million (USD 3 million) to support returnees. Returnees are given a three-year tax break and an especially favourable tax rate for another two years. Shanghai now has six high-tech parks designated for returnees, and every enterprise in the parks is entitled to an interest-free loan up to RMB 150,000. Returnees in Shenzhen, Guangdong Province, can apply for a grant of RMB 100,000–150,000 to start a firm once their project proposals are approved by the municipal government. Returnees have attracted so much attention that they have become a special social group – 'sea turtles' as they are called – a term in Chinese pronounced in the same way as the shorthand for 'return from overseas' (Xiang 2007).

162   *The Asian urban contract*

'Freeing' rural labour towards the 'factory of the world' is a translation of Marx's first volume of *Das Kapital* on primitive accumulation into the context of modern China. Here status (*hukou*) and contract ('free', low-wage labour) are two sides of the same coin. Only a minority of the rural migrants have labour contracts when they arrive, hence a new underclass is created. In Shenzhen, 80% of the de facto urban population is without Shenzhen *hukou*. Changes in legislation later introduced temporary (six months) and resident passes (10 years), thereby creating a new social stratification process. Moreover, it is calculated that half of the migrant population (probably 6 million people) are not registered at all. In 2007, Shenzhen had about 2.1 million local residents and 6.5 million non-*hukou* residents with a temporary residence card; however, the city's Family Planning Bureau calculated a population of around 12 million migrant workers, meaning that half of all migrant workers in Shenzhen were unregistered at that time (Fu and Pasquali 2015).

In 2012, new Implementation Measures for Recruitment of Talents were introduced to attract college students, investors and high-income employees. A social engineering urban process has been implemented in the same vein as in the Western global cities, but directly managed by the state. The *hukou* registration law is used as a legal instrument according to the shifting needs of the government-led economic development strategy (Fu and Pasquali 2015).

Spatial segregation is one of the main consequences of the *hukou* system. It is not, however, a market-led process: the state hierarchy and governmental top-down system are always in charge. 'Despite significant devolution of administrative powers to lower-level governments in the last three decades, the multi-tier hierarchy, consisting of five main levels of government (central, provincial, prefectures, counties, and towns and townships) has remained the same throughout the last half century' (Chan 2009).

Conclusion

The best recent sociological literature on China (Keith et al. 2014) underlines the need to take a non-Western point of view on development, sovereignty and power to understand current capitalist and, specifically, urban changes taking place in Asia. Such changes go, both in China and in India, in the direction of creating a new global geopolitics of sovereignty based on neo-tributary relations within new empires. This trend is in direct contrast with the Western (Weberian and Schmittian) conception of European nation-states based on treaty, property and the contract law of civil society.

Our research goes in a partially different direction. It shows that the contractual logic of capitalist urban development is growing, even in different forms, in the East as well. This does not mean that capitalism is homogenizing the world, as a naïve interpretation of current globalization might assume. Rather, it means that the ongoing transformative patterns of

The Asian urban contract   163

planetary urbanization (Brenner 2014) are destined to mix and contaminate the grand theoretical traditions of both Western and Eastern civilizations.

On the urban ground, we have seen cities, in both China and Japan, experimenting with new forms of 'community building' that can be traced back to concepts of contractual relations. Contracts between national and local states and capitalist groups (including real estate developers, banks and other financial investors), as well as between the national and local states and citizens' groups (*neighbourhoods, machi, shequ* are practically synonymous terms) have been traced back and analyzed on the basis of secondary sources growing out of the best urban research. The case of India, according to the findings that we have analyzed in depth here, derived from relevant empirical research by Indian scholars, is different, and 'community building' or urban contractual forms are far from emerging.

Scott Lash, Michael Keith and colleagues are certainly original in their interpretation of the impact of the Chinese cultural heritage of Confucianism and Daoism on current capitalist development. Not the transcendent but the situated sacred, not civil society but *sittlichkeit* (ethical attitude), not purposive action but situated activity: these are some of their main suggestions. To read Chinese capitalism we need less Weber and more Durkheim and Mauss. Gift exchange, the social network (*guanxi*), experimentalism and other keywords of economic sociology and neo-institutionalism are among their preferred explanatory tools. However, with reference to the economic ethic, the authors admit that 'Weber's China that did not work at the turn of the nineteenth century seems to be eminently successful at the start of the twenty-first century' (Keith et al. 2014, p. 3).

Agreeing with much of their analysis, we have found in the urban contract a powerful logic in interpreting much of the Asian modernization processes. Driven by state capitalism, developmental state or local state capitalism, the logic of state-market interaction is growing. It is therefore natural that the contract logic will emerge as well, producing hybrid forms of regulatory regimes 'neither market nor hierarchy'. But this is only one side of the story, commonly defined as the private contract. Another contractual logic is gaining ground, and it is social in nature. It is the unavoidable need for governmental actors – even in non-liberal democratic regimes – to legitimate their action vis-à-vis their constituencies, groups of citizens and local social interests which is at stake here.

The Asian cities emerge from these contractual arrangements (negotiations, deals, compromises) as a force always able to resist both capitalist and state logics, and to have something to say about their own future development. Experimentalist as it is, such a contractual approach is destined to bring about innovations in the past political traditions of representation, introducing new forms of flexible, adaptable capacities of cities to integrate the many diverse populations flowing into their enlarged enclosures of past 'walled cities'.

164   *The Asian urban contract*

The trajectories followed by the four Asian cities considered here certainly differ also due to their respective life cycles. The centuries-old Tokyo (moreover inhabited by an elderly population) is difficult to compare to the 30-year-old Shenzhen (with a young population, average age 28). The highly innovative (in term of business models and economic wealth) but also socially responsible (with 50% of the population living in public housing) Hong Kong has little in common with Mumbai, with its ambition to follow the Shanghai or Singapore models while 50% of its population lives in slums.

If no single model can be detected among Asian cities, certainly a common growth trend is characterizing Asia's explosive urbanization. The future of our common world is more than ever linked to the ways in which the Asian cities will – or will not – be able to reverse past attitudes (both colonial and postcolonial) and effectively drive the urban change towards socially, economically and ecologically sustainable development.

Notes

1 The following data are extracted from the Center for Spatial Information Science Database, The University of Tokyo, various years.
2 However, the term *shi* also translates into the concept of municipality (autarchic territorial entity).
3 Capital crimes, *The Economist*, July 12–18, 2014.
4 Design/Curial interview: Kengo Kuma – Sharing the Same Shadows, November 11, 2013. www.designcurial.com.
5 According to the 74th amendment, municipal functions include: 1. Urban planning, including town planning. 2. Regulation of land use and construction of buildings. 3. Planning for economic and social development. 4. Roads and bridges. 5. Water supply for domestic, industrial and commercial purposes. 6. Public health, sanitation conservancy and solid waste management. 7. Fire services. 8. Urban forestry, protection of the environment and promotion of ecological aspects. 9. Safeguarding the interests of weaker sections of society, including the handicapped and mentally retarded. 10. Slum improvement and upgradation. 11. Urban poverty alleviation. 12. Provision of urban amenities and facilities such as parks, gardens, playgrounds. 13. Promotion of cultural, educational and aesthetic aspects. 14. Burials and burial grounds; cremations, cremation grounds and electric crematoriums. 15. Cattle pounds; prevention of cruelty to animals. 16. Vital statistics including registration of births and deaths. 17. Public amenities including street lighting, parking lots, bus stops and public conveniences. 18. Regulation of slaughter houses and tanneries.
6 In Bangalore, a substantial number of the poor voted in support of politicians who may have played some role in the real estate politics that moved them out through resettlement policies.
7 Taking urbanization as a whole, it has been seen, over the past few decades, that migration has not been the dominant component of urban growth. For the 1961–71 decade, net rural-urban migration accounted for 18.7% of urban growth. It was 19.6% and 21.7% in the following two decades. For the decade 1991–2001, the percentage remained the same, around 21%. Natural increase has been the principal component of growth at 60% (Sivaramakrishnan 2006).

The Asian urban contract 165

8 The Urban Land Ceiling and Regulation Law of 1976 has been revoked in most states, except West Bengal and Andhra Pradesh.
9 Proceedings of Consultation on Proposed Urban Studies Programme, NIAS, Bangalore, September 18, 2007.
10 Some Chinese scholars observe that, in certain periods in the history of the Chinese Empire, the cities assumed de facto the role of states conflicting with each other given the lack of effective centralized power. However such cities never assumed the self-governing role attributed by Weber. I thank Prof Li Si Ming for fruitful discussion during a seminar held at the David C. Lam Institute for East-West Studies, Hong Kong Baptist University, December 4, 2015.
11 In Marx's primitive accumulation theory (*Capital*, vol. I, VII, 24), the expropriation of the rural population and its expulsion from agricultural land in the long period of the 17th–19th centuries in England is accurately explained. It was a key process in order to 'free' the rural population to make it into the industrial proletariat. Marx analyzes the main tools of the process:

  i   enclosure of commons, making the land which was previously communal property a 'property right' with the eviction of rural populations from their homes;
  ii clearing of estates, so that the agricultural labourers did not even find on the soil they cultivated a site necessary for their own housing;
  iii laws of settlement, making statutory the document proving domicile of the poor in order to control movements from one parish to another, and the consequent poor relief obligation.

12 These findings were presented by urban scholars participating in the 'High-density development and social justice' international workshop of the Department of Geography, Hong Kong Baptist University, December 3–5, 2015, chaired by Prof Wing Shing Tang.
13 Logan and Fainstein (2008) are very cautious when it comes to comparing Chinese and other cities and underline factors that make Chinese cities unique, including the 'distinctive Chinese phenomenon that differentiates the native urban population based on legal status' (p. 19).
14 Youqin Huang and Si-ming Li (eds.), *Housing Inequality in Chinese Cities*. London, Routledge, 2014.
15 *The Economist*, November 1–7, 2014.
16 Paola Pasquali, PhD candidate in Beijing, personal communication.
17 Wong King Lai, PhD candidate in Hong Kong, personal communication.

5 The urban space and deliberative democracy

Lefebvre and Schmitt

In this chapter, I will propose a common understanding of two separate and even opposite bodies of thinking: the traditional contractarian literature (starting from Hobbes' *Leviathan*) and the contemporary global urbanization literature (culminating in Neil Brenner's very promising *Implosions/Explosions*). This will be possible taking as a starting point a comparative reading of two major 20th-century authors, Carl Schmitt and Henry Lefebvre. Schmitt, the modern legal philosopher and staunch Hobbesian, wrote *The Nomòs of the Earth* in 1950, already announcing the end of the epoch of the nation-states and the advent of a stateless global economy. We can say that he saw in advance the coming globalization as a matter of the 'end of the political'. Lefebvre, the most creative contemporary interpreter of Marx, wrote *The Urban Revolution* in 1970 heralding the advent of the urban as a transformative force, an act that assembles and distributes, and hence creates. The subsequent urban literature on 'assemblages' owes much to him.

Finding a meeting point between the two is no simple task, given the very diverse ideological constellations in which they found themselves. Lefebvre was a French philosopher who inspired much of contemporary neo-Marxist urban theory, Schmitt a German philosopher of law known for his dangerous relations with the early National Socialist movement but whose later political theory has influenced non-standard theories of European philosophical circles. Yet if we start deciphering their texts, we find much in common.

I will start with this quotation of Lefebvre (1970):

> The urban (urban life, the life of urban society) already implies the substitution of custom for contract. Contract law determines the frameworks of exchange and of reciprocity in exchange. (. . .) However, use, in the urban, comprises custom and privileges custom over contract. The use of urban objects. (. . .) is customary, not contractual, unless we wish to postulate the existence of a permanent quasi-contract or pseudocontract for sharing those objects and reducing violence to a

minimum. This does not, however, imply that the contract system cannot be improved or transformed.

Here is a basic assumption about our sharing the urban. It is a system which we share, using it and contributing to it collectively. It is a common pool of resources. The permanent quasi-contract is no more (but also no less) than the social contract which binds us together. Custom and social norms regulate our urban life as a community: whenever we use a street we have no need to be regulated by contractual norms; we just follow custom and social routines.

But what about 'assembling' and 'distributing', the distinctive transformative force of the urban, according to Lefebvre? Here the polymorphic nature of the urban emerges. It can assemble and distribute not only people, the diverse inhabitants or citizens, but also space and time: in Lefebvre's words, the time of exchange and the space of values. And he concludes that 'creating space-time unity would be a possible definition, one among many, of the urban and urban society' (ibid.).

In this creative nature of the urban, a conflictual attitude towards the state emerges. There is competition between the two, and something more than that: the incompatibility between the state and the urban is radical in nature. As the urban presumes to exercise self-management within its territorial units, the state can only prevent the urban from taking shape. The state has to retard (a term largely used also by Schmitt in his political philosophy) urban development, and it does so by pushing it in the direction of institutions that extend to society as a whole, through exchange and the market, types of organization and the management of enterprise (ibid.).

This is the same diagnosis Carl Schmitt made in *The Nomòs of the Earth* (and Karl Polanyi in *The Great Transformation*). Both derive from Max Weber and his Western rationality theory, whose influence on Schmitt (as his student in the Weberian inner circle in Munich) is directly documented. Assembling and distributing are attributes of the urban very similar to what Schmitt defines as *nomòs*. In fact, *nomòs* is normally understood and translated as 'norm' or 'custom', but Schmitt's genealogy of the term reveals its polysemic, tripartite meaning. *Nomòs* means 'to occupy' and 'to pasture' land, and to produce its 'development'.

The epistemological turn

Our line of argument challenges a tradition of thought which commonly understands space as an *a priori* container, within which actors move, guided by precise borders, signs and demarcations. However, today a new idea is emerging within the social sciences: it is the actors who freely create their own space, scale and context, in a non-defined, infinite space. This marks a shift from conceptions of the state as predefined power-container attributed to Max Weber (Brenner 2004; Brenner and Elden 2009). It is true

168   *Urban space and deliberative democracy*

that Weber defined the state as a monopoly of violence over a defined territory; but he also noted that the power of the market can be much greater and similar than the 'power of authority' conventionally attributed to the state. An *Empire State* like New York in America – Weber noted – can exercise a much wider, even despotic hegemony, even if it does not hold the formal power of command typical of the authoritarian state. Nevertheless, it is a site of great financial powers (Weber 2003). On this assumption we can credit Weber with foreseeing the dominance of contemporary global cities. Thus Weber's observation on state dominance over a pre-given territory has to be reinterpreted, one century later, as a 'negotiated' process of territorial ordering and localization. It has become even more 'fluid' and 'elusive' (both Weberian terms) than in Weber's time.

The state monopoly over space has come to an end as territorial frontiers are crossed by economic agents (Krugman 1998) and indeed any 'agent' more generally freed from state sovereignty, which is increasingly limited nowadays (by international laws, super-state powers and de facto global market autonomy). The agent's point of view becomes a 'spatial' point of view. And society too reassembles itself starting from such interactions, as Bruno Latour observed in *Reassembling the Social* (2005). Space is no longer geometrical, but fluid and foamy: like spheres where individuals are encapsulated as monads or, as Sloterdijk puts it, as *Ecumes*, *Spheres* (2005). Neither hierarchical nor vertical, but rather, reticular and horizontal. It is now coexistence between subjects which makes space possible, not the other way around. It is a *we*, reunited in a relationship constituting space through the force of coexistence. As French philosopher Emmanuel Levinas (1964) puts it: 'Experience, like language, no longer seems to be made by isolated elements lodged somehow in a Euclidean space where they could expose themselves, each for itself, directly visible, signifying for themselves. They signify from the "world" and from the position from which one is looking.'

As a matter of fact, then, the actors literally 'construct' the space of interaction. This applies not only at the micro level. Indeed, even on the macro level, space appears as a horizontal scansion, an assemblage of infinite micro-spaces. This view has certainly been fostered by globalization, whose spatial implications converge into a unification, and simultaneous multiplication, of the many 'locals'. I will be looking into some key texts of contemporary thought in the light of this spatial revolution, with particular attention to the force of law. How does the law, written to dominate space, react to the growing 'spatial freedom' of its subjects?

Nomòs and space

Saskia Sassen's *Territory, Authority and Rights* (2006) presents itself, from its very title, with the ambition to achieve historical re-reading of the role of space in the global era, when city limits extend beyond national frontiers, creating 'assemblages', forming a planetary constellation. In doing so,

Urban space and deliberative democracy 169

the cities project their sphere of influence by way of occupying a 'glocal' territory and performing a role that is itself 'glocal': although not entitled to any 'right', they aspire to command the world. However, their 'authority', which is, literally, their capacity to grow and produce something new (*auctoritas* comes from the Latin verb *augescere*, to grow) is so strong as to appear undisputed. Hence the essential meaning of the keywords in Sassen's book (*territory*, *authority*, *rights*) in their genealogy. The concept of 'assemblage' is not sufficiently investigated in the book, and Sassen herself warns us of her descriptive, rather than theoretical use. So, given that we are dealing with assemblages of territory, authority and rights, *how are they related*? Even if Sassen never mentions it directly, it seems to me that her text should be considered in relation to the significant work Carl Schmitt dedicated to *The Nomòs of the Earth* (1950) in the middle of the past century. The *nomòs* of the Earth is a 'terrestrial' right, involving the occupation of soil, its demarcation and enclosure. On it the Earth bears fences, delimitations, walls, houses and other buildings. Here, orderings (*ordnung*) and localizations (*ortung*) of human coexistence become apparent. The empty Earth is marked with the signs of occupation, and destined to be discovered and occupied. This applies to the ancient world of city-states and empires, to the transition from feudalism and the territorial state to the New World after 1492 (the '*conquista*'), to the American frontier (Tocqueville's empty continent), and even to the world of today – after land and sea, the conquest of space already predicted by Schmitt. Occupation of land (*sedium occupatio*) implies for Schmitt a twofold direction, both inwards and outwards. In its first 'inwards' meaning, it defines the first rules and regulations of the group occupying that land, upon which any form of property and possession, measurement and distribution will follow. The 'outwards' sense, on the other hand, has to do with the foundation of international law, between 'occupying' (or else, occupied) groups. Clearly, it makes a difference whether the land occupied had hitherto been free or not. What remains true is that its occupation and subdivision are foundational of any public *imperium* or private *dominium*.

Whilst territory, authority and rights are analytically distinct and articulated in Sassen's book, they are subjected to various assemblages, from the form typical of the Middle Ages to the current global phase. According to Sassen, empire and church in the Middle Ages would develop an authority which is not territorial: neither of them, in fact, recognized territorial boundaries to their authority, even as both organizations found themselves within vast networks anchored in territorial units. The nation-state was eventually the first to elaborate a territorial dimension, territorializing authority and rights, and leading the way was the Capetian kingdom. Here Sassen sees at work the historical forces preparing the following phase: medieval cities going through the territorial state-form, much like the way today's global forms find accomplishment through international assemblages. Or, better, through a partial 'de-nationalization' activated by global processes.

170   *Urban space and deliberative democracy*

However, Schmitt's celebrated text presents us with a different reading: the concept of *nomòs unifies* territory, authority and rights. *Nomòs* implies both dividing the occupied land and turning it into pastureland, and from this the concept of *norm* derives: in it, measure, rules and spatial ordering meet. What is involved, then, is always a singular, but always new, act of spatial subdivision. Therefore, *nomòs-pasture* stands for territory, *nomòs-norm* for authority and rights – the powerful common radix of what will later be separated. After all, both the logic of space and the logics of law have to do with physics: they occupy a void. Sassen sees the assemblage promoting exclusive authority over a territory as a process not confinable to a sovereign state, as an example reminding us that it was states and cities that signed the Westphalia Treaty. In other words, the winners (nation-states) and losers (free cities) of the national historical phase. So today's global cities would also be de-nationalized territorial formations which, even if belonging to a national realm, are characterized by a significant regulative autonomy, thanks to the rise of global governance private regimes: international law firms, multinational corporations and so on. In short, the *nomòs* of the Earth would be, in the past as in the present, the result of such combinations, or assemblages, of actors intersecting within the territorial domain.

Schmitt concluded his book anticipating the global lines, following the first global lines, which accompanied international European law from the first discoveries to the world wars, between the 16th and the 20th centuries. His thinking in terms of global lines implies that the new *nomòs* of the Earth will elaborate the dualism between an interstate law and a common economic law in different ways. For now, it is the new law of global markets that literally make space among the residual powers of international law. This is after all the conquest of a void, left by the retreat of the international order based on states. New assemblages are to come.

Today modern technology has made possible the complete unity of the world. The utopia (*u-topos*: no place) of technology is based on the abolition of space and de-localization, on the 'no-longer-being-linked-to-space' of human cohabitation. The process of *Entortung*, de-territorialization and decomposition of former orders of the world, has been brought on by the ongoing globalization of our *globale Zeit* (global time). Hence the displacement of politics within contemporary globalization, and the emergence of an apolitical space inspired by the image of a network, a fully contingent and elastic system whose 'nodes' need no unitary, transcendental foundation. A world governed by technical, functional networks in a permanent conflict and crisis situation. A thoroughly Weberian fate, indeed.

Sassen's research shows how these assemblages are happening *cross-border* and *trans-boundary*. It is about processes which are not, at least in the old meaning of the term, 'international'. As a matter of fact, they are not established by the interaction among nations anymore, with community-states exercising legitimate and exclusive rule over their own territories. Here, instead, we are dealing with processes 'in between' the local and

Urban space and deliberative democracy 171

the global, mixing domains and *milieux*. However localized in national or subnational environments (cities-territory), these processes participate in globalization, in that they involve *trans-boundary* networks and entities which connect processes and manifold actors (local-national) or imply the recurrence of issues or particular dynamics in a growing number of countries and places. These processes are, for example, seen in: trans-boundary communities, global cities, global value chains, phenomena of space time-compression.

Global cities organized in transaction networks are the emerging phenomena. The services localized within them are becoming ever less national: it is as if there were free zones within which the languages spoken and communities' practices were essentially trans-boundary. Perhaps these – increasingly dense – networks will end up by forming trans-boundary urban systems. London-New York or London-Paris might work as the same track, although 'hosted' within different nation-states. In some ways, it is already like that.[1] In fact, there have been cases, for example between Silicon Valley and Taiwan, of tracks formed by entrepreneurs belonging to both regions, Californian and Chinese. They spend their time like modern Argonauts, travelling between the two worlds (Saxenian 2006). Political, cultural and linguistic factors will be at work to maintain the national traits of these transnational sites. Global cities are sites of power and arm-wrestling between economic and political groups. No longer deep-rooted locally, economic and technical elites living in global cities are now only 'anchored' to that place from which they can weigh anchor at all events (Veltz 2005). There is, however, another viewpoint, at least for Europe, considering the upper-middle classes as globalized in mind, but rooted in the city (Andreotti et al. 2015).

The flows those elites are developing have no precise nationality: if we could measure these flows, we would see that cities and regions are essentially 'doors', through which they transit, but not without contributing to modify that place through the attraction of functions and people, construction of new settlements, mobility of phenomena connected with consumption, artistic and cultural tourism. Global flows are in fact *sticky*, in that they stick to the territories they transit through. They are also *lumpy* and *thick*. This gives rise to mixtures and hybridization, but also global disorder.

Global flows do not transit freely within national territories – they are, in fact, subject to many types of restrictions and checks. Still, to a large extent these checks have to be reviewed by the states, under the pressure of global enterprises. Being competitive is the main condition of survival within a given frame of the global market rules: and the states cannot let themselves be abandoned by the global enterprises. Thus, state institutions undergo continuous invasion by other – economic, but also juridical – agents, who reduce their sovereignty to a large extent.

There is, furthermore, a second invasion: politics too transcends the borders that used to surround it in the era of the rule of law – borders that had hitherto defended each individual from the incursion of interests and

172 *Urban space and deliberative democracy*

communicative networks within his/her own vital world. Nowadays, both the body's and the soul's individual domains are exposed to the incursions of expansive politics: an 'anonymous matrix' violating individual borders and individuals' rights.

A third source is at work, equally insidious. Hybrid rights come to be originated, which elude both regulatory institutions and individual control. Reference here is to the rights of digital networks and the Internet, of the new virtual spaces of the new technologies of communication: quite often more similar to borderlands to be plundered than new fields of expression.[2]

Space of interaction

As a matter of fact, the city is a crucial ground of application of these ideas, being more than anything else a 'system of networked organisation, where every part impacts upon the whole, or better, a system of dynamic networked organisation which evolves in space and time' (Cramer 1999, p. 53). This, then, is the form that the city is assuming – a provisional order in constant chaotic movement, but also a fabric of relations constantly in balance, a creation of spontaneous orders in perennial adaptation, conscious sociality mixing with a quasi-biological substratum.

The many meanings of the city are reflected, in our research, within the many meanings of world. The latter is 'mundus', originary of the city of foundation, an ordered cosmos, a mundane society (this world as opposed to the heavens) – the place which fills our existence with meaning but also indifferent, isomorphic globe, a pure agglomeration.

The same applies to the meanings of space: defined by a border, empty space to be filled, 'site' to be occupied, open space to be created, but also, now, virtual space. Most of our view of the past and therefore of the future is within the city. Simone Weil, in *Venice Saved*, wrote: 'The city does not only evoke the social. Roots are very different from the social. A city . . . is a human habitat, of which one is aware to the same extent one is of the air one breathes. It is a contract with nature, the past, tradition, a *metaxy*.' This ancient Greek word means intermediary, a bridge between different worlds.

Sociology has, especially with Simmel, investigated the formal nature of the relationship. The mutual relationship involving the idea of understanding, love, common work is, therefore, foundational of the association of society. This association has no analogy with what Simmel defines as the *spatial world*, where every being occupies its place, which cannot be shared with anybody else. This is the world of nature, the objects of which are distant among themselves. Only the observer composes those fragments of the spatial being into a unity, and society is therefore *my* representation. Only the fact of the *I* and of the *You* exist by themselves, in a fundamental and unconditional way. While things belonging to the spatial world exist only within my representation, the relationship I–You is constitutive of the synthesis 'society'. The union of processes occurring within individuals and which condition their being in society are ultimately the processes of a reciprocal action. Here we have, albeit implicitly, the epistemological shift of space as a construct of interaction.

The forms of association are the ways in which we see the other(s): as Simmel explains, we see each other as if through the veil of social cohabitation. It is also the way in which being-associated is determined, or at least co-determined, by its non-being-associated: the figures of the stranger, the enemy, the poor, find here their origins. The fact is, societies are formed by beings which are at the same time within them and without. Hence we are continuously within, but also outside them. Everyone is a member of society and at the same time, even if preserving the same content, lives according to his/her centre and for his/her centre.

In the end, society is formation of inequalities, a world, a *Kosmos* within which every point is bound to the configuration of the whole, originating a configuration totally functional within which the I, understood as individuality, now remains completely outside the domain. Society flows here as if all its elements were in a unitary relationship, and each of them had found its collocation and correlation within this purely exterior network. The juridical implications of Simmel's analysis are important. The relationship of I–You reciprocity is a *completion of the juridical order*: indeed, while the juridical system imposes the giving and getting of services and considerations, innumerable relationships exist in which the juridical form does not intervene, and gratitude substitutes the law.

Conflicts over space

Space is not a smooth surface on which activities take place, but it is at the same time the condition, the means and the result of social relations. The space of the state too is not filled, as if it consisted of a territorial container previously empty, but rather it is the product of such interactions and is transformed through projects of regulation. The static vision of the Westfalian state, as a confined and self-contained arena, is then to be substituted by a dynamics and process where state-spaces are continuously reproduced.

From this point of view, the city is a socio-spatial battlefield, where forces meet and confront one another – each interested in its own prevalence or hegemony. The interests fragmented and diffused within societies hide distributive games: as Lefebvre put it, 'Is not the secret of the State, hidden because it is so obvious, to be found in space?'.

Within the interactions playing out on the ground, cities appear fragmented among different political jurisdictions, each of them entitled to taxation and to supply services. Specifically, we could visualize cities as tax-service packages, confronting each other, with individuals moving in search of the most advantageous ones.

The state intervenes in the play in two respects: in a strictly spatial respect, through the reconfiguration of its own territorial boundaries within the new

174   *Urban space and deliberative democracy*

world system, but also and crucially, through internal differentiation of territories. On both sides, spatial conflicts are taking place: regions claiming autonomy or independence, new institutional forms of local government and so on. Geopolitical variables are here continuously experienced, sometimes through real conflicts. There is also an integral sense of spatiality, that of the regulatory forms of social relations through selective geographical policies. Through the latter, the state determines, often unconsciously, social geographies, promoting some areas and slowing down others. The state did so during the phase of urbanization, through the infrastructuralization of the world. And it is doing so today, designing axes, corridors, poles, nodes and networks meant to drive development. The fact that such action is conducted by the state (as in the past) or rather, by larger political units, such as the European Union, does not change the approach analytically. As a matter of fact, it is in any case government forms, once national, now multi-scalar, that occupy space, following changing patterns. Two forces are at work, according to Brenner: on one hand, a tension between centralization and decentralization, on the other, a clash between concentration and re-balancing. This double vector of forces is composed differently according to phases and cycles. Hence, on a phase of relative readjustment, where states and supranational governments monitored that regions and underdeveloped territories would not 'lose' too much, has followed a phase of a more evident reopening of territorial inequalities, both on a macro and micro scale, to the advantage of the 'winning' territories. Upon a phase of centralization of resources by the states seems to have followed a phase of larger decentralization towards regions, territories and cities. Within such competitive interactions, the areas which come out most strengthened appear to be those which most affect the distribution of resources, such as metropolises. However, missing is an institutional design able to combine the forces involved on the ground. The occupation of space endures, in ever-changing forms, with no global reflection on the sense and direction of the entire process. On the ground, the 'losers' and 'excluded' remain, while the occupation of empty space by dominant forces continues.

Plenitude and plurality

Simone Weil in her philosophical texts considered ancient Rome as an 'artificial city, made of fugitives' (Weil 1985, p. 249), social without roots, a place of unrooted population in the modern, Foucauldian sense of the term. In other words, an artificial construction, the outcome of statistics and power. Venice and Troy, on the contrary, are cities of roots; they represent that rootedness to which 'the social without city' is opposed, a mere agglomerate of contractual individuals, related to each other only by the satisfaction of appetites and moved by a social force.

The city makes us feel at home, which is why one ought to acknowledge being at home in exile. In order to see reality, detachment is needed, while attachment causes illusions. Many do not feel deep in their soul that there is a big difference between the annihilation of a city and their irreparable exile far from it, Weil observes. The city here is really an intermediary, a *bridge* in the symbolic sense Guénon attributes to it: 'the two worlds represented by the two shores are, in a more general sense, heaven and earth, united in the beginning and then separated' (Guénon 2008, p. 331) – bridge as passage and ascent, to the effect that that passage and ascent are free from the previous stages. This implies 'a continuous destruction of the bonds which unite one to the stages already passed through, up to the moment where the axis is ultimately reduced to a unitary, all-containing point, which is the centre of total being' (Guénon 2008, p. 333). This quotation seems to indicate an ascetic direction, that of uprooting, or better, 'being radicated in the absence of a place' (Weil 1985, p. 252), which appears definitely to close every possible social direction. Yet the negation of the 'I' and of 'We', of possessive individualism and of the social as 'prince of this world', is made in the name of a man (or woman) who remains 'in relation'. Clearly, another anthropology is needed here, inspired by another idea of the city. Still, society has its own force, which works as a barrier to evil, and we need to try to limit evil. The discourse here once again becomes *juridical*. The theme of social order is continuously evoked as the only alternative to unlimited power: 'Fortunately there is social order. Greatness of Laws, even the most inhuman' (Weil 1982, p. 126).

The law of the city

Between order and disorder, the former is to be preferred, *in any case*. It is the soul itself which is in need of order, which is 'a pattern of social relations made in such a way that nobody is constrained to violate rigorous obligations in order to fulfil others' (Weil 1990, p. 19).[3] Greed and gold, ambition and power are constituents of the collectivity. But the remedy lies within the relationship. The relationship breaks away from the social: it is the monopoly of the individual. It is what cannot be taken away from us. As Weil put it: society is the cave; the exit from it is solitude (Weil 2002, p. 284ff.). The cavern is where we stay immobile, as within Plato's myth, without any knowledge, without any relation. Instead, in the Timaeus, 'the city is inhabited as in a state of watchfulness. The world is no longer a subterranean prison. The world is beautiful' (Weil 1985, p. 227). The relationship pertains to the solitary spirit. And everyone, if bearing with him/ herself a superior, transcendent order, participates in this dimension of the social order, which is harmony, equilibrium of forces, geometrical sameness. Where all injustices are punished by each other. Where the state intervenes with a minimum pressure, at the first sign of unbalance. A de-centralized society. A sort of spontaneous order, a harmony among orders. 'The citizen's love for the city would need to be a supernatural love' (Weil 2002,

176   *Urban space and deliberative democracy*

p. 284ff.). A *cité* (the city in philosophical terms) understood as a moral order, like the model of moral orders inspiring Luc Boltanski and Laurent Thévenot in their research on the 'plurality of cognitive formats and engagements' of human beings in interaction and communication (in its original sense of 'to be commonized') (Thévenot 2007).

This idea could be compared with that of Jean-Luc Nancy in *Being Singular Plural:* that of 'being-with'. The concept of world, Nancy observes, is not comparable with that of a room which one could enter, nor with that of one whoever who is in the world. The world consists, rather, in an *originary* 'being-with'.

Our discourse on the city starts out again from this point, from the idea that the relationship, the I–You relation, also in our own times characterized by eradicament and spatial crisis, still finds its form of expression. Of course, it is a mobile city, in endless movement and extension. But an extension, Nancy has explained, whereby space retreats into itself, turning out to be a point, a product of spatiotemporal compression as the node of a network. The fact that the single word dominating contemporary social sciences, its new paradigm is the *network*, also points to the path to follow. And then, what about the law: where would it end up in this world of relations? Where, in other words, will relations between subjects leave the state the *least space possible*? Perhaps it will take the form of an extreme juridical pluralism, in which the interests and expressions of civil society are constitutionalized (constitution without a state, as Teubner suggests). Or it could wait for the end of history, the advent of a universal and homogeneous state whereby the human group has ceased to be exclusive and has englobed humanity as a whole (as Kojève explains).

Deliberative democracy

Government through discussion: thus democracy is frequently defined, and many acknowledge the definition. But of what exactly does this discussion consist? And how are we to single out the differences between the classical models and our present democracy?

In fact, 'building a city with words' has always been considered the task of those who govern a city. Plato's *Laws* (III, 702 D) make much the same point: 'let us select from the statements we have made, and build up by arguments the framework of a State (polis), as though we were erecting it from the foundation. In this way we shall be at once investigating our theme, and possibly I may also make use of our framework for the State that is to be formed.' Since then, every city planner has first developed the idea and built the essential picture, only subsequently setting to work on the physical transformation of the city. In Plato's dialogue between the three ancient philosophers, Athenian, Spartan and Cretan, comparing their constitutions and agreeing together on the constitution of the new city, lies the beginning of every pursuit of political understanding through words.

Urban space and deliberative democracy 177

Thus the dialogue of laws gave rise to the first city model, a product of forward-looking design. The design itself emerges from meticulous survey of the resources and the conditions of the environment: from analysis of the strong and weak points, as we would put it today. It is a matter of the physical resources of the territory, such as the conditions of the soil, convenient closeness to the sea, the availability of timber for shipbuilding, but also of intangible, moral resources. Indeed, the structure of the laws is the principal moral resource of the city: it includes the institutions – rules to define the right population mix for the city, its dimensions and every other relevant aspect. Moreover, the design is not only based on such dialogue but also needs the consensus of the citizens. Plato's was what we would now call a 'bipartisan' project for the city, avoiding the risk that in a power struggle the winners take all, leaving no powers to the losers or their descendants. In that case (Plato, *Laws*, IV 715 a, b): 'Where offices of rule are open to contest, the victors in the contest monopolize power in the State so completely that they offer not the smallest share in office to the vanquished party or their descendants; and each party keeps a watchful eye on the other, lest anyone should come into office and, in revenge for the former troubles, cause a rising against them. Such polities we, of course, deny to be polities, just as we deny that laws are true laws unless they are enacted in the interest of the common weal of the whole State. But where the laws are enacted in the interest of a section, we call them feudalities rather than polities; and the "justice" they ascribe to such laws is, we say, an empty name.'

Equally significant is the way envisaged for direct involvement of the citizens. Plato asks, 'May we not assume that our immigrants have arrived and are in the country, and should we not proceed with our address to them?' (Plato, *Laws*, IV, 715 d). This is argued in terms that evoke what we now call participatory democracy. Plato insists on the need for conviction, persuasion and knowledge of the laws. Of course, the limited dimensions of the planned city facilitate this participation, and care must therefore be taken to control its growth, which must not exceed certain limits. This applies not only to the ancient city but also to modern city planning, where the approach is still based on modular settlements. Furthermore, deliberative democracy is possible only for restricted forums and arenas, and for circumscribed cores of citizens.

It is equally essential in Plato's view on planning for the technicians (the wise ones) designing the city not to live in separation from the citizens, in immunity as it were. The bond between them rests on the distinctly ethical content of city planning, behind which still lies the sacral sense of the site.

Progressive departure from this tradition began well before the modern age, but in our age that expertise, shaking off constraints, has taken on the task of determining and guiding decisions on the city through planning. It is now based on abstract treatment of space as location for functions. City planning has generation upon generation of plans to show, the effectiveness of which we may reasonably doubt, but it has not reduced the distance of

178   *Urban space and deliberative democracy*

regulatory choice from the original context of dialogue. The story of city planning has been analyzed (Choay 1997) in terms of rules that are crystallized in models and then dissolved through processes. This is another aspect of the more general rise of expertise as functional rationale lying behind the entire production of norms. The technical know-how of the experts exercising *command and control* has made isolation from the citizens customary, and with it their claims to be able to decide themselves what is in the public interest. It is an outcome that the art of planning has always sought to avoid, although it has often ended up accepting it, handing power over to the experts.

The myth of neutral experts able to identify the public interest has come in for criticism, beginning with Charles Lindblom (1986). He denies that democratic discussion takes place at the level of cooperative pursuit in the light of common values, arguing that the discussion paradigm is, rather, based on the 'partisan' intention of persuading the others that the policies pursued on one side are in accord with their values. Discussion based on acceptance of radical pluralism serves to identify the best possible solution through partisan debate. The criticism pluralism has come in for over the past few decades does not question the soundness of this approach, but points out that it is not sufficiently practised in our liberal democracies. In fact, according to Lindblom, in public discussion the lip service paid to nonpartisan pursuit of the public interest actually covers up a downright sabotage of competition between ideas, preventing innovations from emerging. Thus it is better to recognize that the discussion proceeds between partisan points of view, each supported by competencies. In this confrontation between arguments advanced by the various interested parties, there is, then, no thinking that one participant or the other has the whole truth, or speaks in the name of the others' values. Rather, through challenges and counter-challenges a 'usable' truth often emerges; it may be imperfect, but it is the only way we have to work towards solving a social problem.

The forms contemporary policy-making takes are based on both 'negotiation' and 'argumentation'. The distinction between these two spheres, which Jon Elster (1991) has made the object of specific study, runs thus (Bobbio 2002): negotiation is a way of bringing together (two or more) distinct and consolidated interests, which work towards a compromise, eventually finding a certain point of equilibrium (usually temporary and partial). Argumentation, on the other hand, is a deliberative process which sees the participation of different points of view which are modified and redefined (the participants' preferences being neither predefined nor constant) in the course of the process on the basis of the points that each of the participants publicly argues out.

Negotiation has certainly predominated in policy-making in the advanced industrial societies, thanks above all to the success game theory enjoyed in the second half of the 20th century, translating the expectations and uncertain behaviours of social actors into mathematical formulas. The theories of

Urban space and deliberative democracy   179

strategic behaviour have then highlighted the conduct of the actors in terms of rational strategies within the limits of a game remaining to be discovered (Raiffa 1982). The negotiation itself is not a single entity, but is made up of various parties re-proposing distinctions previously made in other forms. In bringing out the contrast between 'integrative' versus 'distributive' negotiation we are in fact referring to two forms: the former translates into the – at least partial and provisional – integration of points of view that have come into confrontation in the process, while the latter consists of distributing the stakes between the players in proportion to their respective capacities to influence the distribution, which is in turn determined by the unequal distribution of chances (investments, education, money, access to information etc.).

More recently, the contrast between the dialogue and contract forms has re-emerged in the area of deliberative democracy (Elster 1998). The deliberative type of process has a certain affinity with the concept of direct democracy, and is based on painstaking construction of the conditions within which dialogue can develop. It presupposes informed 'speakers' and a favourable setting, as well as procedures guaranteeing equal access to the different representatives of interests. Various examples of deliberative democracy have been documented; for example, by Eric O. Wright and his collaborators with reference to local politics, both in mature democracies and in developing countries (Fung and Wright 2003).

In fact, Wright examines a wide range of cases, including: the 'participatory budget' of a city like Porto Alegre in Brazil, where the residents play their part in defining the municipal budget allocations; the 'neighbourhood governance councils' of Chicago, where the citizens take part in planning the local school syllabus; the 'Wisconsin Regional Training Partnership', which brings together organized labour, enterprises and local government to thrash out workforce development issues; the Panchayat reforms in Bengal, entrusting the villages with administrative and fiscal powers; and the 'Habitat Conservation Planning', which empowers local interested parties to work on agreements to preserve the threatened ecosystem.

Different as the policies and human ecologies involved in the experiments may be, they are essentially a matter of equal distribution of opportunities for deliberative power, that is empowerment, and developing procedures to ensure the right time and forms for direct dialogue. In fact, all the cases considered have to do with real, concrete problems upon which the common citizens are invited to deliberate together with the officials and politicians. Indeed, public policy is devolved to the local units attributed with powers to take practical action. These units are, in turn, interconnected to develop a common learning process, and the decisions thus arrived at are eventually adopted by the reformed public institutions rather than civil society or the market on a voluntary basis.

According to Wright, the various forms of deliberative democracy (or empowered participatory governance) have three essential principles in

180 *Urban space and deliberative democracy*

common. They are oriented towards practical, concrete ends, which consist of supplying provisions of goods and opportunities for intervention in sectors of society disadvantaged at the decision-making level. These are bottom-up forms of participation, through which the knowledge and social intelligence the citizens and various groups share can be brought to bear on finding solutions that could not have been arrived at with expert know-how alone. Finally, in these deliberative forums the ultimate goal is not total conviction or maximization of the participants' advantages, so much as joint planning and a problem-solving strategy. The superior efficiency of policies thus thrashed out, as compared with the classical forms of *command and control*, is also due to the greater legitimation of the decisions taken, the shortening of the feedback cycles and the proliferation of control centres engaged in simultaneous operation by groups working autonomously but not in isolation from one another.

One outcome of these experiments in deliberation is to offer, in practical and concrete terms, opportunities for various parties to agree together on policy areas or specific issues, limited as they may be in some cases. In this way parties whose interests differ, or even clash, in broader areas can eventually arrive at some agreement in tackling clearly delimited points of contention, enjoying the advantages of cooperation which would otherwise have been denied them.

In a sense, deliberative democracy harks back to the concept of Habermas' communicative action and with it the twofold form of policy that Elster pointed out: on one hand, the market, on the other, the forum. While the market offers policy the instrument of the contract, with the advantages of an automatic mechanism and swift decision-making, but with the risk of undermining the ethical basis of policy, the forum offers a return to the classical idea of the democracy of the polis, although the advantages must be weighed against the costs of participation and slowness in decision-making.

Recently Saskia Sassen (2013) has proposed an analysis of the 'speech' of cities, that is the linguistic actions they perform, working in a rather different direction. Here it is a matter not so much of deliberative democracy in the form of arenas and forums for discussion as, rather, assemblages of the various points of view through an 'underground', infrastructural process of association, virtually 'objectified' in urban forms. Assembling many, diverse parties, cities express a particular urban capability: the capability to lead persons who differ (by class, religion, race etc.) to share the same living space even for considerable lengths of time. In the contemporary cities we have analyzed, this capability is seen in community building: the capability – 'underground', at times – to achieve the appropriate cohesion and resistance to stand up against projects (large-scale urban transformation, global enterprise investment etc.) that risk de-urbanizing the city, depriving it of its cityness. In the following chapter, we will see whether and how the cities we have considered develop one or the other form of cityness: that of deliberative democracy, or that of speech capability.

Notes

1 In the case of a global city, the surrounding territory incorporates even other global cities: New York belongs to the London territory and vice versa, according to demographer J. Véron or to geographer P. Taylor.
2 A pessimistic and critical view can be found in Teubner (2006). A more optimist stance, although critical, appears in Castells (1996).
3 Society is a screen, and thus a defence inasmuch as it is a filter between people and their actions. There is an evident ambivalence vis-à-vis the social; Weil's idea seems to wish to bring to the individual that which the collectivity has been able to produce: 'to individualize the machine'.

6 The common matrix

United in diversities

In my own city, Venice, on top of the Doge's Palace, a statue of Justice holding a sword and a balance looks at the statue of Fortune, standing on top of the Punta della Dogana (the former customs house), holding a sail, symbol of shifting volatile fortunes. The legitimate power of the city and market uncertainty stand confronted, and the former keeps control over the latter. This has been for centuries the foundation of the local urban contract. Yet contemporary globalization processes call for a global dimension of the urban contract today.

In his theory of global justice, Thomas Pogge (2001) asserts that a global social contract would be necessary to drive current globalization in the direction of justice, going beyond the Rawlsian theory of justice limited to (and self-contained in) national societies. He underlines that a two-fold transformation of the traditional realm of international relations has taken place: the proliferation of international, supranational and multinational actors, and their profound influence on the domestic life of national societies.

In this book, we have followed a similar path regarding cities seen as collective global actors, as well as partners in contractual relationships with global players. This novelty helps explain why 'global' is displacing 'international' in both explanatory and moral theorizing, as well as in conceptual, explanatory and policy tools of social sciences. This terminological shift reflects that much more is happening across national borders than before. Moreover, it also reflects the fact that the very distinction between the national and international realms is dissolving, as Pogge pointed out. He concludes that with national borders losing their causal and explanatory significance, it appears increasingly incongruous and dogmatic to insist on their traditional role as moral watersheds.

The global justice approach is challenged by a 'global pluralistic' approach underlying the plurality of systems of value facing current globalization. Martha Nussbaum, among others, has spoken of individual *capabilities* seen as the individual's control over his or her political and material environment: yet, in both Western and non-Western societies, it can be misleading to assume that principles of individual control over the environment can capture the effective conditions of social interaction.

In Western tradition, at least as from Spinoza, 'free' and 'subject' are not contrasted: both follow reason as the guiding principle. There is a great difference, Spinoza asserts, between the 'slave' and the 'subject': the former is obliged to obey a lord's order; the latter does what is useful for the community and therefore for himself or herself, following the superior power (*summa potestas* in Spinoza's words). We can discuss the applicability of such an approach to non-Western societies. In non-Western cultures, reason and rationality can follow different paths.

Take the case of neoliberalism and urban governance. It has been said that Western neoliberal principles have guided the recent evolution of market growth in Eastern societies, like China and India. Yet, elaborating on Isin (2002), Tang (2014a) has pointed out that the rationality of governing is different: the role of the state in China cannot be confused with its role in Western liberal democracies. This is also true in the case of urban governance. While in the West, 'governance without government' prevails today as the main explanatory concept, in non-Western societies like China, this is not the case. 'Cities have continued not to be legally autonomous, and there is no separation between town and country. As a result, the related concepts of inter-city competition and urban governance must be rejected as inadequate' (Tang 2014a, p. 58).

Another case is the urban contract and urban planning law in India, where a large part of the urban population is excluded, and a great majority of dwellings are illegal: in this case, we should look for different forms of contracts, based on occupancy, forced illegality (where no legal options exist?) and informality and daily negotiations. We should here be aware that capabilities vary according to their contexts, and that (as Jane Jacobs teaches) cities have the capability of providing something for everybody only if they are created by everybody. This means that any 'rational planning' to cancel slums or illegal occupations of urban space is violating this capability principle. On a more operational ground, Amartya Sen (2009) suggests that, given the great difficulties of a Rawlsian cosmopolitan perspective, a *comparative evaluation* would be followed among the different solutions given to the problem of justice, and the concrete social realizations.

Our work on global (or globalizing) cities can therefore follow the comparative evaluation exercise Sen suggested, taking into account a number of common variables facing different *cities seen as contractual agents*: their global network connectivity, contractual environment, power capabilities, commercial ethos, governance structures and legal regulation regimes will be taken into account.

The many names of the city

The origin of the word 'city', its polysemy, traverses the whole of political, philosophical and historical tradition. One interpretative key, among

184 *The common matrix*

others, is offered by René Guénon in *The Divine City* (Guénon 2008), where, drawing on the Greek *polis*, Latin *civitas*, Sanskrit *pura*, he contrasts two dimensions (see Table 6.1). The first dimension indicates the idea of plenitude (Sanskrit radix *pur* becomes within Indo-European languages *ple* or *pel*, from which *pleos*, *plenus* derive). The city is plenitude and the dilemma between plenty and empty is eventually synthesized in this connection: we know that fullness and emptiness, considered as correlatives, are among the traditional symbolic representations of the complementarity of the active and passive principles (Guénon 2008, p. 392). The city is at the centre of being and is where the divine principle resides: without it, the city would be an empty field, pure potentiality. Likewise, the Latin word *civitas* comes from *kei*, involving an idea of rest, the residence, the fixed dwelling. The city is residence, stability: the palace where the king resides is also the centre and the heart of the city, of which all the rest is extension (another meaning of the radix *kei*).

But a second meaning of the word 'city' leads us to a different outcome. The same Sanskrit radix signifies also the idea of plurality (Greek *polys*, Latin *plus*). The city exists by virtue of the plurality of individuals inhabiting

Table 6.1 The many names of the city

	Greek/Latin	*Anglo/Saxon*	*Sanskrit*	*Chinese*	*Japanese*
City	*polis* (political city)/ *asty*(physical city) *civitas* (political city)/ *urbs*(physical city) *kosmos-polis* (world-city) *megalo-polis* (big city)	city/town burgh/ borough metropolis megalopolis global city global city-region	*pur, pura* (walled city) (root *shi*): he who resides	*cheng, or chengshi* (walled city and market) *xian* (county) *shequ* (district)	*shi* (city) also *ichi* (market) *machi* (city, urban quarter) *cho* (city or fraction of city)
Citizen	*polites* *civis* *ekklesìa* (parliament open to all citizens)	burgher citizen civil society	*paurah* *seva* ('dear')	*shimin* (private) *gongmin* (public) *minjian* (public sphere)	*chōnin*
Contract	*hòrkos pactum*	pact or covenant	*pasu* (religious offering) *swaraj* (self-rule)	*shequ jianshe* (community building)	*machizukuri* (community building)

Source: Author

The common matrix   185

and populating it, of its *populus*. Such etymology leads us to the idea of conflict, of *polemos*, of permanent risk of civil war (etymology already examined by Vico). Therefore, not plenitude and harmony, but rather, clash among 'plurals' reunited within the city.

Among Indo-European cultures, in Greek (and only in Greek) 'city' means 'polis' and 'state' at the same time, whereas *asty* is the term to define urban physical expansion. In the ancient Greek city, the citizen is *polites*, a term derived from *polis*, whereas in Latin, *civitas* (the political community) derives from *civis* (the citizen) and *urbs* (hence the urban) is its spatial expansion. This duality of meanings is indicative of the historical turn from the collective to the individual as the ontology at the basis of the Western city life. This is well explained in the fundamental text by Emile Benveniste on the Indo-European institutions, and was later elaborated by Pierre Bourdieu.

In the Western medieval city, the individual was a free citizen joining others in a brotherhood through a sacred act of oath (the Latin term *conjuratio* is expression of such 'joining forces'), according to Max Weber. It is the freedom of the city, its 'air', which makes the individuals 'free' from the lords and autonomous (able to give their own law to the city's collective life). In Albert Hirschman's famous elaboration on the rival interpretations of market society, it is the market which helps create such freedom, hence 'civilizing' society.

The attribute of 'autonomy' and the conception of 'freedom' are not associable with the Eastern city. In Chinese, the city is *cheng* or *chenshi*, a walled city and market as opposed to the *xian*, or county. The divide between city and country is not so clear as in the Western case. The Chinese cities were never isolated from their natural surroundings or located in dominating positions, like the Greek acropolis (the city on top of a hill) or the image of the good government within the city walls in the Siena municipal palace. Instead, the locations were selected in such a way that urban features could be interwoven with nature to form an organic whole (Han 2015). Water and mountains were always integrated in the urban landscape. Examining ancient Chinese maps of cities like Hangzhou, with an urban history 2,200 years old and once the capital of the southern Song dynasty (an era that saw the beginnings of intense commercial and urban culture), such integration of city and nature is of the utmost importance. The walled city was the place of the imperial functionaries, but it was not separated from its context.

Also, in Japanese, *shi*, the city, has the same linguistic root as *ichi*, the market, hence the mix of the two dimensions. It is interesting to consider the city as a marketplace, a fluid and relatively changing environment: an assemblage of dwellings much more than an ordered structure like the Western medieval city (in which the marketplace was initially separated and located 'outside the borough', hence the French *faubourg*). The complex relationship between the city and the market is witnessed in the Japanese emergence of the *chōnin*, urban inhabitants with a status similar to Western merchants.

186   *The common matrix*

In ancient Indian civilization, the city was *pur* or *pura* (the wall, the walled city) similar to *polis*, probably having the same root. However, the Sanskrit term *paurah* (citizen) does not hold the same meaning as the Greek *polites*. The Latin *civitas* (city) comes from a root *kei*, similar to the Sanskrit root *shi*, hence *shaya* (he who resides).

Are such historic differences destined to disappear due to the ongoing model of 'planetary urbanization' (Brenner 2014)? Looking at current new towns in China, it seems that this is the case. Any traditional environmental ethics has been lost, water and soil are polluted and mountains are flattened to obtain more land. In thousands of high-density new towns like Qianjiang near Hangzhou, any cultural diversity value of the past has been cancelled (Han 2015). Yet in Japan, looking at Tokyo's suburban development, we can find a fusion of history and ecology: plateaus, sloped green tracts, springs, rivers, archaeological remains, shrines and temples, medieval mountain castles, old roads, villages, large residences, stone walls along roads, residential forests, farmland, trees, small shrines, great roads and relay stations (Jinnai 2015). This astonishing list of cultural and historical products of stratified layers in Tokyo suburbs sheds new light on the distinctiveness of an Eastern capital city as contrasted with other cases of world urbanization.

If we go on now to consider the web of affiliation of citizens in different cultures, the importance of the contract emerges. Its place was the political assembly able to deliberate; in Aristotle's words (in the *Nichomachean Ethics*), *politics is the city's practical sagehood directing action and able to deliberate.*

The city, and later the state, would always be based on this imprinting of direct participation. It is collective, political. The following civil society would be formed much later, only in modernity, but its role is only partially different: it is the public sphere able to counter-balance the state representative power. Criticism made of this Western 'invented tradition' (Isin) fails to offer an alternative construction, and rightly limits itself to pointing out that such images of citizenship are increasingly incongruous with contemporary practices.

We now have to trace a comparative account of similar principles in Eastern cultures. According to Western tradition, the main difference is twofold: embracing both ethics and politics. Both in China and India, the ethical drive of the individual is based on religious principles instead of political ones. In Chinese Confucianism assumed as state-controlled moral conformity, the ruler's moral integrity is the precondition of good government, and ceremonial aspects (*li*) are essential to the government (Wei-Ming 1989). In neo-Confucianism, the goal of sagehood and self-cultivation is expressed by the individual overcoming selfish interests and aspiring to realize the nobility of mankind. In this way, it is the sage who is able to act, changing the outer world. No collective action or equivalent of a public sphere derives from this vision. This line of thinking is in support of centralization and despotism, according to most Western observers of ancient Chinese history, like Hegel. A different interpretation lies in Gary Hamilton's assumption that Chinese neo-Confucianism is ready to develop social conditions favourable to capitalism, if only imported from outside (whether from Hong Kong or Singapore). This rival interpretation is better suited to understand the current state-led capitalist transition in China.

In India, the religious base of action is found in the dilemma between acting and abstaining from action, which is as old as the *Bhagavad Gita*. The warrior (Arjuna) is justified to act by his Lord (Krishna) as far as his action aims at self-control and integration into a superior order. Later, in the *Dharmashastra*, this same justification of action is based on the warrior's protection of the community, overcoming the duty of *ahimsa* (not to kill living things) (Love 2000). This dialectical dilemma is, interestingly, the basis of a legal autonomy similar to Western principles of political ethics. However, in the East, no collective dimension of action is theorized. The political consequence is patrimonialism: the domination of a ruler in the patriarchal household and local clans, and later in the patrimonial state.

Hence the different conception and execution of the contract. In the West, it was a pact or covenant among free men holding citizenship rights, be it the Hobbesian or Rousseauian version of the social contract. In the East, it was almost a religious offering, and religious communion boundaries reinforced pre-existing group or caste divisions. This was later incorporated in the ceremonialism of traditional society. In modern society, this finally takes the form of collective action, like Japanese contractual obligations in the firm.

The contemporary processes are hybridizations of Western and Eastern structures. Take the case of 'translation' of British common law in Hong Kong, giving rise to mixes of British and Chinese law and custom, or indeed of contract law 'incorporation' through China's entry into the WTO commercial treaties.

These are not only the products of colonial mixes, but also of postcolonial thinking about categories of interpretation. Law, rights, contracts are no longer interpreted as nationally bounded but also as the products of interlegality blurring the domestic–foreign demarcations (Ruskola 2002).

Hence the Weberian causality chain (Collins 1980):

citizenship + bureaucratic state > calculable law + methodical economic ethic > rationalized capitalism

should be rewritten in the light of the comparative sociology of Gary Hamilton and Nicole Biggart. In their revised neo-Weberian approach, concepts like authority in business groups and networks, reciprocity and trust find the appropriate basis to interpret the rise of Asian capitalism. The developmental state can make use of former Confucian ethics, life conduct and social discipline in the rise of urban social networks based on connections

188　*The common matrix*

(*guanxi*) and the development of small and medium-sized enterprises in small and medium-sized cities and villages.

The pressure this background is under due to China's intensive mega-urbanization lies behind the massive change under way today and tomorrow. It has freed up the mobility of labour (actually a Weberian precondition for capitalism) and created a second-class citizenship through the *hukou* system (Whimster 2015).

When it comes to contemporary cities, can we find collective action in the form of pact or contract? Both in Japan and in China, the answer is positive, in the form of 'community building'. In India, it is less clear, as it takes the form of 'occupancy urbanism'.

Contractual technologies

The urban contract is a complex phenomenon of social organization, multilevel and multi-actor in nature (see Table 6.2). The 'technologies' of the urban contract are as many and varied as the legal obligations and norms, the negotiation and planning processes, the writing of contracts between the city administration and its private subcontractors, the social dialogue and its variable inclusive/exclusive extensions. The multilayered nature of the phenomena incorporated into contemporary cities is such that it makes the state, the region and supranational bodies, as well as private global and local players, active players in the game.

This general framework can be adapted to different contextual urban entities, as the Chinese case witnesses (see Table 6.3):

Table 6.2 Types of contracts

Government national/local: *institutional accord*	Government (national + local)/global and local capitalism: *quasi-contract*	Government (local)/ collective group interests and citizens: *constituency relation*

Source: Author

Table 6.3 The Shenzhen–Hong Kong cases

Shenzhen	Government national/ local: Special Economic Zone (SEZ)	Government national/ local and global/ local capitalism: Growth coalition	Government (local) and internal migrants: *hukou* system
Hong Kong	British government and Chinese government: Convention on sovereignty	Government national/ local and global/ local capitalism: Growth coalition	Government (central/local) and citizens: conflict over the electoral system

Source: Author

The contemporary urban contracts

Comparative research on cities has to avoid a major mistake, namely evaluating cities without their context, and thus coming up with measurements between non-comparable values. Actually, this lies behind the mistaken presumption leading architects and city builders to disseminate the same buildings and projects in different cities around the world. But, at least in the social sciences, such a mistake should be avoided.

We start from the strategic network connectivity of cities (Taylor et al. 2014), which evaluates cities on the basis of selected global companies in advanced services (law, consultancy, finance, advertising etc.) making their locational choices (see Table 6.4). This clearly means that only some aspects of cities will be selected; many others will be ignored. Interestingly, many of our selected cities rank in the first 20 positions (except Boston, being somewhat smaller than the others; Mumbai ranks 25th, and Shenzhen does not feature in the leading group due to Hong Kong's pre-eminent position). But this does not mean that, for instance, the capital intensity of Boston is any less: on the contrary, its knowledge-based economy is rather higher than the others in our group of cities. The ranking selects on the basis of advanced services firms' capital accumulation, which in turn guides the companies' locational choices. The result is a 'hub and spoke' vision of the world which clearly fits well in some aspects (logistics, finance etc.), but not in others (knowledge, skills etc.). The knowledge of a city is also based on several aspects (schooling, creativity, social and cultural ties) which are necessarily ignored by the ranking logic. The 'hub city' logic is interesting (Conventz et al. 2014), albeit limited to some aspects of cities: capital, mobility and flows.

Also the quality of living ranking (Mercer 2015), assessing the quality of living for expatriates in cities around the world, is biased towards companies' choice to compensate their mobile skilled workforce in the case of delocalization of enterprises in different world cities (see Table 6.5). Interestingly, in this case, our selected cities are clearly polarized: on one side the affluent northern cities, on the opposite side the poorer southern cities, with Tokyo and Hong Kong in an intermediate position.

The urban contractual tools vary with the socio-economic and socio-political variables (see Table 6.6). In London, forms of structured urban participation and interest group consultation emerge, with dominant elites in a better position to influence city deals and strategic plans. In Paris, a multilayered contract among public partners (state-region-city) is dominant, and many contracts are negotiated at local/territorial levels, whereas the private collective actors' influence is weaker. In Milan, a functional governance led by public and private partnerships in different sectors of the economy has been created in the absence of a metropolitan government. In Boston, a long-lasting elitist alliance between government, university and industry prevails. In New York, the fragmented government is a sponge for

Table 6.4 Strategic network connectivity

	London	Paris	Milan	Boston	NYC	LA	Tokyo	Hong Kong	Mumbai	Shenzhen
Strategic Network Connectivity Rank	2°	4°	12°	39°	1°	17°	10°	5°	25°	106° (global network connectivity)

Source: Taylor et al. (2014)

Table 6.5 Quality of living

	London	Paris	Milan	Boston	NYC	LA	Tokyo	Hong Kong	Mumbai	Shenzhen
Quality of Living Rank	40°	27°	41°	34°	43°	48°	44°	70°	152°	139°

Source: Mercer (2015)

Table 6.6 Urban contract tools

	London	Paris	Milan	Boston	NYC	LA	Tokyo	Hong Kong	Mumbai	Shenzhen
Urban Contract Tools	Strategic plan; City deals	Contrat de Ville; Projet 'Grand Paris' et Contrat de development territorial	Functional networks (PPP) waiting for Milan metropolitan city strategic plan	University-Industry-Government Alliance	NYC Housing Plan, with in Tri-state 1,600 governments	CEQA's impact on communities	Machi zukuri community building (bottom up)	High-density town planning, building and design regulations	Fragile social contract, poor excluded	*Shequ jianshe* community construction (top down); *hukou* migrant population

Source: Author's elaboration on various sources

competition and bargaining between private-sector interests. In Los Angeles, the regulatory environmental issues have had a major impact on urban governments and urban communities. In Japan and China, different forms of community building emerge: bottom-up in the Japanese case, top-down in the Chinese one. In India, the fragile urban contract is based on exclusion of the poor, whose only strategy is occupancy urbanism, and the dominance of a select global elite.

The preferences of such cosmopolitan elites (Sassen 2007) in terms of housing, mobility, amenities and consumption styles are clearly biased, and it is therefore difficult to consider cities like New York and Mumbai, or Milan and Shanghai in an appropriate comparative logic. The rhetoric of benchmarking is a major obstacle to understanding cities in their variable essence. Other aspects of the city, from culture to environment, from urban heritage to other immaterial assets, will possibly be neglected. Sassen's vision is rightly critical: she underlines that elites are not genuinely cosmopolitan; rather, they follow the logic of their own interests. Yet the upper-middle classes in Europe (Andreotti et al. 2015) seem to follow a different logic (see Table 6.7). They are global in mind, yet deeply rooted in their cities and invested in their urban fabrics through social, educational and value-oriented behaviours.

If we now go on to consider the contractual logic of cities, the neat north–south demarcation vanishes. Positions are more mixed and convergences or similarities are less biased. The urban contract is a matter of degrees of endowment of urban contractual tools, national frameworks of contractual rights, capabilities on both personal and social group basis, governmental structures, commercial ethos and legal structure. The capability of providing something to everybody, as Jane Jacobs puts it, is a concept able to measure the variable capacity of cities to react and interact with external and internal pressures and challenges.

On examining these multidimensional measurements, the results are surprising (see Table 6.8). North American and Asian cities are more similar in terms of weakness of national contractual rights, as compared to European cities (Tokyo again is in an intermediate position). Does this mean that they are united in neoliberal deregulation? Clearly not.

Table 6.7 Upper-middle classes vs local poor

Upper-Middle Classes vs Local Poor	*Cities*
Self-segregation and urban secession	North American cities
Partial exit, distance and co-presence	European cities
Active mobilization against the poor as 'encroachers'	Indian cities
Compliance (and protest)	Chinese cities (and Hong Kong)

Source: Author's elaboration on various sources

Table 6.8 National framework of contract rights

	London	Paris	Milan	Boston	NYC	LA	Tokyo	Hong Kong	Mumbai	Shenzhen
National Framework of Contract Rights: work, human, criminal, environment and health	High 34 Conventions	High 34 Conventions	High 34 Conventions	Low 11 Conventions	Low 11 Conventions	Low 11 Conventions	Medium 23 Conventions	Low 16 Conventions	Low 15 Conventions	Low 16 Conventions

Source: Laidi (2005)

Table 6.9 Property rights

	London	Paris	Milan	Boston	NYC	LA	Tokyo	Hong Kong	Mumbai	Shenzhen
Property rights of land and housing	+	+	+	+	+	+	+	-		-	-

Source: Author's elaboration on Angel (2000)

It simply means that European cities are more endowed with civil rights due to their democratic and inclusive tradition of civil society, whereas American cities are less endowed due to their individualism, and Asian cities due to state control. This is not explained by Acemoglu and Robison (2012), who contrast inclusive institutions and extractive institutions. In fact, inclusive institutions based on pluralism can also, as in the case of the United States of America, be weak in protecting the collective and social rights of citizens. On the other hand, living in inclusive and socially protective institutions can be a strength but also a weakness (consider the weaker citizens' security or the cities' weaker competitive attractiveness for worldwide economic activities).

Land and housing property rights constitute different regimes in our cities (see Table 6.9). As Angel (2000, p. 85) puts it: 'In a well-functioning property rights regime, such rights are respected and acknowledged by all both formally and informally. In the absence of such a regime, land and housing are usually either in some form of common ownership, in state ownership, or in informal occupation by squatters of common, unused, underutilized, or disputed lands. For better or worse, in the active and growing urban agglomerations where there is a strong competition for land and housing, none of the alternatives to a private property regime provides the right combination of incentives to the main actors in the housing sector.' In our cases, while property rights are clearly settled in Western cities and Japan, in China and India, they are not. One reason lies in the manifold property forms coexisting: private, collective, cooperative and so forth. There is in fact strong competition for land and housing (including land grabbing and various forms of resistance) in Mumbai, as well as in other Indian cities. In the Chinese cases, a complex, stratified system of property emerges due – according to some Western observers – to the ambiguous, plural nature of property boundaries (Keith et al. 2014, p. 4). This complexity is even greater in Hong Kong due to its historical path. As Tang (2014b, p. 87) clearly explains: 'the Chinese customary land practice entails non-dualities between ownership and tenancy, between transferability and perpetuity, between individual and collective (that is, ancestral), between urban and rural. It is difficult to accommodate these non-dualities in the duality-informed common laws.' According to Tang, therefore, it is not a case of ambiguity of property rights, but a completely different case of non-duality: a kind of ontological difference between Western and Eastern cultures.

Another key variable considered here is the 'right to the city' based on housing affordability, measured both by the stock of social or affordable housing in each city as a percentage of the total housing stock, and by the affordability index based on the median housing price and the median household income of each city (see Table 6.10). In the first ranking, Hong Kong comes first with 50% of public housing, followed by London with 24% of social or affordable rental housing (26% some years ago). Boston

Table 6.10 Social and affordable housing

	London	Paris	Milan	Boston	NYC	LA	Tokyo	Hong Kong	Mumbai	Shenzhen
Social housing or affordable rental housing or public housing as % of total housing	24%	17%	10%	22%	17%	8%	7.7% owned by local government or Urban Renaissance Agency	50% including rental and ownership	7% of total households	13.6% (national average gov.-supported affordable housing 1999–2008)
International Affordability Rank	368°			311°	331°	363	280°	378°		

Source: Author's elaboration on various sources and Demographia (2015)

Table 6.11 Capabilities, enabling and control

	London	Paris	Milan	Boston	NYC	LA	Tokyo	Hong Kong	Mumbai	Shenzhen
Capabilities, Enabling, Control over one's environment	Strong for selected interest groups and lobbies	Strong for public vs private	Strong for selected functional networks	Strong for university-industry urban regime	Strong for corporate urban regimes	Strong for landowners vs homeowners	Strong for corporate and community-based activism	Strong for social welfare organizations	Weak for citizens without city: 60% of buildings 'illegal' (slum/encroached city)	Weak for immigrants without *hukou* (up to 80%)

Source: Author's elaboration on various sources (Sen, Angel, Nussbaum)

ranks third, and comes first among the great US cities, with 22%. Paris and New York rank fourth with the same percentage, 17%. Both mayors announced a strategic plan to increase affordable housing in the coming years: up to 30% in Paris, with 200,000 more affordable units in New York. Chinese cities are at 13.6% based on the national average of government-supported affordable housing as a percentage of total dwellings built in the 1999–2008 decade (Wang 2013). Milan, with 10%, ranks in a lower position, although it is high in Italy (the national average being only 4%). Los Angeles (8%), Tokyo (7.7%) and Mumbai (7%) rank in the lowest positions for different reasons.

Capabilities (in the sense Sen attributed to the concept of empowerment) are enabling processes (as Angel puts it) widely distributed in the urban worlds considered here (see Table 6.11). There is heavy polarization and power selection between strong and weak capabilities of distinctive interest groups and the urban poor, who are engaged in survival strategies. However, the underprivileged groups can (as in Western cities and Hong Kong) have the support of social welfare organizations. The enabling process is meant to enable participation in the distributive policies of land, revenue and services. This is not the case in Indian cities like Mumbai, where alliances among the poor at the moment constitute the only survival strategy. Capabilities are also lacking among the massive migrant populations, as in the case of Shenzhen and more generally in urban China, where the *hukou* system has created a huge underprivileged class of workers. Visiting Shenzhen, it is not unusual to come across shacks for construction workers in the shadow of sparkling office towers, and homeless people in the subway tunnels, as in New York or Paris. In Chinese urban villages, the local residents' committees have become developers of the land.

Governmental structures of our cities are also influenced by historical national differences (see Table 6.12). In terms of decentralization/fragmentation of governmental structures, North American cities are at the top, followed by Indian cities, while European and South-East Asian cities are much more centralized. China's centralized rule has the exception of Hong Kong, a Special Administrative Region. In general terms, political centralization has been considered a measure of inclusion: as Acemoglu and Robinson (2012) put it, inclusive systems are both centralized and pluralistic. In the absence of one of these conditions, we can speak of extractive institutional systems. However, in the case of federal systems decentralization is not necessarily a bad thing.

Elected mayors are a distinctive feature of cities (see Table 6.13). Directly elected mayors, as in Paris and London, or the governor of the Tokyo Prefecture, are more empowered and able to influence the central/local power distribution of resources and public-private negotiations. However, the fragmentation of the governance system can be considerable also in a centralized system like Paris: building permits and social housing are the responsibility of the 1,281 municipalities, hence the lack of coordination. In the case of

Table 6.12 Governmental structures

	London	Paris	Milan	Boston	NYC	LA	Tokyo	Hong Kong	Mumbai	Shenzhen
Governmental structure	High Central some decenter. since 2000s	Very high central	Mixed	Decentralized	Decentralized	Decentralized	High central some decenter since 1980s	High central Special Administrative Region	Decentralized/ fragmented	High central

Source: Author's elaboration on Bevir (2013)

Table 6.13 Elected metropolitan mayors

	London	Paris	Milan	Boston	NYC	LA	Tokyo	Hong Kong	Mumbai	Shenzhen
Elected Metropolitan Mayor	Directly elected Greater London mayor	Directly elected Grand Paris mayor	Indirectly elected Milan metropolitan mayor	No metropolitan mayor	No metropolitan mayor	No metropolitan mayor	Governor	2017 election	No metropolitan mayor	No elected mayor

Source: Author's elaboration on various sources

Table 6.14 Culture of commercial ethos

	London	Paris	Milan	Boston	NYC	LA	Tokyo	Hong Kong	Mumbai	Shenzhen
Culture of commercial ethos	++	+	+	+	++	+	+	Confucian hypothesis	-	Confucian hypothesis

Source: Author

Milan, the city mayor is elected directly, but indirectly elected as metropolitan mayor. North American mayors are not metropolitan mayors. Hence, a city like New York depends on forces (like the suburbs and the suburban commuter workforce) beyond its control. China has a one-party system with indirect election: local voters elect the representatives to the People Congresses who have the right to elect the officers of local governments. The exception is the lowest level, the residents' committees (urban) and village committees (rural), where direct elections take place. Here a form of urban-rural management can apply.

The commercial ethos culture has been associated with the commercial moral syndrome of economic agents as opposed to the guardian moral syndrome of governmental political agents (Taylor 2013). We might therefore assume that the higher the commercial market values are, as in the financial global cities, the weaker the governance political values are. But this is not the case (see Table 6.14). Market values, which are ethically meaningful in an intrinsic way, are always tied to political guidance. Only in London and New York have the market values of neoliberal financial capitalism fully occupied the commercial ethos. Yet our findings indicate the existence of communities (ethnic, but not only) holding their distinctive commercial ethos. Elsewhere, in both Western and Eastern cities, the ground is still occupied by an ethical mix of values: relational and selfish, family and individual, group and self-identities and orientations are intermeshed. In the case of India, the overwhelming web of transactions in the domain of the urban informal economies cannot be translated into the language of law and private property forms (Nigam 2011). The actual influence of the culture of commercial ethos in China, simply defined as the 'Confucian hypothesis' here, is an open question. An amalgam of immanentist (Confucian and Daoist) ethics has been observed in contemporary China, and various authors have underlined the actuality of the Weberian assumption for 21st-century China (Keith et al. 2014).

Last but not least, we come to the legal framework of cities (see Table 6.15), which divides into two sides: common law predominates in North America and the United Kingdom and is still alive in mixed, hybrid forms in former British colonies in Asia, whereas civil law is the rule in continental Europe and Japan. The influence of the system can hardly be overlooked by urban contract agents. The common law based on judgements as opposed to the civil law based on codes are not simply formalistic features. There can be no direct transferability of either system to the emerging nations of Asia: a more complex amalgam of customs and laws is the rule here. A specific aspect has to be analyzed with regard to the governmental and legal functioning of the selected cities on the basis of their national governance indicators.

The vexed question of the rule of law returns here, a truly endless debate (see Table 6.16). The high scores of Hong Kong and Tokyo and the low scores of Mainland China and India are of course signs of different patterns

Table 6.15 Legal framework

	London	Paris	Milan	Boston	NYC	LA	Tokyo	Hong Kong	Mumbai	Shenzhen
Legal framework	common law	civil law	civil law	common law	common law	common law	civil law	common law, socialist and Chinese customs mix	common law (hybrid)	Ongoing transition

Source: Author

Table 6.16 Governance indicators

Worldwide Governance Indicators 2013	Rule of Law	Control of Corruption	Voice Accountability	Government Effectiveness	Regulatory Quality
Hong Kong	91	92	69	95	99
China	39	46	5	54	42
India	52	35	61	47	33
Japan	89	92	85	93	83
Italy	62	57	75	64	74
France	88	88	88	89	85
United Kingdom	92	93	92	89	96
United States	90	85	83	90	86

Source: World Bank (2014)

coexisting in the contemporary Eastern world. In the Western world, the lower scores of Italy and (to a much lesser extent) of France against the very high scores of the United Kingdom and United States are possibly indicative of a neoliberal bias, although the institutional fitness of Latin countries is clearly higher in France than in Italy.

Our matrix ends with 'context variables' to be taken into account in evaluating the cities' performance (see Table 6.17). Common to all are immigration, violence and protest: our cities are characterized by both conflict and integration (with some exceptions: Tokyo without foreign immigration, Milan and Shenzhen without violence or voice). Population density is also a key variable: its value is comparable among Western cities, whereas Eastern cities are clearly characterized by high-density development. This is a matter of institutional regulation and a social process, not one of scarcity of land per se. The pro-homeownership policy of Hong Kong is of the utmost significance here: by increasing the homeowners to 70–80% of the total population, it reduces the public and private rental housing supply.

Common to most of our cities is the strength of financial capital and the erosion of social capital and welfare. There is no direct correlation, however. And many differences emerge. In some cases, again like that of Hong Kong, things are rather different, with both high financial capital *and* highly developed social welfare organizations. And in Los Angeles, an ethnic quilt has emerged. The United States has been reported as a case of declining social capital and welfare. London and Paris were the birthplaces of social welfare with the 1942 Beveridge Report and the post-war French state direct provision of welfare, but both have seen their welfare systems eroding since the 1980s. Milan offers an example of third-sector (private sector, churches, foundations) provision of welfare goods and services. In Tokyo, welfare policy is oriented towards the elderly and childcare, in a country of

Table 6.17 Context variables

	London	Paris	Milan	Boston	NYC	LA	Tokyo	Hong Kong	Mumbai	Shenzhen
Violence, voice and protest	2005 terrorist attack	2005 *banlieue* revolt 2015 terrorist attacks		2013 terrorist attack	2001 terrorist attack	1992 urban riots	1995 terrorist attack	2014 political protest	2009 terrorist attack	
Immigration mix	High: 27% born outside Concentrated in eastern boroughs	High: Concentrated in periphery Banlieues	Mixed distributed	High	Very high: 35.8% born outside Concentrated	Very high 49.8% white 33% Hispanic 9.2% Asian 8.5% black	No foreign migration	Very high: 40% born outside	Very high internal from country to city in slums	Very high internal from country to city in urban villages
Population Density (people/ square mile)	4,200	9,800	5,200	2,200	4,600	6,200	11,300	67,000	82,000	17,600
Social capital § welfare	Strong Recently eroded	Strong Recently eroded	Third sector	Bowling alone	Bowling alone	The Ethnic Quilt	Priority Elderly Child care	Social welfare organizations	Encroaching City	*Guanxi* social networks vs rational-legal
Financial Capital	++	+	+	+	++	+	++	++	+	+
Special Economic Zones							ERZ Emergency Redevelopment Zones; Special Zone for Asian Headquarters	Invest in Mainland China SEZs	SEZ	SEZ
Environment PM10 annual mean, ug/m3 (source: WHO 2014)	22	24	37	16	23	33	40	45	136	57 (2005)
Global Events	Olympic games 2012		Expo 2015					Olympic games 2020		

Source: Author's elaboration on various sources

The common matrix   201

high demographic stress. In China, *guanxi*, or social network connective-ness, is of the utmost importance, although signs of relative decline exist. In India, the main phenomenon is the encroaching city, the informal settlement and the tolerance or opposition it is met with by the privileged. Special Economic Zones as poles of new explosions of economic-demographic growth are typical of Eastern cities only: Shenzhen comes first, but all of China, India and Japan are adopting this type of policy.

Environmental quality is a universal matter of concern for world cities, and also a matter of the Western–Eastern divide, as the 2015 Paris Conference on Climate Change clearly stated. The yearly environmental value permitted by WHO (World Health Organization) for PM10 is 20, a value only respected by Boston. London, Paris and New York perform better than the others. Milan is the worst among Western cities. Hong Kong and Tokyo have values two times more than the permitted value, while Shenzhen (in 2005: more recent data are not available) had values three times more, and Mumbai seven times more. Chinese and Indian cities are much more heavily polluted – a challenge for the future development of world urbanization. How urban contracts will be able to include environmental protection among the policy issues to be addressed in the future remains an open question.

7 Conclusions
Tools for the globalizing urban world

Towards a theory of urban social contracts

In Chapter 1, we started our research journey, investigating the state of the art regarding contemporary urban theory, the main challenges we are confronted with and the responses so far given. In Chapters 2, 3 and 4, we followed a research path based on the empirical accumulation of data and analyses regarding three different, and each internally articulated, urban contexts: the European, the North American and the Asian. No implicit evolutionary theory is embedded in this research strategy, based on the historical 'linear' evolution of the urban models across time and space. Instead, there is a basic assumption that such urban forms taken in a diachronic sequence tend to maintain their distinctiveness and not to coalesce in an undistinguishable urban universe. In Chapter 5, we looked into the theoretical body of literature that we consider useful to understand the changing patterns accounting for the empirical phenomena observed. In Chapter 6, a common matrix was designed, based on a number of selected indicators in order to give a measure of the commonalities and huge differences among the 10 cities of our research. In this final chapter, we will evaluate some conceptual, explanatory and policy tools growing out of our research, and their theoretical and political implications (see Figure 7.1). In the meantime, we have traced out a genealogical tree of the fundamental theoretical approaches and paradigms confronted in the past century around the question of world urbanization forms (see Figure 7.2).

The Western modernization theories starting from Weber have produced at least two main streams. On one hand, the theories of globalization and their articulation in the urban field, culminating in the planetary urbanization theory. On the other, a reaction to the modernization theories, assuming the variety of development paths as a radically critical approach to any world theory. In the urban field, this approach has produced a theory of worlding cities (not reducible to the world city or global city approach) and a critique of Lefebvrian interpretations of the planetary urbanization process. A new field to address is that of the urban social contracts needed by (and produced by) social movements and actors in their search for encounters

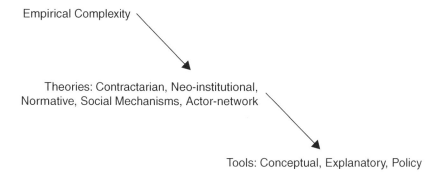

Figure 7.1 The research strategy

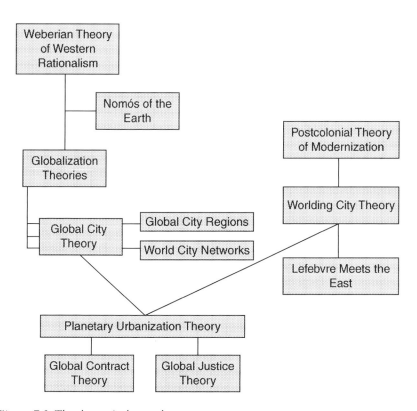

Figure 7.2 The theoretical genealogy tree

204 *Tools for the globalizing urban world*

in cities seen as hubs or crossroads of current planetary urbanization. An overall theory of global justice would be necessary, yet its proponents are few and their arguments are at an early stage of elaboration.

The urban social contract

The *city as a cohabitation of strangers*; thus runs the concise definition by Bauman (2003). The ancient term *synekism* (which means cohabitation, union of habitations) has been revived in contemporary urban theory of the post-metropolis (Soja 2000). Behind cohabitation, which finds ever new configurations from the point of view of urban form (*city, suburb, territory*, terms which apply equally well to the ancient city – *urbs, suburbium, territorium* – and to the contemporary one), lies the assumption that an 'urban social contract' is in place, binding together the various urban populations, and preventing human society from disintegrating and fragmenting to the point of exploding or imploding. The cases of violent explosion (marking here and there the life of the cities of America, Europe and Asia, from Los Angeles to Mumbai, from Paris to Hong Kong, and from Beijing to Taiwan, to confine our survey to the past two decades) revealed the criticalities and weaknesses of the urban contract, calling for immediate response – often not forthcoming – on the part of the elites in command of the respective urban societies.

In modern times, the 'urban social contract' has been built around two keywords: inclusion and individualization (Wagner 2012). Apparently contradictory, these terms are in fact complementary, indicating what has long been the cement of society. On one hand, inclusive social norms have been brought in and accommodated within urban society the successive waves of emerging and conflictual layers (the working class in the 19th century, extranational immigration in the 20th century, and the new poverty of rural origin in the 21st century). At the same time has emerged a growing individual autonomy as an indispensable requisite of the new modern sociability. These tremendous processes have so far made it possible for deracination – the loss of one's native country and roots – to be superseded with the construction of a 'common world' (Arendt 1958) enjoying stability. It was in fact Arendt who formulated the concept of 'contract' to explain how, from ancient times to the present day, bridges have been built creating connections between islands otherwise separated, scattered in a sea of uncertainty and unpredictability. Our research has led us to an understanding of how the urban social contract has come into place even among the diverse situations of Western (European and North American) and Eastern (Japanese, Indian, Chinese) cities. And yet, how is it that these very different situations all call for an urban social contract?

On one hand, it is a matter of the cities' capacity to stand up against pressures brought to bear upon them, above all by the economic agents (real estate, finance) of global capitalism. These forces are today among the major owners of the cities, exercising extraordinary powers in urban

Tools for the globalizing urban world 205

transformation and homogenization. It is these forces that are raising sky-scrapers the whole world over, creating urban infrastructures and services for enterprises and persons, all following the same criteria of capitalistic exploitation in terms of rents and profits. Their language is that of the *private contract*. These are the forces of modernity and rationalization, whose universal language produces alienation, disorientation and disenchant-ment. They apply the same rationale for action and the same city-building techniques everywhere, albeit taking into account the diverse institutional frameworks.

Nevertheless, the cities are also able to absorb these forces into their metabolism, showing the innate urban capacity to metabolize and include contradictions while reasserting the cities' own social dimension. This amounts to proposing a new and different combination between moder-nity and tradition, between inside and outside, between town and country, between indigenous population and immigrants and so forth. A wide range of solutions is found in the 10 cases we have analyzed. What is striking in all of them is the capacity of the city to speak its own distinctive language (speech). This capacity is reinforced by a further factor, which lies in the need for the city authorities to come to agreements (pacts, contracts, deals) with their respective constituencies (diverse urban populations, economic interests, civil society). Their language is that of the social contract. What-ever the urban government – democratic or autocratic, capitalist or socialist, nationalist or cosmopolitan, conservative or progressive – it is driven to seek consensus and thus to arrive at agreements with the society it is called upon (and legitimated) to represent.

Hence the dialectic that we have found in the cities, between political representation and community building. It emerges that all the cities gov-ern through more or less complex and fragmented forms of representation: agencies, utilities, proxies to private governments and so forth. In many cases, urban government is conditioned, and at times even guided, by strong lobby interests (whether in London or Mumbai) which can condition gov-ernments' strategic plans. In others, there is a predominance of concerted action and conflict between the levels of government (as in Paris), while private interests find less representation in the governance process. In yet others (as in the case of Milan), forms of functional government prove even stronger than the forms of institutional government. However, all urban governments need to engage in dialogue with 'their' communities, the sole source of legitimation, and should there be no community as such, it must be built. Among the major findings of the analysis conducted here, we have that in Asia community building is bottom-up in the case of Japan (*machi-zukuri*), top-down in the case of China (*shequ jiiantse*). In North Amer-ica, the ethnic cleavages remain very marked, to the extent more or less of imposing a pattern of community building on this basis (majority-minority communities), influencing every attempt at inclusionary zoning. In the case of India – amongst the most complex – we see a range of responses to the

206 *Tools for the globalizing urban world*

same problem of occupancy urbanism on the part of the marginalized, negotiated participation in urban transformation through alliances between the poor and, finally, mobilization of middle-class communities.

In conclusion, the tools considered here in summing up the research we have carried out may be applied for a transversal reading of our findings. Given their applicability to the various cases analyzed – albeit ruling out an approach looking to convergence or assimilation of unsurmountable differences – they can be of use in constructing a common lexis for world cities.

There are in fact three types of tools. The conceptual tools, coupled together here, serve primarily in *understanding* the urban phenomena we have analyzed, while the explanatory tools can be applied with the hope of *accounting for* the connections between the phenomena observed, using an *explanans* to explain an *explanandum*, and their implications. Finally, the policy tools serve to *indicate* the possible alternatives with which the cities and their urban communities find themselves faced.

Conceptual, explanatory and policy tools

Conceptual tools

Made in the world/worlding

In the early decades of the 20th century, the 'global' idea emerged within a limited core of philosophical thought envisaging the possibility of a unified globe in essentially speculative terms. It was only in this environment that thinking along global lines began to make headway: the term 'global' then came to apply to both the planetary-comprehensive and territorial-geographical nature of this current of thought. It was only in the early 1980s that the neologism 'globalization' began to find strong circulation in the specialist literature (social-economic, territorial-geographic and juridical-political) with increasing potential for representation. However, the concept had yet to enter everyday language with all the connotations – economic, political and symbolic – it entails. With the new millennium, the word found prominence at the world level, looking to anticipate the future developments of a unified world, a great many of which are, moreover, coming about.

In more recent years, these developments have concentrated mainly in the sphere of economic globalization. The idea of creating a global market, driven by the activities of global multinational enterprises, and of organizing flows of production, goods, know-how and, above all, financial capital, has represented the leitmotiv of economic research. On the other hand, few authors have concentrated on the subject of the global society, that is the creation of an interconnected world community, albeit divided by deep-reaching and growing inequalities. In the middle, as it were, we have research – above all in the field of political and juridical studies – on the difficulties of global governance, given the evident and indeed dramatic lack

Tools for the globalizing urban world   207

of common institutions and sets of rules able to regulate not only the global market, but also the world as home to all.

The term 'local' has also found vigorous circulation in the past two decades. In part, this is a matter of rediscovering political and cultural dimensions as a reaction to globalization by 'premodern' social groups (small marginal enterprises, individual trade, informal work etc.). These groups represent a minority in Western cities, but the vast majority of the populations of cities in developing countries. In the West, this has at the outset led to a defensive, localist raising of barriers by social sectors feeling threatened by the delocalization of production towards the less developed countries (offshoring) and the flow of immigration towards the more developed countries. However, this localist response to globalization should not be over-estimated and is likely to wane, at least over the medium term. While, in fact, return to closed economic systems and community-type social-ethnic segregation is unthinkable, the more evidence-based research has focused on the interconnections and interrelations between global and local. The past few years have seen a neologism, 'glocalization', gaining ground, representing the interdependence between the two phenomena. The global contains within itself the local, and indeed the local contains within itself the global: the idea Jean Petitot (1979) formulated at the epistemological level has been taken up and applied in the fields of economics, sociology and political sciences, anthropological-cultural research, territorial-geographical studies, and yet further afield.

The term 'governance' brings the local and global together; emerging from the science of international politics to deal with a world system of inter- and transnational relations increasingly adrift from solid principles of international law. Governance, then, is the system of networks linking up the actors on the world scene, where global law and legitimacy have long been in abeyance (according to most observers, since the disappearance of the bipolar balance that emerged from the Second World War, and that had ruled the world from Yalta to the fall of the Berlin wall). Meanwhile, a new pole has emerged in Asia, driven by the striking growth of China and India. This new pole lacks the references normally associated with the history of the West, and yet the work of 'provincializing Europe' (Chakrabarty 2007) has only just begun. This Asian path to modernization throws the key concepts of Western modernity into perspective: citizenship, state, self-rule, human rights, the individual, popular sovereignty and so on. This path to non-Western modernity includes criticism of any 'abstract human occluding questions of belonging and diversity', as well as criticism of the tendency to 'evacuate the local by assimilating it to some abstract universal' (ibid., p. 17). We must, however, remember that the major objective critic (be it explicitly or implicitly) of this non-Western path, namely Karl Marx, observed in the Grundrisse (as if in answer to his future postcolonial critics) that even the most abstract categories, albeit applicable to all periods, are nevertheless the product of historical conditions and apply only within such conditions.

208 *Tools for the globalizing urban world*

While global governance shows the pursuit of forms of government not based on sovereignty of the state type (according to some authors, 'rule without sovereignty'), local governance reveals the same processes that work at the local level. In this case too government no longer functions on the basis of state-type authority, but of pursuit of consensus and the implication and involvement through networks of various different actors, public and private, each representing interests that are reformulated and reconstructed in the different local contexts. Here the focal point upon which debate would seem to converge is definition of globalization as global network. From this point of view, globalization is a complex network of interactions between different actors and diverse geopolitical areas of the world economy which, while conserving distinct structures and their own cultural identities, share in broader processes of integration. Such, in fact, is the point of view that emerges from the research by Suzanne Berger (2006) through the concept of *made in the world*. The world product conceived, designed, created and assembled in different places, and eventually taken to the global markets, corresponds to an increasing interrelation between distinct social, organizational and cultural segments.

At the cultural level, this is a matter of the 'worlding' process, in the sense of 'diverse spatializing practices that mix and match different components' (Ong 2011). These apparently weak definitions of globalization can represent an intermediate point of view between economic theory stressing the standardizing forces of globalization and the social-cultural theories which, by contrast, highlight the historical dependence of the national paths (path dependence). With the definitions proposed here, however, it is possible to take a broader view of world society as open 'field', in the sense that Pierre Bourdieu (1975) attributes to the term, where independent but interrelated actors take part in a game whose rules remain largely yet to be written.

The theme of 'made in the world/worlding' has continually cropped up in this research, associated with different contexts which, however, show common features: world city-building projects (in London, Paris, New York and Tokyo), investments of global capital in SEZs, relations between cities in the process of worlding (Hong Kong and Shenzhen) and standardizing strategic plans (e.g. Vision Mumbai). What has also emerged, however, is the continuous capacities of cities to react and reaffirm their own reasons and speech, staunchly resisting the standardizing intentions of the globalized economy.

Global/globalizing cities

Everywhere we find a new conceptual model of economy-territory emerging, far more complex than the old pattern described by international trade theory. The old hierarchy of national economies and centre–periphery relations has given way to a growing multipolarity and interdependence between global and local. Behind this phenomenon lie the contextual nature of knowledge, over and above the codified aspect, the relational and systematic

Tools for the globalizing urban world 209

nature of competition and – above all – the role of uncertainty. A multipolar world comes to light, made of flows and links in all directions between the various poles, and a set of networks, both horizontal and vertical, within the framework of global risk and disjointedness. The nodes consist of cities and regions, global city-regions as Scott (2006) puts it, which thus reacquire a central role in globalization. The dynamics of the new territorial amalgams rests on the variety of their economies entering into global value chains (Gereffi 2006). However, only an elite of these nodes forms that exclusive club Saskia Sassen (1991) defined as global cities, control centres of the world economy. Actually, the dynamics of the 'archipelago-economy' (Veltz 2005) multiply on a wider scale the opportunities and new possibilities for the territorial systems to enter into extended production networks. Such is the case, in the countries of the Global North, of the industrial districts, which produce essentially 'off district', keeping on the premises only the service functions of coordination and planning of production delocalized in the world (in Asia above all). From here we must extend our view to the Global South.

In China, in particular, the literature on global cities has been taken up and applied to the conditions of that country. However, as Zhou (2014) points out, 'these studies successfully use ideas and methods of foreign research as a source of reference, better understanding the special nature of the construction of modern international metropolis in China, which give them practical pertinence. But the domestic research on the global city began late, focusing more on empirical analysis, comparative study between individual cities, and study of corresponding countermeasures, with the theoretical framework not established, resulting in relatively weak theoretical guidance.'

Here we come to a more critical viewpoint, addressing the globalizing cities and the worlding cities (Roy and Ong 2011) in Asian terms. These authors criticize 'the frequent use of world-class cities as a talisman to endorse varied kinds of partnership, justify mega-projects, and denote the necessity of dislocating inconveniently sited poor residents' (Ong 2011). In the case of India, this use of global cities translates into Vision Mumbai, to make of it a Shanghai or Singapore, according to the inter-referencing method. In contrast with this approach, researchers taking a critical line have evidenced just how different is the 'development' generated by systems of 'neighbourhood as factory' (Benjamin 2014). These are informal production systems based on small firms finding niches in the great cities, like Mumbai, where up to 85% of the urban workforce is employed in informal economy sectors.

Community/citizenship

Given this state of affairs, we can better understand the paradoxical revival of the concept of 'community' in the age of globalization: behind it lie various circumstances. Defence of the community as an area of protected

210 *Tools for the globalizing urban world*

identity is only one, partial explanation. In fact, it is only if the political community is seen as an integrated crew sharing a moral and religious viewpoint that localism or even fundamentalism arises. However, the tendency in much of neo-community thought is to reject this viewpoint, stressing, rather, the expressive, non-instrumental aspects of the community sphere, and even its inoperative nature (Nancy 1992). If, on the other hand, the community is seen, as in this book, in the perspective of deliberative democracy, then it is a place of political autonomy requiring those who are governed to find acceptable bases for collective decisions, even though they may disagree on the details of a decision. The choices analyzed in our research, where it is the community that is at stake (e.g. choices regarding 'zoning' in New York, Los Angeles and Boston, but also in different forms in the community building of Mumbai and Shenzhen), must be made involving the various representatives of local interests. The local development strategies are promoted with the choices of the various actors – local and regional, national and supranational – and must, difficult as it may prove, be conducted in terms of multilevel governance (an example is to be seen in Paris).

Participation in global networks through delocalization of production towards countries with low costs is but one of the possible variants that make a local community fragile. Then we have cases of integration between supralocal communities, of opening up new productive districts, of specializations and corporations between territories. In some cases, the development of actual supranational commuting has been observed (Saxenian 2006), as in the case of Californian enterprises promoted by Chinese entrepreneurs who have gone on to create indigenous enterprises in Taiwan, and more recently in the case of similar integration between Silicon Valley enterprises and globalizing cities like Bangalore in India. Ong (2005) uses the expression 'flexible citizenship' in this respect. In our research, we have found, above all, the figure of the non-citizen or second-class citizen: immigrants in the cities of North America, 'non-*hukou*' residents in Chinese cities, dwellers with insecure residential status in the cities of India. The challenge of citizenship is now playing out in new forms, all to be explored, in the claims of budding civil society in Asia: the strike launched by dismissed temporary workers and labour unions of the retail chain E-Land Group in Korea (2007), hunger strikes of family members of the victims of Sewol Ferry disaster in Seoul (2014), the Sunflower Protests in Taiwan against China trade deal (2014), the protests against introducing Mainland China's moral and national education in Hong Kong (2012), the 79 days' Umbrella Movement for democratic elections in Hong Kong (2014), and the three days' demonstrations against the enactment of the legislation introducing self-defence in international conflicts in Japan (2015).[1]

Delocalization/diffusion

While centralization implied a monopoly of regulatory functions excluding all competition from regional or sectoral powers in the age of national

Tools for the globalizing urban world 211

states, this no longer necessarily characterizes the behaviour of the post-Fordist productive and regulatory systems, which in fact allow for a considerable degree of decentralization in both the economic and regulatory systems. Delocalized production centres, but also local systems, SEZs as at Shenzhen boosted by the investments of Hong Kong, regional clusters, small regional states, city states (e.g. Singapore), multi-localized agencies – a burgeoning of non-central actors characterizes the evolution of today's numerous productive and regulatory systems.

There certainly are good reasons for decentralization, including competition between local systems and communities, stimulating competition also in terms of performance, and thereby enhancing the supply of public and private services. The more efficient local communities will be rewarded with investments from outside, and indeed new residents, at least where conditions favour mobility. In our research, however, we have found strong local resistance to importing models devised elsewhere.

These are points that enter by right into the strategic planning of cities in both the United States and Europe, with the aim of rendering them competitive on the global scale. Asia has proved ready to receive the powerful flows of productive delocalization from the multinationals of the most developed countries, and indeed to generate flows of its own towards the developed and emerging countries alike, with a singular reversal of perspective. In fact, China does not delocalize, but takes on work from the rest of the world, to the extent of becoming the major global manufacturing platform. Thanks to the differentials in the direct, and above all direct+indirect, cost of labour between Asian and Western production, the process has become irreversible, even taking into account the prospect of a gradual increase in wages (and possible development of union protection) in the countries of Asia. The prospect for the advanced industrial countries, on the other hand, is of a nonmanufacturing future.

The state's retreat from the market and decentralization of production operations have been matched by the diffusion of world economic power. The progressive shifting of power from the state to the market has clearly been among the major events at the turn of the new millennium, the process looming particularly large in the sectors of production, trade and finance. Among the most evident effects we have seen the increased power of the multinationals, or transnationals, and their networks. It can therefore be argued that the diffusion of powers has coincided with a concentration under a significant number of global enterprises or global players (somewhere in the region of 30,000 to 100,000, according to the method of estimation).

The process has also had repercussions on the domestic enterprises. Thanks to economies of scope, these have been able to compete on various product markets through network connections. Parts of production are shifted abroad, but above all what remains at home is a factory with fewer workers. Predominant are the strategic managerial and technical functions, with white-collar staff controlling the global cycles of outsourcing and subcontracting.

212 *Tools for the globalizing urban world*

The systems of flexible production are recognized in the world, as in the case of Italy's productive constellations and sectors summed up with the expression 'made in Italy', but by now largely 'made in the world'. In the past, these systems were localized in a single industrial district. Now enterprises are worldwide: near Bologna, the company world leader in the design and manufacture of automatic machines for the processing and packaging of pharmaceuticals, cosmetics, food, tea and coffee, has a consolidated turnover of €1 billion, exports 91% of it in 80 countries, and has 4,600 employees (500 are designers committed to product innovation), more than half based overseas in 34 manufacturing sites in Italy, Germany, France, Switzerland, Spain, the United Kingdom, the United States, India and China.

In Asia, the Hong Kong model of dispersed manufacturing has since the 1980s–1990s created a supply-chain management organized around a front end (design, engineering, planning) and back end (quality control, testing, logistics) in Hong Kong and the geographical spread of manufacturing production through suppliers in Mainland China, and then in Vietnam, Bangladesh, Sri Lanka and so forth.

The productive systems can go on representing a source of competitive advantage in the sophisticated global economy of variety, but only on condition that they recognize that they will have to change. They will have a future in globalization choosing between two alternative paths of development. They can aim at hierarchical solution, becoming network-firms that internalize strategic planning, design and marketing, while entrusting most of the manufacturing production to outside firms, and often delocalization to low-cost areas. This is the trend that appears most evident at present. Alternatively, they can aim at non- (or less) hierarchical solutions, becoming federative networks or planned constellations, without centralizing key functions within the firm but multiplying forms of horizontal and lateral cooperation. This alternative seems to be followed mainly in the more sophisticated productive sectors with know-how, creativity and design representing the major contents.

The federative approach can be seen to throw a bridge between the post-Fordist economic systems and the post-national political systems at the present stage. However, comparable as the organizational-institutional models underlying both may be, there are great differences in the resources they respectively have at their disposal. Nevertheless, both the productive federations and the institutional federations follow common principles, reducing the role of the centre, favouring processes of mutual adaptation and learning between the system components and adopting the logic of joint exploration and dialogue rather than command and control.

Globalism/governance

From a critical viewpoint, the positions of the globalists can be seen to boil down to two different interpretations. What the two positions have in common is a profound scepticism vis-à-vis nation-states, deemed incapable of guiding macroeconomic policies, and even welfare policies. As Saskia Sassen

Tools for the globalizing urban world 213

put it, they are 'losing control'. From the point of view of the globalists, the nation-states are hostages of the global market. However, their new orthodoxy develops along the lines of at least two rival schools. The neo-medievalists argue that the local and regional networks and transnational enterprises will develop without the state (somewhat like the case of the empire in the Middle Ages) being able to play any crucial role; the global governance that eventually emerges will consist of interconnected networks, whether in terms of enterprises, regions, political or social institutions, or non-governmental organizations (NGOs). On the other hand, the liberal internationalists hold that the existing institutions will continue to exercise their power within a new world government.

And yet we are still waiting for a critical view of globalization to come to the fore, whether we mean by this something that unites the protest movements emerging as from the 1990s from contestation of the WTO (World Trade Organization) in Seattle and the Rio de Janeiro Conference on the environment and development (movements clearly on the wane today), or whether reference is to geopolitical blocs of countries and economic systems that remain onlookers if not, indeed, losers. At the same time the old winners-losers pattern representing respectively the developed and developing countries has now been overturned by the facts. India, Brazil, South Africa and Russia, as well as China, are among the obvious protagonists of the globalized economy.

The progressive conceptual drift from government to governance that occurred at the turn of the millennium is indicative of the exhaustion, or mere sterilized survival, of the old hierarchical power, and the rise of networks of economic and social actors alongside the political and institutional counterparts, seeking a new capacity for government through negotiation and agreement. The concept widely applied to interpret transitions in the West is not so applicable in the case of the East, above all in the forms taken on by the strong national government in China (and to a lesser extent in India).

From the institutionalist point of view, democratic governance means something more than mere management of political coalitions or exchange of benefits within set limits. Governance also means influencing the process through which the limits are defined, aiming at developing citizen and group identity, deploying new institutional capabilities, and experimenting practices through dialogue to gain control of and responsibility for the democratic systems, and ensure their flexibility in matching up to the new demands. Essentially this would be a decalogue of objectives which could inspire a positive critical view of globalization, and not only one of protest. In fact, the development of new collective identities could give rise to new forms of solidarity over and above those delimited by the old national borders. This idea of global or cosmopolitan forms of solidarity to be constructed goes, once again, hand in hand with the emergence of the local governments of cities, which may be defined as the capacity to bring together diverse interests, actors and organizations and to give them expression within the ambit of the local community. Thus local governance translates into the capacity

214 *Tools for the globalizing urban world*

to develop a strategy and a community project, able to reach out from the single local dimension and enter into dialogue with the other levels. What is envisaged, then, is multilevel governance: it represents transition from the legitimacy of the institutions anchored on input (and so supported by the strong collective identity of the community) to one based on output, or in other words on the economic performance of the institutions, and so on highly differentiated, limited and contingent mechanisms of legitimation.

Moreover, an output-oriented identity can easily embrace the coexistence of manifold, interconnected collective identities, in part overlapping on specific issues that call for collective solutions. Such is the case of Europe's multilevel governance in its present configuration (despite the crisis now under way): hence the contribution to globalization that could emerge from Europe's experience, in the sense not of standardization, but of the new pluralism and multipolarism, both economic and political.

Local/national/regional

As we have seen, in the literature on globalization, the concept of global is usually contrasted with national, while 'local' occupies a more ambiguous position, in some respects converging with global. In fact, the global/local antinomy disappears when we consider the spatial-temporal distance, looking to the example of Anthony Giddens. Giddens references the complex interrelation that comes about between local implications and remote interaction (Giddens 1990). In our day and age, spatial-temporal distance has become far more reducible than it used to be, and a sort of 'stretching' has developed between local and remote forms and events. Relations form between them by virtue of which they become parts of one and the same world network despite belonging to different regions and social environments. Globalization is in fact this intensification of social, cognitive and productive relations on a world scale, with the result that local events are shaped reciprocally by other local events occurring in remote situations. This reciprocal action is part of what we may call 'reflexive' modernity, in which the world acts reflecting on the actions it is performing, and so is continually remodelled by them.

Local, in the sense of locale, can also mean a place that sees interaction, be it a room, a street, a region, the territory of a state or indeed the world. Here it has a contextual meaning, referring to the context of interaction, and eloquently evokes the fixity of the institutions. Moreover, each locale appears to be internally regionalized, in that it has a front space and a backstage, both essential in creating contexts for interaction.

We have seen a significant addition to the literature on the 'local' (both *local* and *locale*) in the early years of this century, thanks to the epistemological work of Bruno Latour (2005, 2013), who stresses the importance of the explanatory tool of 'local sites' where the structures said to be global take shape, with modification of the entire topography of the social world.

Tools for the globalizing urban world 215

Macro no longer designates a larger site which the micro level locks into, but another place, also micro, also local, connected to others. Rather than being configured initially, the scale is defined by the actors who scale, space out and contextualize themselves reciprocally, thanks to their specific characteristics. Latour proposes a three-step procedure: 1) localizing the global: the global is patterned ground, where flows cross and tangles form; 2) redistributing the local: the local structure is preformed by 'other things' (sites, times, actors). Rather than starting from the place, we start from circulation between the places; 3) connecting the sites: the sites of the global and local consist of the coming and going of entities in circulation. In the foreground, we no longer have the structure or subject, but the flows of behaviours, circuits that provide the actors with the necessary tools to interpret the given situation. The cognitive faculties are neither within the individuals nor emerge from the context, but propagate in the environment formatted through patches and plug-ins (connections).

The objects, modes of existence, contents and attachments, the mediators are entities, beings, objects, enunciation systems that populate the world and form collectives. Society is not the great everything which the rest locks into, but that which travels through all the rest. In the flat, reticular topography Latour designed, the social circulates within its own metrological chains. But what about all that which remains outside, not connected by the network? Latour calls it plasma – for example, the population before it is transformed into figures through statistics: a vast hinterland that supplies the resources necessary to perform any action, a fluid, unknown material that a new sociology of associations can begin to explore, as an unknown land.

According to some authors, the debate on globalization has radically disrupted the explanatory power of the idea of nation, although other authors take a less wholesale approach. Timely reference has been made to the theory of the anthropologist Benedict Anderson on *Imagined communities* (1980). Anderson sees the nation as a community 'imagined' in time and space, resulting from the selection of certain languages and their predominance over others, from technology (printing, to begin with), which has been able to create readerships united by the same language, from capitalism, and from a fair degree of chance. One answer given to the Marxist Anderson is that class too, the main competitor of the nation, is also an imagined community and that nation and class have grown together within the same process of modernization. So are we, then, to conclude that nation and class declined together at the end of the process? Some historians are rather more wary about the decline of the nation, following the example of Michael Mann (1997), who proposed the distinction between five sociospatial and interaction networks: local, national, international, transnational and global.

The local and national networks are included in the nation-state, while the international networks link up among themselves. In these three cases, the national dimension is never questioned. Only the transnational networks

216 *Tools for the globalizing urban world*

operate ignoring national borders, but they are not necessarily global. Only these latter operate on the world scale, covering a vast range of elements, from social movements to the financial markets (Mann 1992).

A balanced view on the relations between the national and transnational spheres is also offered by the authors who find a place in the 'variety of national capitalisms' school. Starting from the variety of institutional forms, from pure markets to enterprises, from the state to formal associations and informal networks, these authors have analyzed the impact of globalization. This, while favouring the pure forms of market and enterprise autonomy, will not necessarily lead to deregulated capitalism. Rather, regimes of regulation at the regional, sectoral and global levels (rather than national) will be favoured. There may well also be a symbolic reassertion of national sovereignty, if only to prevent forms of supranational governance. Actually, when we speak of national economies, we are always thinking of countries like France or Germany, but in the 21st century we should, rather, be thinking of China and India, whose economic nationalism is indisputable. So much is amply evidenced by the 'production of the nation' (Goswami 2004) in the case of India. The use of Benedict Anderson by postcolonial authors (Ong 2005) shows how important it is to reappraise the notion of imagined community and nation building in the diverse contexts of modern China, India and Asia in general.

In the 20th century, the region received little or no attention in some of the major disciplines of the social sciences, economics in particular. We have to go back to the 19th century to find a theory of economy taking a regional approach, as in the districts of Lyon, Sheffield and Solingen, Saint-Etienne and Birmingham, studied by Alfred Marshall, and rediscovered by Charles Sabel and Michael Piore as historical examples of districts and regions with flexible specialization. But as from the 1950s, at least, the region dropped out of economic analysis, remaining only as an administrative entity for jurists to address. As unit for economic analysis, the region was replaced by the nation, on one hand (the new industrial state), and the Fordist enterprise on the other.

As the 20th century came to an end, however, growing international competition made the markets increasingly volatile, and enterprises more dependent on new forms of flexible organization. This has led to rethinking about the region as explanatory tool for phenomena of organization of integrated production, and about firms as belonging to a regional dimension. According to authors like Michael Storper and Robert Salais (1997), the regions (more than the nations, which are often merely the sum of heterogeneous parts) have economic identities of their own insofar as their products are the result of contracts (or 'conventions') between the respective economic actors: the reputation of certain products depends on the frames of activities which guarantee (or fail to guarantee) their success. This applies to the textiles and footwear of the Italian districts, just as much as the Californian software of Mountain View or the Dutch logistics of the Port of

Tools for the globalizing urban world 217

Rotterdam. The economic identity of a city-region, even more than an often heterogeneous nation, also depends on its capacity for innovation which, in turn, is the fruit of effective coordination between the objects (again, as Latour noted) and actors necessary to bring in the innovation.

Alongside this analysis, we also have the analysis of sociologists of metropolitan space like Neil Brenner (2004), who identifies in the new dimensions of the metropolis and the city-region the outcome of a rescaling process on the part of states, creating or supporting new spaces in the global competitive contest. The greater the capacity for coordination enjoyed by region or global city-region, the greater will be its comparative advantage over other competing regions. The enterprises may, then, be seen to be integrated within regional institutional contexts that influence their behaviours, and even their strategies and structures. These latter are only partially the outcome of deliberate choice by the managements of the firms located there. To some extent, they reflect the productive culture of the region, and its accumulation of skills and distinctive competencies. From this point of view, doing finance in the City of London is no different from doing design in Milan, to take two examples from the cases analyzed in this book: the regions bring out the characteristics of that specific and highly idiosyncratic 'doing enterprise'. They do so through the store of know-how accumulating over time, and through the concrete urban and regional institutions, which include organizations representing interests and universities, local governments and foundations, professional schools and lobbies, informal clubs of entrepreneurs, and even places of entertainment (serving for fluid exchange of personal know-how and product culture). It is the – more or less dense and integrated – networks of these actors, both economic and institutional, that account for the comparative advantages and diversity of performance of enterprises and their respective regions. All this literature has, moreover, come up against the challenge of capitalistic financialization and the financial crisis of 2007–8, which highlighted the destructive logic in the regional anchoring of world production.

Speaking of regions in the emerging countries of Asia, however, means reckoning with a different relationship between urban and rural, between industry and agriculture. Here a continuum prevails – the non-otherness we have seen in this book in relation to Hong Kong and Shenzhen. These are *desakota* regions (Mc Gee 2014), a mixture of urban and rural showing their continuum. We see highly intensive agricultural regions alongside great urban centres. To begin with, there is the type of this phenomenon characterizing countries that have seen a decline in agriculture and migration towards the cities, while the use of agricultural land remains an important source of income if protected by public policies. Examples of this are seen in Japan (examined here in relation to the mega-region of Tokyo) and South Korea. The Japanese term is *konjuka*. Here we see a mixture of small plots of agricultural land and residences, relay stations and major roads, archaeological remains and natural water sources, medieval sites and early modern

218 *Tools for the globalizing urban world*

villages. We have agricultural landscapes where most of the activities are non-agricultural.

The second type we come to is characterized by regions in which the gains in productivity have been both industrial and agricultural, and the shift from agricultural to non-agricultural has taken place in the urban centres of the contiguous regions. This type is associated with growing income, good infrastructures and transport. Examples of this second type of development are found in certain coastal regions of China (including Hong Kong-Guangzhou), Thailand and India.

The third type is characterized by high-density regions with slow agricultural development. These regions are often in the neighbourhood of secondary urban centres with slow economic growth, marked demographic growth, surplus labour and low productivity both in agriculture and in extra-agricultural activities. The examples here are Java, southern India and Bangladesh. This literature can give rise to a new perspective freeing us from the dichotomy logic and opening the way to a different understanding of the urban–rural relationship in the contemporary world, characterized by what is now called 'planetary urbanization'.

Explanatory tools

Contracting cities

> *(explanans: the expanding contractual form, explanandum: the uneven extended urbanization)*

The idea of the contract city has been applied in the American city of Los Angeles to define the forms of incorporation that have led to urban growth through successive associations of local communities with a central city. In this book, however, we take the expression in a broader sense. It is also through contracts that diverse communities are brought together within one great urban conglomeration, as in the region of Ile-de-France or the Prefecture of Tokyo. The state, the region and the city draw up contracts to establish key investment choices, as in London and Paris with their strategic plans, and Shenzhen or Mumbai with the Special Economic Zones (SEZ). It is contracts that define the participation of the community (of groups of dwellers, residents, districts, urban villagers) in the life of the city. Urban governments and global enterprises draw up contracts to determine forms of strategic collaboration, the use of local resources, the supply of services and public utilities. Thus the city is wrapped in a swathe of contracts, taking the form of legal and regulatory tools, but also social and citizen networks and instruments of power.

There is a part of the city that is not regulated by contracts – the informal mega-city, predominant in India but widespread the world over (Pain

Tools for the globalizing urban world 219

2014). The decisive elements here are reciprocity, exchange of favours and promises, necessarily illegal behaviour and expectations of regularization, squatting and eviction, informal negotiation and pork-barrelling, survival and voice.

Virtual cities

> *(explanans: the digital revolution; explanandum: the growing urban virtuality)*

The web society is ever extending the scope for virtuality. This is what Manuel Castells calls the culture of real virtuality, in the sense of a system in which reality itself – the material and symbolic existence of persons – is entirely captured in the world of figment. Is it, indeed, the virtual city, disjointed and geared down in the web, that this complex of processes has been leading to, making places – in the sociological and symbolic sense of the term – and even spaces inessential?

A power is exercised in the information circulating in the web or the images appearing on our screens at home or indifferently remote that – as observed by the anthropologist Marc Augé (1992) – by far exceeds objective information. This power without personality or localization fully reflects the preponderance of technology. And the images, overlapping and converging (information, publicity and fiction), composed before our eyes are relatively homogeneous universe, for by now all messages are enclosed within the technological medium.

Thus place is increasingly replaced with non-place, defined by Augé as the installations necessary for the expedited circulation of persons and goods, or even the means of transport necessary for our universal mobility, or indeed the great shopping centres for the consumption of global merchandise. The advantage of this viewpoint, in comparison with the broadband dematerialized city, is that it takes in the materiality of the spaces and the subjects passing through them. Both, however, have by now lost the personality and significance of places.

Network cities

> *(explanans: the new network paradigm; explanandum: cities' interactive disconnectedness)*

The cities are turning into new social-economic amalgams, which are spreading, waiting to find representation and take on political form. Whether global cities or city-regions, these are mega-metropolitan areas challenging the traditional way of understanding political responsibility, participation,

220 Tools for the globalizing urban world

and even administration itself. The answer can no longer be localism or communitarianism: the dichotomy between a universal economy and technology and the policy of local identities is an oversimplification of the issue.

Today, in fact, we are faced with a challenge with the proliferation of network forms in the archipelago-economy made of nodes of global web firms and the emergence of a space of flows (Castells 1996). And behind the challenge raised by the global sphere of the economy lies technological rationale, a potentially unlimited and now entirely self-referential force. Thus we have to reformulate the classical question: what sort of society is possible in the age of webs? An age which sees not only single innovations, but a new technological-economic paradigm arising with the pretence of unifying the world, straining the rationalization process but without any view to ends. At the same time, it is changing the form of reciprocal interaction, the I–other relationship, into the form of virtual reality. The web redesigns space: it changes the sense of being together, redefines the limits of society, making local absence and belonging equivalent, increasing indifference to the spatially near and reinforcing relations with the spatially remote. Thus space no longer means the possibility of being together. The web has come into its own, the spatial-temporal operator that links up heterogeneous fields which the actors enter and exit not on account of scheduled situations, but only as action in the present moment (Sfez 2003). What space is left when places lose their cultural significance and are reintegrated in functional networks and collages of images (Castells 1996)?

And yet, in the age of its alleged extinction the city is coming back into play, for it is the place in which technological civilization and the modern individual meet. In essence, it is a meeting between global and local, between macroscopic social phenomena and the irrepressible individual dimension of societies. The city is precisely that commutator that integrates global knowledge and technology and local contexts of action, that device that connects direct and remote interaction.

This core, represented by the city, returns to the centre of the scene in the 21st century at the very moment when the leading actor who occupied the scene in the previous centuries – the nation-state – is compelled to withdraw. Or perhaps it has taken on a new structure with various levels, leaving more room for manoeuvre, and at the same time exerting greater pressure at the level of the city. In Castells' definition, the state too becomes network state, including supranational institutions deriving from the interaction between states that are weakened but still viable, regional and local bodies and non-governmental organizations. Essentially, the idea is that government as hierarchy and authority is willy-nilly extending the field to governance, consisting in self-organization and a capacity to manage complex networks of languages, interests and actors through dialogue, and so to represent them.

This intertwining of global, national and local is under way, but as yet we do not know where it will lead. For the time being, however, some critical observations can be made. The picture of a world becoming virtual city or

Tools for the globalizing urban world   221

bits (Mitchell 1995) does not seem able to take on the new dimension. It assumes possession of the universal translator of languages in the technical power of the new digital economy, but on the contrary every language refers to a text, and every text relates to a process of individuation. Governance is not a standard language, as modernist thought might ingeniously take it, but interdiscursive plurality. The virtual city does not stand up to the test of deconstruction, which reflects the polysemic complexity of the world.

However, also the classical political-institutional issue needs reappraising. Taking reference once again from Castells, it is time to rethink the concept of public space to take in the connection between physical spaces and the spaces of flows. Public space is to be identified as a basic medium of communication, taking in the new social practices beyond the institutional limits. If we then contemplate the new institutional forms, we again arrive at a picture of the city of networks. However, underlying this rediscovery of the city is radical rethinking of the very concept of local. On one hand, it is no longer limited, but at the same time it has no precise limits. Georg Simmel noted this aspect long ago in his *Soziologie* (1908), observing that the significant reach of a city within a state does not finish with its geographical limits, but extends and expands throughout the state. Today, this expansion is no longer limited to the territory of the state, but reaches out to the world. This 'local', moreover, accords with virtuous competition between systems. The idea goes back to Tocqueville, who saw in American democracy two distinct and interlocked societies, two separate and almost independent governments, federal and state. These are at the same time in rivalry and solidarity, they demand autonomy but yield only when there are interests to share with others. This picture foreshadows the concept of reticulate governance.

Mobile cities

> *(explanans: mobility increase; explanandum: cross-border territorial expansion)*

Thus a new geography of territorial governments is being drafted. In part, it ties in the lines of the old world network of cities brilliantly reconstructed by Peter Taylor (2013), but not as return to the city-state of the past. The Mediterranean area circulation Fernand Braudel described is now a network of largely new flows, differentiated and to a great extent immaterial: knowledge, logistic networks, culture. A new map of network 'glocal' systems is encroaching on the old map of national states, albeit more through restructure than substitution. Even the approaches to action in the new cities belonging to global networks are very different from the traditional lines followed by the states. Today, besides proceeding on the basis of norms and other regulatory forms, the cities prefer to produce contracts in the form

222 *Tools for the globalizing urban world*

of strategic plans, perspectives and projects, no longer seeking sole control over their territorial limits but rather to render them obsolete. This is the 'mobile city' (Estèbe 2008).

When we look at the old European city, we see a twofold movement. On one hand, the city re-centres itself, returning to the centre to revive it with economy and finance command functions, cultural facilities and political power. We now see returning to the city centres (but had they really left them?) the strategic functions and cosmopolitan populations of city-users, bearing out the old idea of Lewis Mumford that, despite all the glass and steel, the modern city is still basically a stone-age structure. At the same time, the mobile city waxes 'delirious' (as *Delirious New York* had foreseen), oozing out of its limits: every city project entails new borderlands, ever less physically set, but resulting from the intersection of flows, both material and immaterial, representing something very close to the invisible city Mumford himself evoked.

This twofold movement of the mobile city is, again, perfectly compatible with the technical effect of decentralizing and at the same time re-centralizing, without the one trend actually clashing with the other. And yet the standardizing development of functions, all equal and equally indifferent in the city centres and the vast, anonymous peripheries, which Mumford labelled anti-city, is perfectly compatible with this technique. Thus the technique appears applicable to both perspectives. The new cities of Asia, in particular, are thrusting forward along these lines.

Policy tools

Community building

Historically, the state and network (at least in Western medieval thought) represent, respectively, the descending dimension of power (from sovereign to subjects) and the ascending dimension of power (from society to state). In the course of history, this has been a long confrontation in which the network has often reappeared with a submerged paradigm, which re-emerges in associative and dissociative models (as in the various versions of federalism).

Today the local/rival association appears in forms of competitive federalism, as competing territories – essentially, great city-regions and city systems. Here too is confrontation between two models: in the old European states, whose local authority centres had been suppressed in the course of modern history, powerful new neo-regionalist or neo-municipalist forces re-emerge in permanent contrast with the new trends towards state recentralization. The 'Europe of cities' may not be the winning option, but it still reaches out into the 21st century as a peculiar formation of 'territorialised capitalism' (Le Galès 2002). In the other cases of formation of a nation that see the state constructed through progressive and prolonged aggregation, as

Tools for the globalizing urban world 223

in the United States, the fabric of the network is more structured and susceptible to institutional flexibility, to the cities' manifold administrations, and yet even there the tensions between these spheres are increasing. Finally, the Asian systems are of a third type: the cities take the form of megalopolises constituting new world productive platforms, while still remaining part of solid national command and control systems.

However, a new phenomenon is developing in Europe: trans-local policy networks, associations of cities and regions, begin to represent what we might call 'territory in action' (in the sense of agency). Here we have networks of actors, both local and multi-located, geared to joint production of public goods and club goods. Governance, in fact: the city of networks at many levels and on many planes, the outcome of simultaneous devolution of state powers upwards and downwards, of the variable combination of global and local public goods (Crouch et al. 2001).

Striking developments in technology favour these policy networks. Without final ends, the technical network is available not only for unlimited economic development of capitalism, but possibly also the use of its potential by governance systems based on self-organization: cities, districts, regions and their variable combinations.

All today's forms of community building, from the local Japanese community protecting itself from pollution by creating pocket parks and town-watching programmes, to the smart cities flourishing in West and East alike to favour intelligent use of services, transport and public utilities – all are answers the city offers to the new social, environmental and political challenges the contemporary age throws out in abundance.

Territorial networks

Territorial networks are policy tools, constructions that unite the cities and regions of the world on new bases, not only of physical proximity but also of strategic alliance. As we have seen in the case of the regions, and indeed of the cities, the economy has kept concepts of the spatial type at a distance: at least until the end of the 20th century, no economics textbooks contained words like locality, space, region and city. The recent interest in spatial economics is obviously connected with globalization. Thus a new economic geography has come into existence, presented by its authors as a form of analysis that seeks to account for the spatial structure of the economy using models based on increasing returns and imperfect competition.

On these bases, the social sciences like sociology and history may, perhaps, seek dialogue with economics. In fact, economic theory that puts its faith in universal laws guiding human action clearly leaves space (and time) out of the main picture. Space, whether physical or political, is merely a parameter added for specific cases. But if we assume, as does the new economic geography, a variety of economies with various working systems, then definition of the spatial and temporal characteristics becomes fundamental.

224　*Tools for the globalizing urban world*

With globalization, territory emerges from the field of interest of certain specialists (urbanists, geographers) and enters into the entire range of thinking in the social sciences (Elden 2013). Thanks to the study by Stuart Elden on 'The Birth of Territory', we can at last understand how the concept emerged, at least in the Western world, between antiquity and the 16th century. A comparative study on territory as a concept in the East remains to be carried out, possibly beginning with the postcolonial thought of Dipesh Chakrabarty (2007).

Territory is a political concept: from its very origin, territory has been associated with the power (terror) of legitimate actors to include/exclude. Paradoxically, however, in some cases this comes about – Bernard Badie offers an example – only to announce the end of territories, the dissolution they have undergone due to the impossibility of defining their limits. We witness the rise of an economy and society of flows, running across the territory in all directions beyond all control by states or other regulatory bodies. However, it hardly seems likely that territory as a category can disappear, if only because the regulatory system, conservative as it is, continues to conform to its principles. But it certainly is a new territory, porous and discontinuous, and above all with geometry as variable as the phenomena that traverse it. State borders themselves are now being contested, as in the sea of China and Japan, or at times outsourced, as in the case of European borders in the Mediterranean of the migrants.

In any case, the territorial principle as basis for international order, the principle the world order has rested on from Westphalia on, is now dissolved. A new world scenario comes to the fore – space in certain respects aterritorial and at the same time subject to the logic of competition between territories which ever less correspond to nations, however. On this point, the order of Westphalia has broken down, as indeed has Max Weber's vision of the state monopolizing legitimate violence over a specific, delimited territory. Relations between nations are increasingly bound up with the functioning of the world scene based on global financial networks, and the proliferation and volatility of alliances that have formed in many and varied spatial ambits. In this respect, Castells may well be the author who has come closest to a theoretical construction which, following through on the lines Weber traced in the early 20th century, rewrites the economy and society of the 21st century.

Global transcalarities

Economics, and above all industrial economics, has so far been leader at the transnational level, studying how the various international industries in diverse sectors have turned into integrated formations on supranational or transnational bases. For example, there was a time when consumer electronics represented the major example of globalized industry, like software and Internet applications today, while other sectors remained

Tools for the globalizing urban world 225

prevalently national, and yet others, like telecommunications, spanned the two. The manager of transnational enterprises like Google, Amazon or Apple seems to be the hero of globalization, just as Werner Sombart's *Der Bourgeois* was of national capitalism in the early 20th century.

And yet, if we take the point of view of the historical sociologists, the process looks very different. As they saw it – as Immanuel Wallerstein saw it – a world economy began to take shape step-by-step as from the beginning of the 17th century, and on up to the 21st century. In this story, the nation-states were not the only actors; indeed, the centres of world capitalism came to be at times something less (metropolises) and at other times something more (federations) than the nation-state. Globalization theory should therefore show greater historical-critical sensitivity, without confining itself to the short span between the late 20th and early 21st centuries, as is so often the case.

In this different perspective, the trend towards the global integration of humanity is only in its earliest stage, as Norbert Elias (1987) pointed out. And we are only seeing the beginnings – doubtful, even, given the fragmentation of our times – of the emergence of a new, global sense of responsibility surpassing the sense based on national, tribal, ethnic or religious identity. The complex topic of cosmopolitanism still constitutes an uncertain political response to economic globalism.

At the present stage, which sees us at the very beginning of the road to globalization, there is something somewhat prophetic about this perspective. And we also seem to have moved very far from the optimism of the years of steady growth marking the long aftermath of World War II. If, then, we had models for a metropolis, today, with planetary urbanization in full swing, we have no model for global humanity. Transcalarity (Scholte 2014) is a promising concept of global democracy seen as fluid mobilizations across scales. Our cities, more than nations or states, are today's loci of such mobilizations.

Note

1 I owe thanks to Prof Wing Shing Tang for the list of social movements in Asia.

Bibliography

Acemoglu, D. and Robinson, J.A. (2012), *Why Nations Fail*, New York, Crown Business.

Ackroyd, P. (2000), *The Biography*, London, Chatto and Windus.

AEP (2014), *CEQA (California Environmental Quality Act) Statute and Guidelines*, California, Palm Desert.

American Institute of Architects (2012), *Architect*. The Mag Guidelines of the American Institute of Architects, Washington, DC, August.

Andreotti, A., Le Galès, P. and Moreno-Fuentes, F.J. (2015), *Globalised Minds, Roots in the City. Upper-Middle Classes in Europe*, Chichester, West Sussex, Wiley Blackwell.

Angel, S. (2000), *Housing Policy Matter. A Global Analysis*, Oxford, Oxford University Press.

Angel, S. (2012), *Planet of Cities*, Cambridge, MA, The Lincoln Institute of Land Policy.

Appadurai, A. (1996), *Modernity at Large: Cultural Dimensions of Globalization*, Minneapolis, University of Minnesota Press.

Appadurai, A. (2001), Deep Democracy: Urban Governmentality and the Horizon of Politics, *Environment & Urbanization*, 13, 2, pp. 23–43.

Appadurai, A. (2013), *The Future as Cultural Fact: Essays on the Global Condition*, London, Verso.

Arendt, H. (1958), *The Human Condition*, Chicago-London, The University of Chicago Press.

Arendt, H. (1968), Walter Benjamin: 1892–1940, in W. Benjamin (ed.), *Illuminations*, New York, Harcourt, Brace & World, pp. 1–51.

Arendt, H. (1995), *Cos'è la politica*, Milano, Edizioni di Comunità (or. Title: *Was Ist Politik?*, Munchen, R. Piper 1993).

Augé, M. (1992), *Non-lieux*, Paris, Seuil.

Banham, R. (1971), *The Architecture of Four Ecologies*, Los Angeles, Harper and Row.

Barabási, A.L. and Bonabeau, E. (2003), Scale-Free Networks, *Scientific American*, 288, 5, pp. 60–9.

Bauman, Z. (1998), *Globalization. The Human Consequences*, Cambridge, Polity Press.

Bauman, Z. (2003), *City of Fears, City of Hopes*, London, Goldsmiths College, University of London.

Benjamin, S. (2014), Occupancy Urbanism as Political Practice, in S. Parnell and S. Oldfield (eds.), *A Routledge Handbook on Cities of the Global South*, London, Routledge, pp. 309–21.

Bibliography 227

Benjamin, W. (1995, or. 1940), Tesi di filosofia della storia, in W. Benjamin (ed.), *Angelus Novus: Saggi e frammenti*, Torino, Einaudi.

Benjamin, W. (2000), *I 'passages' di Parigi*, Torino, Einaudi.

Benjamin, W. (2007), *Immagini di città*, Torino, Einaudi.

Benjamin, W. (2012), *Charles Baudelaire: Un poeta lirico nell'età del capitalismo avanzato* (or. title: *Das Paris des Second Empire bei Baudelaire*), in G. Agamben, B.Chitussi and C.-C. Haerle (a cura di), *Charles Baudelaire*, Vicenza, Neri Pozza, pp. 7–927.

Berger, S. (2006), *How We Compete: What Companies around the World Are Doing to Make it in Today's Global Economy*, Cambridge, MIT Press.

Berger, S. and Piore, M. (1980), *Dualism and Discontinuity in Industrial Societies*, Cambridge, MA, Cambridge University Press.

Berta, G. (2014), *Oligarchie*, Bologna, Il Mulino.

Bevir, M.(2013), *A Theory of Governance*, Berkeley, GAIA Books.

Bidou-Zachariasen, C. (sous la direction de, 2003), *Retours en ville*, Paris, Descartes et Cie.

Bjorkman, L. (2014), Becoming a Slum: From Municipal Colony to Illegal Settlement in Liberalization-Era Mumbai, *International Journal of Urban and Regional Research*, 38, 1, pp. 36–59.

Blank, Y. (2006), The City and the World, *Columbia Journal of Transnational Law*, 44, pp. 875–939.

Bluestone, B. and Harrison, B. (1982), *The Deindustrialization of America*, New York, Basic Books.

Bluestone, B. and Stevenson, M.H. (2002), *The Boston Renaissance: Race, Space and Economic Change in an American Metropolis*, New York, Russell Sage.

Bobbio, L. (2002), Come smaltire i rifiuti. Un esperimento di democrazia deliberativa, *Stato e Mercato*, 1, pp. 101–42.

Bognar, B. (1997), *Tokyo*, London, Academy Editions.

Borraz, O. and Le Galès, P. (2010), Urban Governance in Europe: The Government of What?, *Metropoles*, 7. http://metropoles.revues.org/4297.

Bourdieu, P. (1975), Campo del potere, campo intellettuale e habitus di classe, *Rassegna italiana di sociologia*, 16, 3.

Bourdieu, P. (sous la direction de, 1993), *La misère du monde*, Paris, Seuil.

Brenner, N. (2004), *New State Spaces: Urban Governance and the Rescaling of Statehood*, Oxford, Oxford University Press.

Brenner, N. (2010), *The 'Cityness' of the City: What Is the Appropriate Unit of Analysis for Comparative Urban Sudies?*, Lugano, Globalization of Urbanity, USI-Lugano, July.

Brenner, N. (2014), *Implosions/Explosions: Towards a Study of Planetary Urbanization*, Berlin, Jovis.

Brenner, N. and Elden, S. (2009), Henri Lefebvre on State, Space, Territory, *International Political Sociology*, 3, pp. 353–77.

Brenner, N., Madden, D.J. and Wachsmuth, D. (2012), Assemblages, Actor-Networks, and the Challenges of Critical Urban Theory, in N. Brenner, P. Marcuse and M. Mayer (eds.), *Cities for People, Not for Profit*, London-New York, Routledge, pp. 117–37.

Brook, D. (2013), *A History of Future Cities*, New York, Norton Co.

Brueckner, J. and Sridhar, K. S. (2012). Measuring welfare gains from relaxation of land-use restrictions: The case of India's building-height limits, *Regional*

228 Bibliography

Science and Urban Economics (Special issue in honor of Jacques Thisse), 42, 6, pp. 1061–7.

Burrows, E.G. and Wallace, M. (1999), *Gotham. A History of New York City to 1898*, Oxford, Oxford University Press.

Calafati, A. and Veneri, P. (2010), Re-defining the Boundaries of Major Italian Cities, Universita' Politecnica delle Marche, Economy Faculty, Working Paper No. 342, June.

Castells, M. (1996), The Rise of the Network Society, in M. Castells (ed.), *The Information Age: Economy, Society and Culture*, Cambridge-Oxford, Blackwell.

Caves, R.E. (2002), *Creative Industries: Contracts between Art and Commerce*, Harvard, Harvard University Press.

Chakrabarty, D. (2007), *Provincializing Europe: Postcolonial Thought and Historical Difference*, Princeton, Princeton University Press.

Chan, K. W. (2009), The Chinese Hukou System at 50, *Eurasian Geography and Economics*, 50, 2, pp. 197–221.

Charmes, E. (2003), Les Tissus périurbains français face à la menace des 'gated communities'. Éléments pour un état des lieux. Recherche conduite pour le PUCA, juillet.

Cheshire, P.C. and Hilber, C.A. (2008), Office Space Supply Restrictions in Britain: The Political Economy of Market Revenge, *Economic Journal*, 118, pp.185–221.

Chipperfield, D., Long, K. and Bose, S. (eds.) (2012), *Common Ground. A Critical Reader*, Venezia, Marsilio.

Choay, F. (1997), *The Rule and the Model*, Cambridge, MIT Press.

City of New York (2015), *Housing New York. A Five Boroughs, 10 Years Plan*, New York.

Collins, R. (1980), Weber's Last Theory of Capitalism: A Systematization, *American Sociological Review*, 45, 6, pp. 925–42.

Conventz, S., Derudder, B., Thierstein, A. and Witlox, F. (2014), *Hub Cities in the Knowledge Economy*, Farnham, Ashgate.

Corbetta, G., Minichilli, A., and Quarato, F. (2014), L'industria creativa, in *Milano Produttiva*, Milano, Camera di Commercio.

Corò, G. and Dalla Torre, R. (2015), *Spazio metropolitano*, Venezia, Marsilio.

Cramer, F. (1999), *Caos e ordine*, Torino, Bollati Boringhieri.

Crouch, C., Le Galès, P., Trigilia, C. and Voelzkow, H. (2001), *Local Production Systems in Europe: Rise or Demise?*, Oxford, Oxford University Press.

Davezies, L. (2008), *La Rèpublique et ses territories. La circulation invisible des richesses*, Paris, Seuil.

Davis, M. (1990), *City of Quartz, Excavating the Future in Los Angeles*, London-New York, Verso.

De Maio, S. (2013), La ricostruzione della città giapponese. Un quadro di riferimento/The Reconstruction of Japanese Cities. An Outline, *Storia Urbana*, 140–1, pp. 17–48.

Demographia (2015), 12th Annual Demographia International Affordability Survey, www.demographia.com.

Derudder, B. (2011), Milan as a 'Digital City': An Assessment of Its Position in the Context of the European Urban System, *Globus et Locus*, Milano, 24 May.

Derudder, B. (2012), "Milano digitale": posizione e potenziale nell'ambito del sistema urbano europeo, *Impresa & Stato*, 95, pp. 41–56.

Donzelot, J. (2004), La ville à Trois Vitesses: Gentrification, Relégation, Périurbanisation, *Esprit*, 303, pp. 14–39.

Bibliography 229

D'Ovidio, M. (2014), Moda e manifattura a Milano, in C. Sangalli, (ed.), *Milano Produttiva*, Milano, Camera di Commercio.

Durkheim, E. and Mauss, M. (1902), De quelques formes primitives de classification, *Année Sociologique*, 6, pp. 1–72.

Elden, S. (2013), *The Birth of Territory*, Chicago-London, University of Chicago Press.

Elias, N. (1987), *Die Gesellschaft der Individuen*, Frankfurt a. M., Suhrkamp.

Elster, J. (1991), Arguing and Bargaining in the Federal Convention and the Assemblée Constituante, Working Paper, University of Chicago, August.

Elster, J. (ed.) (1998), *Deliberative Democracy*, Cambridge, Cambridge University Press.

Elster, J. (2009), *Alexis de Tocqueville, The First Social Scientist*, Cambridge, Cambridge University Press.

Esherick, J. E. (ed.) (1999), *Remaking the Chinese City*, Honolulu, University of Hawai'i Press.

Estèbe, P. (2008), *Gouverner la ville mobile*, Paris, Presses Universitaires de France.

FIAS (2008), *Special Economic Zones*, Washington, The World Bank.

Foucault, M. (1984), What Is Enlightenment? in Paul Rabinow (ed.), *The Foucault Reader*, New York, Pantheon Books, pp. 32–50.

Foucault, M. (2004), *Sécurité, Territoire, Population*, Paris, Seuil-Gallimard.

Freeman, A. (2010), Working Paper 40: London's Creative Workforce (2010 update), London, Greater London Authority.

Friedmann, J. (2014), Becoming Urban: On Whose Terms?, in N. Brenner (ed.), *Implosions/Explosions: Towards a Study of Planetary Urbanization*, Berlin, Jovis.

Frug, G. (1984), The City as a Legal Concept, in L. Rodwin and R.M. Hollister (eds.), *Cities of the Mind*, New York and London, Plenum Press, pp. 233–90.

Frug, G. (2007), A 'Rule of Law' For Cities, *LSECities*, November.

Frug, G.E. and Barron, D.J. (2006), International Local Government Law, *The Urban Lawyer*, 38, 1, pp. 1–62.

Fu, Q. and Pasquali, P. (2015), Legal Instrumentalism in China: The Case of Hukou Legislation in Beijing and Shenzhen, in S. Miyazawa, W. Ji, H. Fukurai, K.-W. Chan and M. Vanhullebusch (eds.), *East Asia's Renewed Respect for the Rule of Law in the 21st Century*, Leiden, Brill.

Fung, A. and Wright, E. O. (2003), *Deepening Democracy*, London, Verso.

Gereffi, G. (2006), *The New Offshoring of Jobs and Global Development*, Genève, International Labour Organization.

Giddens, A. (1990), *The Consequences of Modernity*, Stanford, Stanford University Press.

Glaeser, E. (2011), *Triumph of the City*, New York, Penguin Books.

Glaeser, E.L. and Gyourko, J. (2003), The Impact of Building Restrictions on Housing Affordability, *Economic Policy Review*, 9, 2, pp. 21–39.

Goldman, M. (2011), Speculating on the Next New World City, in A. Roy and A.Ong (eds.), *Worlding Cities*, Chichester, Wiley-Blackwell, pp. 229–58.

Goswami, M. (2004), *Producing India. From Colonial Economy to National Space*, Chicago, The University of Chicago Press.

Greater London Authority (GLA) (2014), The London Plan. Further Alterations to the London Plan, January.

Greater London Authority (GLA) Economics (2014), Current Issues Note 41, Regional, Sub-regional and Local Gross Value Added Estimates for London, 1997–2014, March.

230   *Bibliography*

Grilliat, S. (2013), Grande Londra e Parigi Ile-de-France: La costruzione dei regimi urbani, *Imprese & città*, 2, pp. 159–65.

Grote, J. (2012), Horizontalism, Vertical Integration and Vertices in Governance Networks, *Stato e mercato*, 1, pp. 103–34.

Gualini, E. (2003), The Region of Milan, in W. Salet, A. Thornley and A. Kreukels (eds.), *Metropolitan Governance and Spatial Planning*, London-New York, Spon Press, pp. 264–83.

Guénon, R. (2008, or. 1962), *Symboles fondamentaux de la Science sacrée*, Paris, Gallimard.

Guthrie, D. (1998), The Declining Significance of Guanxi in China's Economic Transition, *The China Quarterly*, 154, pp. 254–82.

Habermas, J. (1989), *The Structural Transformation of the Public Sphere: An Inquiry into a Category of Bourgeois Society*, Cambridge, MIT Press.

Hall, P. (1984a), Hong Kong, in P. Hall, *The World Cities*, London, Weidenfeld and Nicolson, pp. 198–213.

Hall, P. (1984b), *The World Cities*, London, Weidenfeld and Nicolson.

Hall, P. (2002), The City of Enterprise: Planning turned Upside Down: Baltimore; Hong Kong; London, 1975–2000, in P. Hall, *Cities of Tomorrow*, Third Edition, Oxford, Blackwell, pp. 414–42.

Hall, P. and Pain, K. (2009),*The Polycentric Metropolis: Learning from Mega-City Regions in Europe*, London, Routledge.

Han, F. (2015), The Traditional Chinese View of Nature and Challenges of Urban Development, in F. Bandarin and R. van Oers (eds.), *Reconnecting the City*, Oxford, Wiley Blackwell, pp. 148–59.

Heidegger, M. (1962, or. 1927), *Being and Time*, London, SCM Press.

Herod, A. (2014), The Rational City, in P. Knox (ed.), *Atlas of Cities*, Princeton, NJ, and Oxford, Princeton University Press, pp. 88–105.

Hirschman, C. and Mogford, E. (2009), Immigration and the American Industrial Revolution from 1880 to 1920, *Social Science Research*, 38, pp. 897–920.

Hofmann, H. (2003), *Repraesentation. Studien zur Wort-und Begriffsgeschichte von der Antike bis ins 19. Jarhundert*, Berlin, Bunker & Humlot.

Huang, Y. and Low, S.M. (2008), Is Gating Always Exclusionary?, in J.R. Logan (ed.), *Urban China in Transition*, Oxford, Blackwell, pp. 182–202.

Inkpen, C. and Pien, W. (2006), An Examination of Collaboration and Knowledge Transfer: China-Singapore Suzhou Industrial Park, *Journal of Management Studies*, 43, 4, pp. 779–811.

Insolera, I. (1975), Europa XIX secolo: ipotesi per una nuova definizione della città, in A. Caracciolo (a cura di), *Dalla città industriale alla città del capitalismo*, Bologna, Il Mulino, pp. 123–32.

Isin, E.F. (2002), City, Democracy and Citizenship: Historical Images, Contemporary Practices, in E.F. Isin and B.S. Turner (eds.), *Handbook of Citizenship Studies*, London, SAGE, pp. 305–16.

Jacobs, J. (1961), *The Death and Life of Great American Cities*, New York, Vintage Books.

Jinnai, H. (1995), *Tokyo, A Spatial Anthropology*, Berkeley and Los Angeles, University of California Press.

Jinnai, H. (2015), Reading the City of Tokyo, in F. Bandarin and R. van Oers (eds.), *Reconnecting the City*, Oxford, Wiley Blackwell, pp. 261–8.

Jünger, E. (1965 or. 1958), *Journal de guerre et d'occupation 1939–1948*, Paris, Julliard.

Bibliography 231

Kanai Ken (2013), Patrimonio costruito e pianificazione urbanistica nel Giappone del dopoguerra/Immovable Cultural Heritage and Urban Settings in Post-war Japan, *Storia Urbana*, 140–1, pp. 95–125.

Kantor, P., Lefèvre, C., Saito, A., Savitch, H.V. and Thornley, A. (2012), *Struggling Giants: City-Region Governance in London, New York, Paris, and Tokyo*, Minneapolis-London, University of Minnesota Press.

Keith, M., Lash, S., Arnoldi, J. and Tooker, T. (2014), *China Constructing Capitalism*, London-New York, Routledge.

Knox, P. (2014), *Atlas of Cities*, Princeton and Oxford, Princeton University Press.

Kojéve, A. (1982, or. 1943), *Esquisse d'une Phénomenologie du Droit*, Paris, Gallimard.

Koolhaas, R. (2001, or. 1978), *Delirious New York*, Milan, Electa.

Krugman, P. (1998), Space: The Final Frontier, *Journal of Economic Perspectives*, 12, 2, pp. 161–74.

Kundu, A. (2007), The Future of Indian Cities, *LSECities*, November.

Laidi, Z. (2005), *La norme sans la force: L'énigme de la puissance européenne*, Paris, Presses de Sciences Po.

Latour, B. (2005), *Reassembling the Social: An Introduction to Actor-Network Theory*, Oxford, Oxford University Press.

Latour, B. (2013), *An Inquiry Into Modes of Existence*, Cambridge, MA, Harvard University Press.

Lefebvre, H. (1996), *Writings on Cities*, Oxford, Blackwell.

Lefebvre, H. (2014, or. 1970), La revolution urbaine, in N. Brenner (ed.), *Implosions/Explosions*, Berlin, Jovis, pp. 36–51.

Lefèvre, C. (2009), *Gouverner les métropoles*, Paris, LGDJ.

Le Galès, P. (2002), *European Cities: Social Conflict and Governance*, Oxford, Oxford University Press.

Le Galès, P. (2011), Urban Governance in Europe. What Is Governed?, in G. Bridge and S. Watson (eds.), *The New Blackwell Companion to the City*, Chichester, Blackwell, pp.747–58.

Levinas, E. (1964), *Umanesimo dell'altro uomo*, Genova, Il Melangolo.

Lindblom, C.E. (1986), Who Needs What Social Research for Policymaking?, in C.E. Lindblom, *Knowledge: Creation, Diffusion, Utilization*, vol. 7, Newbury Park, Sage, pp. 37–58.

Logan, J.R. and Fainstein, S.S. (2008), Introduction, in J.R. Logan (ed.), *Urban China in Transition*, Oxford, Blackwell, pp. 1–23.

Logan, J.R. and Molotch, H. (1987), The City and a Growth Machine, in J. Logan, *Political Economy of Place*, Berkeley, University of California Press, pp. 50–98.

Logan, J.R. and Zhang, W. (2013), *Separate but Equal: Asian Nationalities in the U.S.*, June, New York, The Russell Sage Foundation.

London First & Turner and Townsend (2014), *Moving Out*, London, August.

Lorrain, D. (2011), Shanghai ou une modernisation publique, in D. Lorrain (ed.), *Métropoles XXL en pays émergents*, Paris, Presses de Sciences Po, pp. 53–138.

Love, J. (2000), Max Weber's Orient, in S. Turner (ed.), *The Cambridge Companion of Weber*, Cambridge, Cambridge University Press, pp. 172–99.

Lynch, K. (1960), *The Image of the City*, Cambridge, MIT Press.

Magatti, M. (2005), *Milano nodo della rete globale: un itinerario di analisi e proposte*, Milano, Bruno Mondadori.

Mann, M. (1992), The Emergence of Modern European Nationalism, in J.A. Hall and I.C. Jarvie (eds.), *Transition to Modernity*, Cambridge, Cambridge University Press, pp. 137–65.

232   Bibliography

Mann, M. (1997), Has Globalization Ended the Rise and Rise of the Nation-State?, *Review of International Political Economy*, 4, 3, pp. 472–96.

Maraini, F. (2000), *Ore Giapponesi*, Milan, Corbaccio.

Markusen, A. (1996), Sticky Places in Slippery Space: A Typology of Industrial Districts, *Economic Geography*, 72, 3, pp. 293–313.

Markusen, A. (2010), *Los Angeles: America's Artist Super City*, Los Angeles, Centre for Cultural Innovation.

Markusen, A. and Gadwa, A. (2010), Arts and Culture in Urban and Regional Planning: A Review and Research Agenda, *Journal of Planning Education and Research*, 29, 3, pp. 379–91.

Marx, K. (1858), Grundrisse. Notebook VII, Fixed Capital and Circulating Capital as Two Particular Kinds of Capital. Fixed Capital and Continuity of the Production Process – Machinery and Living Labour (Business of Inventing), in K. Marx and F. Engels (eds.), *Collected Works*, vol. 29, online edition, Marxist Internet Archives, pp. 634-6.

Mc Gee, T. (2014), The Emergence of Desakota Regions in Asia: Expanding a Hypothesis, in N. Brenner (ed.), *Implosions/Explosions. Towards a Study of Planetary Urbanization*, Berlin, Jovis, pp. 121–37.

McMahon, E.J. and Siegel, F. (2005), Gotham's Fiscal Crisis: Lessons Unlearned, *The Public Interest*, 158, Winter, pp. 96–110.

Meny, Y (1992), La Republique des fiefs, *Pouvoirs*, 60, pp. 17–24.

Mercer LLC Consulting Company. (2015), Quality of Living Survey, www.uk.mercer.com/newsroom/2015-quality-of-living-survey.html.

Miller, G.J. (1981), *Cities by Contract*, Cambridge, MIT Press.

Mitchell, W.J. (1995), *City of Bits*, Cambridge, MIT Press.

Morrow, G. (2013), The Homeowner Revolution: Democracy, Land Use and the Los Angeles Slow-Growth Movement, 1965–92, Phd in Urban Planning, University of California, Los Angeles.

Mumford, L. (1962), The Future of City: the Disappearing City, *Architectural Record*, CXXXXII, October, pp. 121–8.

Nakajima Naoto (2013), La ricostruzione postbellica e il paesaggio urbano storico di Tokyo/Post-war Reconstruction Planning and Historic Landscape in Tokyo, *Storia Urbana*, 140–1, pp. 127–53.

Nakane, C. (1972), *Japanese Society*, Berkeley, University of California Press.

Nancy, J.-L. (1992), *La comunità inoperosa*, Napoli, Procopio (or. *La communauté désœuvrée*, 1986).

Nancy, J.-L. (2002), *La creation du monde ou la mondialisation*, Paris, Galilée.

Nancy, J.-L. (2011), *la Ville au Loin*, Paris, La Phocide.

Nel.lo, Oriol (2002), *Cataluna, Ciudad de Ciudades*, Leida, Milenio.

Nel.lo, Oriol and Blanco, I. (2015), *La segregaciò urbana a la Regiò Metropolitana de Barcelona*, Barcelona, Pla Estratègic Metropolità de Barcelona.

Nigam, A. (2011), *Desire Named Development*, Haryana, Penguin Books India.

Nguyen, T. (2013), Governing through Shequ/Community: The Shanghai Example, *International Journal of China Studies*, 4, 2, August, pp. 213–31.

Ong, A. (2005), Anthropological Concepts for the Study of Nationalism, in P. Nyíri and J. Breidenbach (eds.), *China Inside Out: Contemporary Chinese Nationalism and Transnationalism*, Budapest, Central European University Press, pp. 1–34.

Ong, A. (2011), Introduction: The Art of Being Global, in A. Roy and A. Ong (eds.), *Worlding Cities*, Chichester, Wiley-Blackwell, pp. 1–26.

Bibliography 233

Owens, A. and Sampson, R.J. (2013), *Community Well-Being and the Great Recession*, Stanford, CA, The Russell Sage Foundation and The Stanford Center on Poverty and Inequality.

Pain, K. (2014), Megacity Dynamics in Globalization: Revisiting Informality, *GAWC Research Bulletin*, 435.

Parolin, L. (2010), L'innovazione nelle relazioni tra i nodi di un network. Il caso dei fornitori artigiani nell'industria del mobile, *Studi organizzativi*, 2, pp. 57–79.

Parolin, L.L. and Mattozzi, A. (2013), Sensitive Translations: Sensitive Dimension and Knowledge within Two Craftsmen's Workplaces, *Scandinavian Journal of Management*, 29, 4, pp. 353–66.

Paul, S. and Sridhar, K.S. (2015), *The Paradox of India's North–South Divide. Lessons from the States and Regions*, New Delhi, Sage India.

Paul, S., Sridhar, K.S., Reddy, A.V. and Srinath, P. (2012), *The State of Our Cities: Evidence from Karnataka*, New Delhi, Oxford University Press.

Pereira, A. (2002), The Suzhou Industrial Park Project (1994–2001): The Failure of a Development Strategy, *Asia Journal of Political Science*, 1, 2, pp. 122–42.

Perulli, P. and Pichierri, A. (a cura di, 2010), La crisi italiana nel mondo globale. *Economia e società del Nord*, Torino, Einaudi.

Petitot, J. (1979), Locale/globale, in R. Romano, (ed.), *Enciclopedia Einaudi*, vol. 8, Labirinto-Memoria. Torino, Einaudi, pp. 429–90.

Pfeffer, F.T., Danziger, S. and Schoeni, R.F. (2013), *Wealth Disparities Before and After the Great Recession*, University of Michigan, April 1, The Russell Sage Foundation.

Pinson, G. (2009), *Gouverner la ville par projet*, Paris, Presses de Sciences Po.

Plato (1967–8), *Laws, in Plato in Twelve Volumes*, Vols. 10 & 11 translated by R.G. Bury. Cambridge, MA, Harvard University Press; London, William Heinemann Ltd.

Plato, *Laws*, online English edition www.perseus.tufts.edu.

Ploeg, van den J. (2013), Introductory Lecture, Nuova agricoltura e sviluppo locale, *Summer School di sviluppo locale Sebastiano Brusco*, Seneghe, 18–23 July.

Pogge, T.W. (2001), *Global Justice*, Oxford, Blackwell.

Praja Org-Making Democracy Work (2014), Report on The State of Affordable Housing in Mumbai, Mumbai, November.

Raiffa, H. (1982), *The Art and Science of Negotiation*, Harvard, Harvard University Press 1982.

Reardon, S.F. and Bischoff, K. (2011), *Growth in the Residential Segregation of Families by Income, 1970–2009*, November, New York, The Russell Sage Foundation.

Rich, B. (2010), *To Uphold the World. A Call for a New Global Ethic from Ancient India*, Boston, Beacon Press.

Rodrik, D. (2004), *Growth Strategies*, Cambridge, MA, Kennedy School of Government, Harvard University, August.

Romano, M. (2014), La volontà estetica nella storia urbana, in M. Della Torre and B. Pedretti (a cura di), *Cittadinanza*, Roma, Donzelli, pp. 67–94.

Roth, G. (2000), Global Capitalism and Multi-ethnicity, in S. Turner (ed.), *The Cambridge Companion to Weber*, Cambridge, Cambridge University Press, pp. 117–30.

Roy, A. (2011), Conclusion: Postcolonial Urbanism, in A. Roy and A. Ong (eds.), *Worlding Cities*, Chichester, Wiley-Blackwell, pp. 307–35.

Roy, A. and Ong, A. (eds.) (2011), *Worlding Cities*, Chichester, Wiley-Blackwell.

Ruskola, T. (2002), Legal Orientalism, *Michigan Law Review*, 101, 1, pp. 179–234.

234   *Bibliography*

Rykwert, J. (1988), *The Idea of a Town*, Cambridge, MA, MIT Press.

Sacchi, L. (2004), *Tokyo. City and Architecture*, Milano, Skira.

Salet, W., Thornley, A. and Kreukels, A. (eds.) (2003), *Metropolitan Governance and Spatial Planning*, London-New York, Spon Press.

Sassen, S. (1991), *The Global City: New York, London, Tokyo*, Princeton, NJ, Princeton University Press.

Sassen, S. (2006), *Territory, Authority, Rights: From Medieval to Global Assemblages*, Princeton, Princeton University Press.

Sassen, S. (2007), *A Sociology of Globalization*, New York, Norton Co.

Sassen, S. (2013), Does the City Have Speech?, *Public Culture*, 25, 2, pp. 209–21.

Sassen, S. (2014a), *Expulsions*, Cambridge, Harvard University Press.

Sassen, S. (2014b), Who Owns the City?, *Governing Urban Futures Conference*, UADelhi, November.

Savitch, H.V. and Kantor, P. (2004), *Cities in the International Marketplace: The Political Economy of Urban Development in North America and Western Europe*, Princeton-Oxford, Princeton University Press.

Saxenian, A.L. (2006), *The New Argonauts: Regional Advantage in a Global Economy*, Cambridge, MIT Press.

Scaff, L.A. (2000), Weber on the Cultural Situation of the Modern Age, in S. Turner (ed.), *The Cambridge Companion to Weber*, Cambridge, Cambridge University Press, pp. 99–106.

Scaff, L.A. (2011), *Max Weber in America*, Princeton, Princeton University Press.

Scholte, J.A. (2014), Reinventing Global Democracy, *European Journal of International Relations*, 20, 1, pp. 3–28.

Schmitt, C. (2006), *Il Nomos della Terra*, Milano, Adelphi (or. title: *Der Nomos der Erde*, 1950).

Scott, A.J. (ed.) (2001), *Global City-Regions*, Oxford, Oxford University Press.

Scott, A.J. (2006), *Geography and Economy: Three Lectures*, Oxford, Oxford University Press.

Scott, A.J. (2008), Inside the City: On Urbanization, Public Policy, and Planning, *Urban Studies*, 45, 4, pp. 755–72.

Sen, A. (2011), *The Idea of Justice*, Cambridge, MA, Belknap Press of Harvard University Press.

Sennett, R. (1990), *The Conscience of the Eye: The Design and Social Life of Cities*, London-Boston, Faber and Faber.

Sfez, L. (2003), Eléments de synthèse pour penser le réseau, in P. Musso, *Réseaux et société*, Paris, Presses Universitaires de France, pp. 43–64.

Shatkin, G. (2011), Planning Privatopolis: Representation and Contestation in the Development of Urban Integrated Mega-projects, in A. Roy and A. Ong (eds.), *Worlding Cities*, Chichester, Wiley-Blackwell, pp. 77–97.

Shieh, L. (2011), *Shequ Construction: Policy implementation, Community building, and Urban governance in China*, Phd Thesis, Faculty of Graduate Studies (Community and Regional Planning), University of British Columbia, Vancouver, Retrieved from https://open.library.ubc.ca/cIRcle/collections/24/items/1.0071650.

Simmel, G. (1903), *Die Großstädte und das Geistesleben*, Dresden, Petermann.

Simmel, G. (2009, or. 1908), *Sociology. Inquiries into the Construction of Social Forms*, Leiden, Brill.

Simmel, G. (2011), *Diario Postumo*, Torino, Aragno (or. title: *Aus dem nachgelassen Tagebuch*).

Bibliography   235

Siu, H. (2011), Retuning a Provincialized Middle Class in Asia's Urban Postmodern: The Case of Hong Kong, in A. Roy and A. Ong (eds.), *Worlding Cities*, Chichester, Wiley-Blackwell, pp.129–59.

Sivaramakrishnan, K.C. (2006), *Growth in Urban India: Issues of Governance*, Delhi, Centre for Policy Research, June.

Skinner, G.W. (ed.) (1977), *The City in Late Imperial China*, Stanford, Stanford University Press.

Sloterdijk, P. (1999), *Sphaeren II. Globen*, Frankfurt am Main, Suhrkamp Verlag.

Sloterdijk, P. (2003), *Shaume, Spharen III*, Frankfurt a. M., Surkamp.

Soja, E. (2000), *Postmetropolis: Critical Studies of Cities and Regions*, Oxford, Blackwell.

Soja, E. and Kanai, M. (2014), The Urbanization of the World, in N. Brenner (ed.), *Implosions/Explosions. Towards a Study of Planetary Urbanization*, Berlin, Jovis, pp. 142–59.

Sombart, W. (1976, or. 1906), *Why Is there no Socialism in the United States?*, London, MacMillan.

Sorensen, A. (2002), *The Making of Urban Japan: Cities and Planning from Edo to the Twenty-First Century*, London, The Nissan Institute/Routledge Japanese Studies Series.

Sridhar, K.S. (2010), Impact of Land Use Regulations: Evidence from India's Cities, *Urban Studies*, 47, 7, pp.1541–69.

Sridhar, K.S and Venugopala, R.A. (2010), *State of Urban Services in India's Cities: Spending and Financing*, New Delhi, Oxford University Press.

Storper, M. (2013), *Keys to the City*, Princeton, Princeton University Press.

Storper, M. and Salais, R. (1997), *Worlds of Production. The Action Frameworks of the Economy*, Cambridge, Cambridge University Press.

Storper, M. and Scott, A.J. (2009), Rethinking Human Capital, Creativity and Urban Growth, *Journal of Economic Geography*, 9, 2, pp. 147–67.

Storper, M. and Walzer, R. (1989), *The Capitalist Imperative: Territory, Technology and Industrial Growth*, New York, Basil Blackwell.

Tang, W.-S. (2014a), Governing by the State: A Study of the Literature on Governing Chinese Mega-cities, in P.O. Olof and E. Bjorner (eds.), *Branding Chinese Mega-cities*, Cheltenham-Northampton, Edward Elgar, pp. 42–63.

Tang, W.-S. (2014b), Where Lefebvre Meets the East: Urbanization in Hong Kong, in L. Stanek, C. Schmid and A. Moravansky (eds.), *Urban Revolution Now: Henry Lefebvre in Social Research and Architecture*, Farnham, Ashgate, pp. 71–91.

Taylor, P.J. (2013), *Extraordinary Cities*, Cheltenham, Edward Elgar.

Taylor, P.J. (2004), *World City Network: A Global Urban Analysis*, London-New York, Routledge.

Taylor, P.J., Derudder, B., Faulconbridge, J., Hoyler, M. and Ni, P. (2014), Advanced Producer Service Firms as Strategic Networks, *Global Cities as Strategic Places*, *Economic Geography*, 90, 3, pp. 267–91.

Teubner, G. (2006), La matrice anonima: Quando 'privati' attori transnazionali violano i diritti dell'uomo, *Rivista critica del diritto privato*, 1, pp. 9–37.

Therborn, G. (2011), *The World*, Cambridge, Polity Press.

Thernstrom, S. (1973), *The Other Bostonians: Poverty and Progress in the American Metropolis, 1880–1970*, Cambridge, MA, Harvard University Press.

Thévenot, L. (2007), The Plurality of Cognitive Formats and Engagements. Moving between the Familiar and the Public, *European Journal of Social Theory*, 10, 3, pp. 409–23.

236 Bibliography

Thoenig, J.-C. (1992), La decentralisation dix ans après, *Pouvoirs*, 60, pp. 5–16.

Tilly, C. (1974), *An Urban World*, Boston/Toronto, Little, Brown and Company.

Tilly, C. (1984), History. Notes on Urban Images of Historians, in L. Rodwin and R.M. Hollister (eds.), *Cities of the Mind*, New York-London, Plenum Press, pp. 119–32.

Tilly, C. (1991), *L'oro e la spada* (or. title *Coercion, Capital and European States, AD 990–1990*), Oxford, Blackwell 1990) Firenze, Ponte alle Grazie.

Tilly, C. (1992), Prisoners of the State, *International Social Science Journal*, 44, pp. 329–42.

Tosi, S. and Vitale, T. (2011), *Piccolo Nord. Scelte pubbliche e interessi privati nell'Alto Milanese*, Milano, Bruno Mondadori.

Veltz, P. (2005), *Mondialisation, villes et territoires: L'économie d'archipel*, Paris, Presses Universitaires de France.

Veltz, P. (2013), Paris-Saclay: un campus per cambiare le relazioni tra università, ricerca, imprese e territorio, *Imprese & città*, 2, pp. 6–16.

Vicari, S. and Molotch, H. (1990), Building Milan: Alternative Machines of Growth, *International Journal of Urban and Regional Research*, 14, 4, pp. 602–24.

Wacquant, L.J.D. (1993), De l'Amerique comme utopie à l'envers, in P. Bourdieu (sous la direction de, 1993), *La misère du monde*, Paris, Seuil, pp. 169–79.

Wagner, P. (2012), *Modernity. Understanding the Present*, Cambridge, Polity Press.

Wakeman, R. (2009), *The Heroic City: Paris 1945–1958*, Chicago, University of Chicago Press.

Wallace, M. (2002), *A New Deal for New York*, New York, Bell & Weiland Publishers.

Wang, F.-L. (2005), *Organizing Through Division and Exclusion.China's Hukou System*, Stanford, Stanford University Press.

Wang, Y.P. (2013), China's Urban Housing Revolution: From Socialist Work Units to Gated Communities and Migrant Enclaves, Glasgow, Glasgow University Working Paper.

Watanabe, J.S. (2007), Toshi keikaku vs. machizukuri: Emerging paradigm of civil society in Japan, 1950–1980, in A. Sorensen and C. Funck (eds.), *Living Cities in Japan: Citizens' Movements, Machizukuri and Local Environments*, Milton Park-New York, The Nissan Institute/Routledge Japanese Studies Series, pp. 39–55.

Weber, M. (1958), *The City*, New York, Free Press.

Weber, M. (1922), Wirtschaft und Gesellshaft (Italian edition Economia e società, vol. IV, sez. VIII, Milano, Edizioni di Comunità).

Weber, M. (1964), *Religion of China. Confucianism and Taoism*, New York, Free Press.

Weber, M. (1978), *Economy and Society: An Outline of Interpretative Sociology*, Berkeley and Los Angeles, University of California Press.

Weber, M. (1997), *Storia economica. Linee di una storia universale dell'economia e della società*, Rome, Donzelli.

Weber, M. (2003), *General Economic History*, London, Allen & Unwin.

Wei-Ming, T. (1989), *Centrality and Commonality. An Essay on Confucian Religiousness*, Albany, State University of New York Press.

Weil, S. (1982), *Quaderni, I*, Milano, Adelphi.

Weil, S. (1985), *Quaderni, II*, Milano, Adelphi.

Weil, S. (1990), La prima radice (or. title *L'enracinement*, Paris, Gallimard 1949), Milano, Studio Editoriale SRL.

Bibliography 237

Whimster, S. (2015), *The Weberian Analysis of Chinese Capitalism in the Light of Contemporary Developments*, London, Global Policy Institute.

Wong, T.-C. and Goldblum, C. (2000), The China-Singapore Suzhou Industrial Park: A Turnkey Product of Singapore?, *The Geographical Review*, 90, 1, pp. 112–22.

World Bank (2014), Worldwide Governance Indicators, http://data.worldbank.org.

World Health Organization (WHO) (2014), Database: outdoor air pollution in cities, www.who.int.

Wu, F. (2015), *Planning for Growth. Urban and Regional Planning in China*, London, Routledge.

Wu, W. and Rosenbaum, E. (2008), Migration and Housing: Comparing China with the United States, in J.R. Logan (ed.), *Urban China in Transition*, Oxford, Blackwell, pp. 250–68.

Xiang, B. (2007), *A New Mobility Regime in the Making: What Does a Mobile China Mean to the World?*, *Idées pour le Débat, 10*, Paris, Institut du Développement Durable et des Relations Internationals.

Zérah, M.-H. (2011), *Mumbai ou les enjeux de construction d'un acteur collectif*, in D. Lorrain (ed.), *Métropoles XXL en pays émergents*, Paris, Presses de Sciences Po, pp. 139–214.

Zhou, M. and Cai, G. (2008), Trapped in Neglected Corners of a Booming Metropolis: Residential Patterns and Marginalization of Migrant Workers in Guangzhou, in J.R. Logan (ed.), *Urban China in Transition*, Oxford, Blackwell, pp. 226–49.

Zhou, Z. (2014), *A Study of Globalizing Cities. Theoretical Frameworks and China's Modes*, Shanghai, The Development Research Center of Shanghai Municipal People's Government, World Century.

Zorbaugh, H.W. (1976, or. 1929), *The Gold Coast and the Slum*, Chicago, The University of Chicago Press.

Zukin, S. and Braslow, L. (2011), The Life Cycle of New York's Creative Districts: Reflections on the Unanticipated Consequences of Unplanned Cultural Zones, *City, Culture and Society*, 2, pp. 131–40.

Index

Abercrombie, P. 16, 44
Acemoglu, D. 193–5
Ackroyd, P. 81
Adiga, A. 117
Africa 6, 9, 18, 23; North 81; South 20, 213
Agamben, G. 55
agglomeration 16, 58, 65, 70, 152
Alberti, L.B. 44
Amazon 19, 225
America: North 2, 6–7, 9, 11–12, 17, 23, 29, 35, 68, 78, 191, 195, 197, 204–5, 210; South 18, 91
American Institute of Architects 84
Amsterdam 17, 77, 122
Anderson, B. 215
Andreotti, A. 171, 191
Angel, S. 107, 193, 195
anomia 19
Appadurai, A. 3, 12, 21, 35, 118, 123, 133, 137
Apple 106, 225
Arendt, H. 14, 37, 64, 204
Aristotle 186
arrondissements 60
Asia 1, 3, 6, 9–12, 17–8, 20, 23, 29, 35, 68, 77, 91, 191, 193, 195, 197, 204, 207, 209, 211, 222
assemblage 21, 26–7
Athens 19
Augé, M. 24, 60, 219
Australia 17
Austria 66
authority 168–9

Badie, B. 224
Baghdad 55
Balearic Islands 29
Bangalore 1, 20, 33, 136, 141–3, 164, 210

Bangkok 134
Bangladesh 39, 212, 218
Banham, R. 84
banlieues 9, 58–9
Barabási, A.L. 31
Barcelona 12, 19, 29, 33, 67
Barron, D.J. 5–6, 8, 23, 35
Basel 76
Baudelaire, C. 55
Bauman, Z. 108, 204
Beijing 18, 29, 62, 146, 204
Bengal 179
Benjamin, S. 10, 137, 139, 142, 209
Benjamin, W. 15, 55–64
Benveniste, E. 36, 185
Bergamo 69–71, 76–7
Berger, S. 154, 208
Berta, G. 42
Bidou-Zachariasen, C. 60
Biggart, N. 187
Bischoff, K. 99
Bjorkman, L. 135
Blanco, I. 12
Blank, Y. 34
Bluestone, B. 87, 88–92
Bobbio, L. 178
Bognar, B. 122
Bologna 67–8, 70, 212
Boltanski, L. 176
Bonabeau, E. 31
border 1
boroughs 39–54, 94
Borraz, O. 61
Boston 1–2, 11, 83, 85–94, 108, 116, 189, 193, 201, 210
Bourdieu, P. 36, 58–9, 185, 298
Braslow, L. 105
Braudel, F. 21, 221
Brazil 179, 213

240 *Index*

Brenner, N. 11–12, 16, 21, 33–4, 61, 65, 120, 162, 217
Brescia 70
Brno 19
Brockton 90
Brook, D. 11, 130
Brueckner, J. 139
Brussels 17, 19, 29
Buenos Aires 18
Burdett, R. 24
Burrows, E.G. 94

Cai, G. 149
Cairo 18
Calafati, A. 28, 36
California 23–5
Cambodia 9
Cambridge (Massachusetts) 89
Canada 91
capabilities 183, 195
capitalism: and Confucianism 12, 144, 163, 187, 197; financial 197–200; global 204–5; and Protestant ethic 96, 144, 151
Caribbean 91
Castells, M. 18, 24, 181, 219–21, 224
Cattaneo, C. 72–3
Caves, R.E. 47
centre 1, 17, 71, 124, 145
Chakrabarty, D. 207, 224
Chan, K.W. 161
Charmes, E. 59
Chelsea (Massachusetts) 89
Cheshire, P.C. 45
Chicago 18, 108, 179
China 2–10, 17, 20, 25–6, 36, 39, 78, 140, 142–63, 183, 186–7, 191, 193, 195, 197, 201, 204–5, 207, 209, 211–13, 216, 218, 224
Chinese Empire 145
Chipperfield, D. 146
Choay, F. 178
citizen 4, 123–5, 177, 185
city 14, 143; central 1; capital 2, 61, 126; *cheng, chengshi, shi* (Chinese and Japanese) 124, 152, 185; *cité* (French) 176; *civitas* (Latin) 184–5; compact 48, 108, 146; contract 14, 20, 22, 64, 107, 218; deals 49; entrepreneurial 26; foam 119; generic 23, 83; global 39, 63, 98, 105, 120, 171, 181, 209; hub 31, 189; mobile 221; network 219–20; *polis* (Greek) 1, 37, 184–5; private 8, 84–5, 128, 133, 141; *pura*

(Sanskrit) 184; relational 29; satellite 74, 124–6, 146; smart 27; *urbs* (Latin) 18, 204; virtual 219; walled 185–6; world 40; worlding 5
city-region 124; global 14, 18; polycentric 44
civil society 38, 84
clusters 109
coalition: growth 146; opposed 110
Collins, R. 187
Colombia 91
communism 145
community 2, 209–10, 222–3; building 92, 111, 142, 163, 191, 205; *machizukuri* (Japan) 7, 127–8, 205; *shequ jianshe* (China) 7, 156–8, 205
Como 79
connectivity 189
constituencies 13
contract 1, 5–8, 187–9; and gift 6; natural 22; private 3, 7, 8, 205; relational 16; social 3, 7, 8, 81, 204; and status 5; of territorial development 63
Conventz, S. 19–20, 189
Corbetta, G. 79
Cordova 55
Corò, G. 23
cosmopolitan elite 133, 191
creative industry 47, 73
Crouch, C. 223
cultural districts 105, 110

Dallas 99
Dalla Torre, R. 23
Daoism 22, 151, 163
Davezies, L. 26
Davis, M. 105, 110
decentralization 97, 146
De Groot, J.J.M. 2
Delhi 1, 5, 18, 137
delocalization 210–12
De Maio, S. 125
democracy 6, 17; deliberative 176–80
Deng Xiaoping 151
Derrida, J. 29
Derudder, B. 19, 68
desakota (town-village) 20, 153, 217
de-territorialization 170
Detroit 99
devolution 49, 140
Dhaka 18
diffusion 210–12
Donzelot, J. 59–60

Index 241

D'Ovidio, M. 79
Dubai 10
Duisburg 76
Durkheim, E. 2, 6, 163

Elden, S. 167, 224
Elias, N. 225
Elster, J. 82, 178–80
Enlightenment 37
environment 111–14, 185, 201
Esherick, J.E. 22
Estèbe, P. 222
Europe 6, 11–13, 15, 20–1, 23–4, 27, 29, 35, 37, 68, 77–8, 140, 191, 195, 197, 204, 211, 222
European Union 4, 14, 78, 174

Facebook 19
Fainstein, S.S. 165
floor area bonus 104
floor space index 139
Florida, R. 79, 97, 101
flows 21, 75–6, 87, 106, 171
Foshan 18
Foucault, M. 15, 37
France 17, 23, 39, 66, 68, 76, 91, 199, 212, 216
Frankfurt 17, 19, 76–7
Freeman, A. 42, 47
Friedmann, J. 118
Frug, G. 5–6, 8, 23, 35, 84–5, 94
Fu, Q. 162
Fung, A. 179

Gadwa, A. 110
Gans, H. 87–9
Genoa 70
gentrification 59–60, 66, 105
Gereffi, G. 209
Germany 17, 23, 68, 76, 78, 212, 216
Ghandi, M.K. 143
ghetto 9, 58
Giddens, A. 214
Glaeser, E.L. 11, 89, 107
global 214: events 43, 57, 200; transcalarities 224–5
globalism 212–14
globalization 3, 202–6
Goldblum, C. 155
Goldman, M. 10, 141
Google 19, 20, 106, 225
Goswami, M. 143, 216
Goteborg 19

governance 20, 61, 155, 183, 207, 212–14
government 195–6, 199, 205
Gramsci, A. 80
Granada 55
Graz 19
Greece 2
green belt 44, 146
Grilliat, S. 62
Grote, J. 30
growth 2, 26, 53, 70
Gualini, E. 29, 68
Guangdong 155
Guangzhou 18, 149, 218
guanxi (social network) 20, 163, 201
Guénon, R. 2, 175, 184
guild 40–1
Guthrie, D. 20
Gyourko, J. 115

Habermas, J. 37, 143, 180
Hall, P. 11, 44, 65, 152, 154
Hamilton, G. 187
Han, F. 185
Harrison, B. 87
Hegel, G.W.F. 187
Heidegger, M. 2
Herod, A. 62–4
Hilber, C.A. 45
Hirschman, A. 27, 185
Hirschman, C. 82
Hobbes, T. 6–7, 37, 39–40, 166, 187
Hofmann, H. 36
homeownership 148
Hong Kong 2, 11, 20, 29, 39, 129, 134, 143–63, 187, 189, 193, 195, 197, 199, 204, 208, 210–12, 217–18; Kai Ching Estate 148; Kai Tak Development Project 152; Kowloon Peninsula and the New Territories 151
housing: affordable 94, 100, 104, 114–16, 193–4; social 9, 43
Houston 99, 108
Howard, E. 44
Huang, Y. 151, 157, 165
hukou (registration) 149, 160–2, 188

ICT (information and communication technologies) 19–20, 47–8
Incheon 18
India 2, 3, 5, 10, 20, 25, 39–40, 129–43, 150–1, 156, 183, 186–7,

242 *Index*

191, 193, 197, 201, 204, 207, 210, 212–13, 216, 218
informal economy 142
infrastructure (transport, digital, water, waste) 49–52, 63, 70–2, 133
Inkpen, C. 155
Insolera, I. 70
institutions: extractive 195; inclusive 100, 195
Isin, E.F. 144, 183
Islam 3
Istanbul 18
Italy 4, 39, 91, 199; Northern 22–3, 97; Third 25

Jacobs, J. 29, 87, 103–4, 191
Japanese Empire 125
Java 218
Jinnai, H. 121, 186
Junger, E. 1, 12
juridical order 197–9
justice 117–18; global 182

Kahn, E.L. 107
Kanai, K. 127
Kanai, M. 36
Kant, I. 37
Kantor, P. 11, 35, 45–6, 53, 58, 61–2, 99, 101
Karachi 18
Kautilya 8
Keith, M. 6, 162–3, 193, 197
Knox, P. 142
Kojéve, A. 5
Kolkata 18
Koln 19
Koolhaas, R. 23–4, 95
Korea 91, 210, 217
Krugman, P. 168
Kuma, K. 129
Kundu, A. 19
Kyoto 18

Lagos 18
Lai, W.K. 165
Laidi, Z. 192
land 70, 140–1, 146; occupation of 142; property system 153
Laos 91
Lao-tzu 151
Lash, S. 163
Latour, B. 21, 26–8, 168, 214, 217
law (common, civil) 198

Lawrence (Massachusetts) 89
Lecco 75
Lefebvre, H. 2, 33, 36, 142, 166–7, 173, 202
Lefèvre, C. 62
Le Galès, P. 11, 18, 20, 40, 61, 67, 222
Legnano 75
Li, S.M. 165
Lindblom, C.E. 178
Lipset, S.M. 85
Lisbon 55
local 25, 207, 214–15; development 24
localization 7, 14
location 70
Lodi 75
Logan, J.R. 86, 99, 165
London 2, 9, 11, 16, 17, 18, 19, 20, 29, 35, 37–54, 55, 60, 62, 69, 77, 80–1, 120, 125–6, 134, 181, 189, 193, 195, 197, 199, 201, 205, 208, 217–18; city of 40; First 44–54, 62, 80; Greater Authority 44–53; Greater Plan 16, 39
Lorrain, D. 35
Los Angeles 2, 5, 11, 16, 18, 25, 99, 105–15, 125, 191, 195, 199, 204, 210, 218; Department of City Planning 112–14
Los Angeles County 105
Love, J. 145, 187
Low, S.M. 151, 157
Low Countries 78
Lowell (Massachusetts) 89, 92
Lynch, K. 83, 86, 107

Madrid 19
Magatti, M. 72
Maharashtra 130; State Legislative Assembly 140
Malaysia 20, 56
Manila 18
Mann, M. 215–16
Mantova 75
Maraini, F. 124
Markusen, A. 32, 156
Marne-la-Vallée 65
Marseille 29
Marshall, A. 216
Marx, K. 19, 162, 165–6, 207
Massachusetts 87
Mattozzi, A. 30
Mauss, M. 2
Mc Gee, T. 119, 153, 217

Index   243

McMahon, E.J. 98
Mediterranean 77–8
mega-cities 18
megalopolis 1, 124–5
Meny, Y. 61
Mesopotamia 2
metaxy (bridge, intermediary) 172
metropolis 1, 45; dispersed 83,
  105–7, 156
Mexico City 18
middle class 9, 59–60, 141–3,
  152, 206
Middle East 23, 77, 81
migration 149, 151–2, 160
Milan 9, 11, 19, 29, 36–7, 55, 66–80,
  189, 191, 195, 199, 201, 205, 217
Miller, G.J. 107
Ming, L.S. 165
Mitchell, W. 221
mobility 20, 159
Modena 70
modernization 3, 125–6, 146, 163, 202
Mogford, E. 82
Molotch, H. 86
Montpelier 83
Montreal 83
Monza-Brianza 68–9, 71, 79
Moscow 18
Mountain View 216
Mumbai 1, 2, 11, 18, 20, 29, 35,
  129–43, 164, 189, 191, 193, 195,
  201, 204–5, 208–10, 218; Advanced
  Locality Management Programme
  137; Metropolitan Corporation of
  Greater 133; Metropolitan Region
  Development Authority 133; Navi
  130–3
Mumford, L. 23, 96, 100, 110, 222
Munich 96

Nakajima, N. 126
Nakane, C. 119, 124
Nancy, J.-L. 18, 36, 107, 176, 210
Nanjing 157
Naples 80, 139
national 214–16
negotiation 178
neighbourhood 90, 108, 130, 146, 150;
  majority-minority 99
Nel.lo, O. 12, 81
network 2, 12, 30, 65–6, 81, 176; actor
  21; territorial 223–4
New England 83, 85, 88

New York 2, 4, 5, 11, 16, 17, 18, 20,
  29, 35, 39, 60, 69, 79, 94–105,
  108, 116, 120, 134, 168, 181, 189,
  191, 195, 197, 201, 208, 210, 222;
  Department of City Planning 101–5;
  Economic Development Corporation
  102
Nguyen, T. 157
Nietzsche, F. 106
Nigam, A. 197
Nigeria 20
nomòs 13, 166–70
North Ireland 39
Novara 69, 76
Nussbaum, M. 182

oikos 4, 14
Ong, A. 3, 11–12, 144, 208–10, 216
Ontario 44
ontology 4, 15, 21, 26
Orange County 105
ordering 7
Osaka 18
Owens, A. 99

Pain, K. 11, 218
Paris 2, 9, 11, 16, 18, 19, 27, 29, 37,
  54–67, 77, 79, 80–1, 126, 189, 195,
  199, 201, 204–5, 208, 210, 218;
  Grand 62–5, 80
Parma 70
Parolin, L. 30, 68
Pasquali, P. 162, 165
Paul, S. 33, 137, 143
Pereira, A. 155
Perulli, P. 22, 36, 67
Petitot, J. 207
Pfeffer, F.T. 98
Philadelphia 99
Piacenza 69, 75–6
Pichierri, A. 22, 36, 87
Pien, W. 155
Piore, M. 154, 216
Pinson, G. 26, 61, 65
planning 71, 125–7, 139; crisis of 26,
  44; strategic 53–4, 71, 100–2, 189
Plato 44, 176–7
Ploeg, van den J. 159
Pogge, T.W. 182
Poland 39
Polanyi, K. 5, 167
polarisation 43
political 38, 122

244 Index

population 1, 3, 82, 88, 96, 108, 120–1, 164; density 200
Porto Alegre 179
post-colonial urban theories 3, 144, 148
postmetropolis 2, 106–8
poverty 134, 142, 150, 191, 206
Praja Org. 140
property rights 193
protest 199
Provence 29
Puerto Rico 91

Raiffa, H. 179
Rawls, J. 182–3
Reardon, S.F. 99
Reggio Emilia 68–70
region 17, 214–18; Baltic 29; Bavaria 67; Catalunya 67; Chubu 129; Danubian 29; Emilia-Romagna 76; Ile-de-France 63; Kanto 120; Liguria 67, 76; Lombardy 67, 78; megacity 119–20; Piedmont 76
representation 34, 205
residential segregation 91, 98, 108–9, 162
Rich, B. 8
rights 191–3
Rimini 70
Rio de Janeiro 18, 134, 213
Riverside County 105
Robinson, J.A. 193, 195
Rodrik, D. 27, 32, 36
Rogers, R. 48
Roissy 65
Rokkan, S. 30
Romania 36
Romano, M. 71
Rome 1, 29, 36, 39, 69, 80, 174
Rosenbaum, E. 149
Roth, G. 84
Rotterdam 216
Rousseau, J.-J. 187
Roy, A. 11, 12, 134, 138, 148, 209
Ruskola, T. 144, 187
Russia 20, 39, 213
Rykwert, J. 2

Sabel, C. 216
Sacchi, L. 122
Saclay 65–6
Salais, R. 216
Salet, W. 18, 27

Sampson, R.J. 99
San Bernardino County 105
San Diego 108
San Francisco 25, 84, 107–8
São Paulo 18, 134
Sassen, S. 11–13, 27, 36, 80, 98, 105, 120, 168–71, 180, 191, 209, 212
Savitch, H.V. 11, 35, 99, 101
Saxenian, A.L. 171, 210
Scaff, L.A. 95, 144
scale 217
Schmitt, C. 7, 13, 34, 166–72
Scholte, J.A. 225
Scotland 39
Scott, A.J. 14, 18, 32, 67, 109, 209
Seattle 213
Seine-Saint-Denis 58–9, 64
Sen, A. 117, 183, 195
Sennett, R. 23, 83, 96
Seoul 18, 128, 210
Sesto San Giovanni 71, 75
Sfez, L. 220
Shanghai 2, 4, 12, 16–18, 20, 22, 29, 35, 134, 142, 146, 150, 157, 164, 191, 209
Shatkin, G. 25
Sheffield 216
Shenzhen 5, 11, 143–63, 188–9, 195, 199, 201, 208, 210–11, 217, 218
Shieh, L. 157–9
Siegel, F. 98
Silicon Valley 4, 20, 25, 171, 210
Simmel, G. 1, 4, 19, 30, 47, 55, 119–20, 172–73, 221
Singapore 20, 120, 128–9, 134, 142, 155, 164, 187, 209, 211
Siu, H. 148
Sivaramakrishnan, K.C. 139–40, 164
Skinner, G.W. 145
Sloterdijk, P. 4, 22, 119, 168
slum 9, 58, 135–8; Dharavi 142; Maharashtra Rehabilitation Authority (SRA) 135; Shivajinagar-Bainganwadi 135
Soja, E. 11, 36, 107, 120, 204
Solingen 216
Sombart, W. 82, 225
Sorensen, A. 126
sovereignty 162, 208
space 2, 4, 166–74; larger 34–6; political construction of 59; public 221
Spain 4, 17, 39, 66, 212

Index   245

SPARC (Society for the Protection of Area Resources) NGO 137–8
special economic zone (SEZ) 9, 128, 142, 154, 201, 208, 211, 218
Spinoza, B. 183
Sridhar, K.S. 137, 139–40
Sri Lanka 212
state 34–5; entrepreneurial 144–5, 150–1, 155; monopoly 168; nation 14–15
Stevenson, M.H. 88
St. Louis 95
Stockholm 19
Storper, M. 11, 16–17, 25, 32, 83, 120, 216
Stuttgard 67
Sudjic, D. 24
Suzhou 155
swaray (self-rule) 143
Switzerland 67, 212
Sydney 16–17, 134
synekism 4, 204

Taiwan 171, 204, 210
Tang, W.-S. 3, 10, 145, 147, 152, 165, 183, 193, 225
Tange, K. 126
Taylor, P.J. 11, 12, 18–19, 29, 32, 37–8, 55, 69, 75, 120, 181, 189, 197, 221
Tehran 18
territory 168–71, 204, 224
Teubner, G. 181
Thailand 218
Therborn, G. 9, 150
Thernstrom, S. 87, 91–2
Thévenot, L. 176
Thoenig, J.-C. 61
Tilly, C. 14, 30, 145
de Tocqueville, A. 2, 82–3, 169, 221
Tokyo 2, 4, 9, 11, 16, 18, 22, 35, 39, 55, 62, 106, 120–9, 164, 189, 191, 195, 197, 199, 201, 208, 217, 218; Business Development Center 129
Toronto 17, 134
Tosi, S. 36, 75
town 2, 82; new 10, 44, 64, 131–3, 149, 152–3
Trento 70
Treviso 68–70
Troy 174
Turin 19, 29, 36, 68, 70

United Kingdom 39, 78, 141, 197, 199, 212
United States 4, 17, 25, 76, 82–116, 129, 140, 142, 193, 199, 211–12, 222
urban 2, 166; regionalization 71; rural continuum 123, 145, 152; village 89, 121, 158
urbanization: colonial 146; planetary 2, 34, 118

Valencia 29
Vancouver 17
Varese 76–9
Veltz, P. 65, 171
Veneri, P. 28, 36
Venice 55, 68, 70, 122, 172, 174, 182
Ventura County 105
Venugopala, R.A. 140
Véron, J. 181
Vicari, S. 74
Vico, G.B. 185
Vienna 19
Vietnam 152, 212
violence 199, 204
Vitale, T. 36, 75
voice 142, 199

Wacquant, L.J.D. 58
Wagner, P. 125, 204
Wakeman, R. 58
Wales 39
Wallace, M. 94, 102
Wallerstein, I. 225
Walzer, R. 16
Wang, F.-L. 149–50, 195
Washington 29
Watanabe, J.S. 127
Weber, M. 3, 8, 12–13, 26, 37, 40–1, 83, 85–6, 95, 123, 143–51, 163, 165, 167–8, 185, 187, 202, 224
Weil, S. 172, 174–5, 181
Wei-Ming, T. 186
welfare 199
Westphalia 224
Whimster, S. 188
Williamson, O.E. 29
Wirth, L. 149
Wisconsin 179
Wong, T.-C. 155
world 34, 175; common 158; environment 2; made in the 206–8; theory 202
worlding 206–8

246   *Index*

Wright, E.O. 179
WTO (World Trade Organization) 187
Wu, F. 25, 146–9, 155
Wu, W. 149

Xiang, B. 159, 161

Yalta 207
yamen (mandarin's residence) 145
Yehoshua, A. 55
Yokohama 18, 125

Zerah, M.-H. 133–8
Zhang, W. 99
Zheng, C. 107
Zhou, M. 149, 209
zone 1, 9; priority urbanization 58–9;
    sensitive urban 58–9; urban free 9,
    58–9
zoning 96, 99–105, 112–15, 141;
    incentive 104; mixed uses 103
Zorbaugh, H.W. 134
Zukin, S. 105